A BRUS
THE C

An artist's search for inspiration along the South West Coast Path

SASHA HARDING

Illustrated edition first published in Great Britain by Sasha Harding, 2015.

This revised edition, of text in paperback format, published in Great Britain by Sasha Harding, 2019.

ISBN: 978-0-9932364-5-7

Book design and layout: Amy Goodwin
Editor: Kath Morgan
Proof Reader: Bee Harding

Typeset in Utopia

Printed and bound by TJ International Ltd, Padstow, Cornwall.

This book is dedicated to the memory of my
Mum and Dad: Jane and Rob Harding.

THE BEGINNING

The summer after graduating from art college, I read a book about a man and his dog, who walked the South West Coast Path in one go. By the time I finished the last page, I'd developed a fully formed vision of myself following in his footsteps, striding over rugged cliffs, the wind in my hair, a faithful hound at my heels. But it remained a vision, a dream, growing fainter and finally evaporating as the years went by; years spent working in a restaurant kitchen at night and painting during the day, fuelled by a diet of cabbage and hand-rolled cigarettes. In the circumstances, taking seven weeks off to go on a walking holiday seemed absurd. But time moved on. I left the kitchen, stopped smoking, adopted a dog and started eating a balanced diet. I became a full-time painter, got married, acquired a second dog, lost the first, and had set a date for a career-enhancing one-man show when … I ran out of ideas.

Thereafter followed weeks of worry, wondering if I would ever paint another picture. I distracted myself by methodically cleaning my studio, and I came upon the book about the man, his dog and the SWCP. As I turned the pages, a sketch of an idea formed in my head. Could I possibly take on the six-hundred-and-thirty-mile walk and, in doing so, find the inspiration I desperately needed?

I discussed the idea with my husband, Jack, breathlessly describing the length and varied terrain of the Coast Path.

"Every day, something new. Imagine how inspired I will be."

"Sash, don't take this the wrong way." He paused. "It sounds … daunting. You won't do a forward roll because you're afraid you might break your neck. Are you sure you're prepared for the physical challenge?"

"It'll be no different from walking a dog every day, and I've been doing that for years. I've probably racked up thousands of miles."

"The thing is, tackling the Coast Path won't be like taking Jess for her daily stroll. What you're proposing will be – "

I interrupted him. "The Coast Path finishes near Swanage."

"Ah," he said, and leaned back in his chair.

After twenty-five years of living in Cornwall, I still refer to Swanage as home. My idyllic childhood could be the reason for this: endless summer days spent on the beach, swimming before breakfast, playing beach boules, searching for crabs, snorkelling and eating chocolate sundaes while wrapped in towels on the steps of our beach hut. Those early years still resonated in my paintings, a tangible connection to my past – and to my mother. She died at forty-eight, leaving behind her seven children, of whom I was the third. When I returned to Swanage, I not only relived my childhood, but I also rekindled precious memories of my mum. And that connection forever makes Swanage my home.

"From the minute I set off," I smiled at Jack, "I'll be making my way home."

THE SOUTH WEST COAST PATH

The South West Coast Path stretches unbroken for an impressive six hundred and thirty miles, from Minehead in Somerset to Poole in Dorset. It was conceived as an ingenious way for the local coastguards to patrol the cliffs between lighthouses, on the lookout for smugglers. Years later, red-socked ramblers would replace the sharp-eyed coastguards, with the formation of the SWCP Association in 1973. Over time, the single sections of footpath have combined to create an entire trail, encompassing National Parks and World Heritage Sites, including the Jurassic Coast of Dorset. No wonder National Trails described the SWCP as one of the best long-distance hikes in the world, and the readers of Ramblers magazine voted it Britain's best walking route.

For those who relish a challenge, there are plenty of tough sections; the combined ascents and descents add up to the equivalent of climbing Mount Everest four times. For wildlife enthusiasts, the variety of coastal habitats provides an opportunity to see a range of mammals, reptiles and birds, including dolphins, seals, basking sharks, lizards, choughs, puffins and even adders. For the botanist there's sea thrift, common vetch, oxeye daisy and acres of heather and gorse. And for the gourmand? An endless diet of crab sandwiches, ice cream and pasties. The SWCP also provides a financial boost to the pubs, cafés and blister plaster vendors along the way, bringing in 300 million pounds annually.

THE SIDEKICK

With the decision to undertake my SWCP quest confirmed, I turned to the question of a companion. My choice was limited to my husband, Jack, and my dog, Jess. I quickly dismissed the idea of asking Jack, who, while fully supportive of my decision to do this, viewed any kind of exercise as a waste of time. Also, unlike me, he held down a proper job and couldn't possibly take seven weeks off. That left one candidate: Jess, my seven-stone Rhodesian ridgeback.

Lithe and sporty, ridgebacks are bred for endurance and stamina – handy when hunting lions – with a calm self-assurance that would be a comfort if the going got tough. So, the perfect sidekick you might say. But Jess is an anomaly. Where most dogs become infused with joy at the mention of a walk, Jess will invariably raise a lazy eyebrow and let out a deep groan of despair. Napping for hours while the world goes on around her, she lives a life of semi-hibernation, only emerging from her bed to eat and relieve herself. But I couldn't be choosy. A narcoleptic dog was better than nothing.

THE PLAN

Plenty of questions still needed to be answered. Where would we stay? Would we camp? What about B&Bs? Would they take dogs? How much would it cost? What about luggage? What did people do before the internet?

After several evenings spent running around the rabbit warren of the web, I settled on a plan. Jess and I would walk – that was the whole point after all – but it didn't need to be harder than necessary, so I booked a luggage transfer company to deliver our suitcases to B&Bs along the way. In keeping with my desire to make life easier, I asked a local walking company to arrange all the details, from booking dog-friendly accommodation to providing maps. They recommended leaving in September, when the weather would (hopefully) still be dry and warm, the kids would be back at school and, with the tourists gone, the B&Bs would be more likely to accept a one-night booking.

As the plan took shape, I pictured the walk in my mind: a carefree, sun-soaked adventure. Each morning would begin with a laid-back breakfast, then Jess and I would walk for a few hours. With all day to reach the next B&B, there would be plenty of time for both exercise and relaxation. I imagined sitting on harbour walls sketching boats. I'd find isolated coves and fish for bass or lie on the sand and read. If the weather became too hot I'd swim. If the weather turned wet we'd find shelter in a pub. The only challenge would be not ballooning in weight from scoffing cream teas, pasties and pints.

PACKING

Head full of idyllic images, I concentrated on the most crucial part of the preparation: buying the right accessories. My usual dog walking outfit consisted of trainers and jeans, but even I realised they'd be impractical for serious hiking. Wet jeans would chafe, and trainers aren't designed with vital ankle support and robust soles. I knew, from meeting plenty of bonafide ramblers on the coast, there existed a specific dress code made up of sturdy boots, thick socks, a plastic folder with a map hanging around the neck, walking sticks, a wide-brimmed hat and a smudge of sun cream on the nose.

Standing in the entrance of my local outdoor activity emporium, my eyes watered at the sheer range of things for sale: coats, hats, tents, torches, freeze-dried food, walking sticks, water bottles, whistles … the list went on. I took a deep breath and crossed the threshold.

Three youngsters in matching fleece tops with name badges were loitering around the tills. They turned their heads, sized me up, and resumed their conversation. Undeterred, I marched up to them. "Hi. I'm going to walk the SWCP and could do with some help."

They collectively raised their eyebrows.

The youngest assistant – once he realised I meant business – took responsibility for making sure I bought everything I needed to give me the best chance of survival: waterproof trousers that turned into shorts, water bottles without the bad-for-you plastics, socks that would let my feet breathe, a backpack that would let my back breathe, and an orange whistle, which the assistant warned me sounded as loud as a jet engine.
The final, and perhaps most important, purchases were a pair of leather boots and five pairs of thick wool socks. Two hours later, laden with bags, I tottered outside. Progress.

At home, I held a fashion show for a bemused Jack. All the fabrics felt completely different from my usual clothes – lighter and comfier, with the benefit of being water repellent. I regaled him with a new word – "self-wicking" – explaining it meant the fabric could actually pull sweat away from my body, thus keeping me cool. Instead of the expected gasp of amazement, Jack shook his head and left the room, leaving me to preen in front of the mirror. From then on, to get into the swing of things, I wore my kit during my daily outings with Jess and began the essential task of breaking in my new boots.

Not yet ready to stop spending, I bought two new suitcases – one for me and a much larger one for Jess, whose travel essentials included her mattress-sized bed, food, treats and a smart blue waterproof coat. And, a beautifully made, five-piece fishing rod, essential for the bass fishing I expected to do.

With a month still to go, I packed.

First my new wardrobe, then watercolours, watercolour paper, pencils, sketchbooks, reading books (x3), travel rod, lures, line, hooks, a selection of energy bars, boot cleaning kit, first aid kit, maps, travel books, MP3 player and – optimistically – sun cream.

Then I counted down to the big day.

THE WALK

DAY 1 – MINEHEAD TO PORLOCK

All too soon, the momentous day arrived. I woke with an itchy feeling of apprehension. Zipping myself into my uniform did nothing to ease my anxiety. I forced down a bowl of porridge and a cup of coffee, and fed a blissfully unaware Jess, who, of course, knew nothing about my objective. She raised an eyebrow when Jack and I carried the suitcases out to the car, but, not realising their significance, innocently jumped into the boot when I whistled. I offered to drive, grateful for something to take my mind off the situation. Just a little jaunt up the coast, I chanted in my head. Don't imagine going all the way back on foot. Don't think about Tintagel, Bude, Hartland and Lynton. Just grip the wheel and drive.

Two hours later, after a short detour to Porlock to drop the suitcases off at the first B&B, we arrived in Minehead and parked near the harbour.

Jack peered up and down the seafront. "What now?"

I put my rucksack on, tightened the straps, and rolled my shoulders to adjust the weight. "Over there, look." We strolled towards an impressive bronze sculpture of a pair of hands holding a map: the official start of the path. The official start of seven weeks of walking. Seven. Whole. Weeks.

Jack insisted on taking a photo while I jiggled from one foot to the other. After the photoshoot, I squeezed Jack tight and reassured him I would be okay. Jess would protect me. I'd ring every night, so he'd know we were safe. Then I walked away, on the look out for the signpost to Porlock.

After a few steps, I turned back to Jack. "I can't see the bloody sign."

"Lost already? Are you sure you're up for this?"

"Just help me look."

We headed for the harbour and happened upon the elusive sign, carved with an acorn. I gave Jack another hug. "Right, Jess, let's go."

Jack called to me, "Sash, just remember to keep the sea on your right."

I attempted a smile, but as he waved goodbye I felt as if the invisible tether tying me to the world I knew had been severed.

The initial climb through woods on the outskirts of Minehead rendered me flustered and short of breath – a swift lesson in my pitiful levels of stamina. My clothes felt tight, my rucksack heavy, and I couldn't settle into a comfortable pace. I took off my waterproof coat and jumper and folded them into my rucksack before having a drink of water. Feeling more composed, I set off again. Jess, in an uncharacteristic burst of energy, bounded in and out of the trees, thrilled to be somewhere new. It didn't take long for her enthusiasm to rub off on me. I stopped focusing on my discomfort. We were on our way!

At North Hill, we left the woods for a broad track cutting through heathland above the sea. I threw a stick for Jess. This was more like it: great views and no intimidating hills, precisely the kind of start I'd hoped for.

It didn't last long. On the other side of Bossington Hill we came to Hurlstone Combe and the treacherous descent of a shale-lined gorge. Taking a deep breath, I inched my way down, knees burning with the effort. Every step set off a miniature avalanche. Midway, the ground beneath me shifted and I fell back, bruising my elbows. Shaken, I scooted the rest of the way down on my bum. When I reached the base, I paused for a moment to let my legs get over the shock, snaffled a handful of nuts, and shared some water with Jess.

From our position I could see Porlock Bay and an ancient shingle embankment. Although going along the shore seemed the obvious route, the guide book warned against it, so we followed the path inland.

At a wooden bridge outside Bossington, we came across a man with two alpacas that were drinking from a stream. Jess let out a breathy woof and leaped back in surprise as one of the alpacas sneezed and pulled back its lips, revealing a conglomeration of teeth. Jess, tail between her legs, fled over the bridge while I waved apologetically at the man then jogged after her into the village. I knew, from reading the guide book, that a tea room existed somewhere in amongst the thatched cottages, but while attempting to find it I became lost – a remarkable achievement in a village of twelve houses.

Giving up on tea and cake, I continued my hunt for the acorn signpost. I turned along a quiet back road and after a time came to a T-junction. Standing on the verge I peered, squinty-eyed, left then right. An old man weaved up the road from the direction of the village. His breath reached us before he did; a pungent mix of beer and whisky. I asked for directions to Porlock and to my surprise he crooked his finger and motioned for us to follow him down a residential street. "This is me," he declared in front of a modest house, "and that's where you go." He showed me an overgrown track at the side of his front garden. We kept to a well-trodden path, around fields and through lanes to the village, and easily found the B&B. I let myself in with the key the landlady had given me, pushing through the oak door into a dark, low-ceilinged hallway, where I spied the grey outline of our suitcases leaning against the far wall.

Hearing noises from a side room, I peeked around the door to see a man lying on the sofa, engrossed in a cricket match. I cleared my throat. When that didn't work, I shuffled about in the gloom, but he ignored my ineffectual attempts to get his attention and kept his eyes firmly fixed on the game. At a loss, I flicked through a stack of pamphlets on a side table until a flood of light heralded the arrival of the female owner, who bustled into the hallway with a brisk: "Hello, did you enjoy your walk?" Not waiting for my reply, she motioned for us to follow, bounded up four flights of stairs to an attic bedroom, opened the door, invited us in, and promptly left.

I slumped onto the bed, shattered despite the relatively short nine-mile walk. Jess crumpled onto the carpet and fell asleep. Trying not to do the same, I opened a window, letting in the sounds of the street and a welcome waft of fresh air. Then I remembered our suitcases. I crept out of the room, not wanting to wake Jess, but as soon as she heard the door open, she hauled herself off the floor and tagged along. I lifted the smaller of the two suitcases up the four flights of stairs with little effort. But moving Jess's piano-sized suitcase drained all my remaining energy as I hauled it through the house, bumping up every step, resting on each landing, and wrestling its bulk through heavy fire doors. I left a trail of gouges, chipped paintwork and expletives behind me, but for all the commotion, no one offered to help.

Exhausted, I took a reviving shower and fed Jess. We ambled into the village for something for me to eat. A few doors down, I found a pub. After ordering a pint of beer, I settled at a table and opened the menu. Anything can appear exotic when you're not used to it, and I ogled over the standard pub fare with as much wide-eyed wonder as a diner in a Michelin-starred restaurant. Over the next seven weeks, pub food would lose its allure, but as I tucked into a plate of scampi and chips on the first evening of my adventure, I felt I'd never eaten a better meal.

The barman cleared my plate and I started a conversation with a couple on the next table. My sturdy boots and obligatory fleece jumper gave me away as a hiker and they asked how far I'd walked. "I've come from Minehead but I'm on my way to Poole." The woman frowned. "But that's in Dorset."

"I know, my dog Jess and I are going to walk the whole way in seven weeks."

The woman clapped her hands. "Marvellous. Aren't you brave?"

I admitted I'd feel less confident without my sidekick, who was taking a nap under the table. The discussion woke the butterflies in my belly, but I left the pub with a swagger, and with their wishes of good luck ringing in my ears.

Ensconced in our room, I unpacked Jess's bed and plonked her toy lion in one corner, then put a couple of bones in her food bowl. She helped herself to one, lay on her bed and methodically chewed it to bits, eyes half shut with pleasure. When she finished, I covered her in a blanket, leaving her nose poking out. She let out a deep, rumbling sigh and fell asleep.

I pulled off my boots, lay on the bed, and closed my eyes. Nine miles. The first of six hundred and thirty miles. And all to be done on foot. Blimey. After years of dreaming about it, I'd taken the first steps on my South West Coast Path adventure.

With effort, I rose, changed into my pyjamas, and slid under the covers.

Nine miles done.

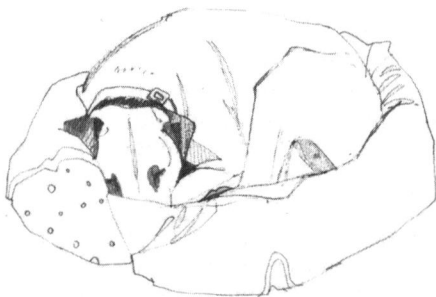

9.3 miles • 23,133 steps • Grading: Moderate

DAY 2 – PORLOCK TO LYNMOUTH

I woke early, after a disturbed night, my mind darting from one scenario to another. My head ached from thinking and my shoulders throbbed from carrying my rucksack, but nothing a couple of paracetamol and a cup of tea wouldn't fix. Sure enough, half an hour later, as the tea and painkillers kicked in, I started to feel better. Turning on the TV, I kept an eye out for the weather while brushing my teeth and getting changed. Then I filled my water bottles, checked for snacks, maps and wet weather gear, painkillers, notebooks, sketchbooks, pencils, watercolours, a fully charged phone, binoculars, camera and lip salve. Ready for day two.

Dogs were not allowed in the dining room of the B&B so I stuck my head around the kitchen door to ask for a takeaway bacon sandwich. The cricket man stood at the oven listening to his beloved game on the radio. He agreed to my request and was about to slide some rashers under the grill when his wife marched in and instructed me to leave Jess in the room and eat a proper sit-down breakfast. Too frightened to refuse, I dashed into the dining room, perched on the edge of the chair and consumed a bowl of cereal, a glass of orange juice and cup of tea, before racing up the stairs to the sound of muffled howling. On opening the door, a desperate Jess greeted me as if I'd returned from a tour of duty. That confirmed it – from now on we would have breakfast together or I would eat on the run.

Before we left, I reread the guide book to prepare myself for the moderate-to-strenuous twelve-and-a-half-mile day. Merely reading the word *strenuous* brought me out in a rash; up until now, my day-to-day walks could be described as ideal for families with young kids, the elderly and wheelchair users. Jess held no such reservations and appeared to be in unusually high spirits. Well, if a narcoleptic dog could rise to the challenge then so could I.

Following Jess's example, I left the B&B with a smile and a cheery "goodbye", determined to face my fears. We strolled through the village, turned left down a country lane and tramped through farmland to the edge of a flooded salt marsh. Ivory coloured trees, long dead, jutted at skewed angles from the marshy ground. A beady-eyed crow, hunched on a branch like a feathered fiend, enhanced their spooky appearance. The marshland butted up against a shingle bank and we scrambled onto it and crunched over the pebbles towards Porlock Weir.

Gathered around an ancient harbour, Porlock Weir is as pretty as a posy of daisies. Some of the cottages date back to the 17th century, with thatched roofs and pointy gables and enough character to make a watercolour artist swoon. I headed to the pub. Not for a drink – a bit early for me – but for the nearby signpost. At the back of the building a flight of steps led to a steeply sloping field. In no time I began to wheeze. I fought the urge to return to the pub for a fortifying shot of brandy and took a swig of water instead. We soon came to the ornate stone arch and thatched roof of Worthy Toll Road gatehouse, and from there strode through tunnels at the entrance to Yearnor Wood. Under the canopy, the air felt warm and still, the only sounds my ragged breath and occasional curse. No birds trilled through the branches, no insects buzzed: it was as if the wood's inhabitants were holding their breath, willing us to leave.

We pushed further into the trees on a path that snaked ever upwards. When we could go no higher, we turned a corner and I gazed down on an unexpected sight: a little church, half hidden in the trees. This, my guide book informed me, was Culbone Church, the smallest whole parish church in England. Eager to look inside, I crossed the churchyard and pushed open the satisfyingly creaky oak door. Immersed in the cool, dark atmosphere, I let my eyes adjust and then took a pew. With whitewashed walls and simple, carved, dark wood furnishings, the interior resembled a monk's cell. The air smelt of soil and mushrooms. Breathing in the history, I couldn't help wondering about the congregation who prayed, wept and celebrated in the intimate interior.

The arrival of two German backpackers interrupted my moment of reflection. Craning my neck, I wished them "good morning" in my church voice: a reverential whisper conveying sincerity and piety. They answered in the same manner before taking a seat. I left them to soak up the atmosphere in peace, woke the napping Jess, and stepped out into startlingly bright sunlight.

Back in the woods, and underway, I caught glimpses of a fellow walker zipping around the path like a manic wind-up toy. Slim and fit, he made me feel like a sloth. Although dressed in the right attire, beneath my self-wicking clothes I remained an amateur, a donkey in the Grand National. Fortunately for my self-esteem, the man cantered around a corner and out of sight, leaving me to plod on with some semblance of dignity.

We tramped through farms, and across fields separated by islands of trees. After weeks of rain, the grass grew knee-high, a vibrant apple green. Jess grazed happily on the juicy stems.

Dropping back into dense woodland, with waterfalls fringed in ferns, we came upon a pair of pillars, each crowned with a boar's head. Sunlight played on the honey-coloured stone and gave the sculptures a magical air, as if they might burst into life. The boars were protecting the entrance to Glenthorne House, whose driveway merged with the SWCP for a while, before the latter turned off onto rhododendron-choked paths.

Eventually, after a morning of dipping in and out of woodland, we stood on a rocky shelf, high above the sea. I glanced back at a series of headlands covered in trees that looked from a distance like broccoli florets. Far below us, waves slapped against the cliffs. Seagulls called to one another and were joined by a man-made noise, a rhythmic splashing and chugging. From out at sea the distinctive silhouette of the Waverley steamed towards us. The last sea-going paddle steamer in the world, she sat low and long in the water, her black and white paintwork and two scarlet funnels gleaming. Had I the energy, I would have sketched her – after all, that was part of the plan – but my body ached and we had miles to go. I watched her chug down the coast to Lynmouth, and slowly followed in her wake.

A mile or so further on, I finally caught up with the Wind-Up Man, only to discover *he* was an androgynous *she*. We began to talk, and I made the grave mistake of agreeing to join her. She accelerated away without a pause in the conversation, leaving me fighting for breath while trying desperately to act cool. Distracted by her chatter, I missed the sign for Lynmouth and followed her on an off-piste trek, a merry jaunt down to the lighthouse at Foreland Point. After taking photos, I expected to carry on around the headland, but no, we retraced our steps. She sped up the hill, still talking, while I lagged further and further behind. By the time I caught up with her, red-faced and sweating, she'd enjoyed a drink, snapped some photos and scrutinised her map. Puffing and panting, I shrugged off my rucksack and shared the last of my water with Jess as the monologue continued. Then, to my surprise, she broke wind. I took a step back, waiting for an apology, or laughter, but she didn't seem the least bit abashed. She maintained a steady releasing of wind as we set off again.

It's interesting how quickly a person can get used to an unusual situation, and after a while the sporadic sound of trumping melted into the background. Her excellent use of walking sticks interested me more. I owned a pair of Norwegian poles, which required a different technique to the arm pumping motion of my speedy friend – more like a cross-country skier without the snow or skis – but I'd put off using them because I thought I looked like a prat. However, after spending time in the Wind-Up Woman's company, I realised long-distance walkers were a breed apart; the standard rules of worrying about being regarded as a twit don't apply, they have a higher purpose. There and then, I made up my mind to start using my own sticks and embrace looking daft.

Near Lynmouth, the Wind-Up Woman grabbed the opportunity to add a couple more miles to her tally by investigating Countisbury's church – some way in the distance. I enthusiastically encouraged her, while muttering something about not being able to tag along because of my frail constitution. She threw me a look of disapproval and stalked off at breakneck speed.

Looking Back Towards Foreland Point

Able to slow down at last, I took the time to look around me. From Countisbury Common I looked back to Foreland Point. The cliffs were bathed in a warm coral blush. Here and there, rosebay willowherb added a hot pink in amongst the bracken and hawthorn. Turning the other way, I could see Lynmouth, hazy in the distance, the sun flashing off the cars as they travelled down the road towards the town. With my destination in sight, I spent the last mile dreaming of a cold drink and a lie down.

During the 19th century, tourists flocked to Lynmouth, lured by the attractive architecture, the local beach and the stunning coast. Two rivers – the East Lyn and the West Lyn – converge in the town before flowing past the harbour to the sea. Jess and I crossed over the East Lyn and I paused to look down at the trickle of water beneath me. Twenty-five years before, my six siblings and I had stood on the same bridge, listening as our father told us about the Lynmouth disaster. On 15th August, 1952 – after days of torrential rain on Exmoor – a wall of water descended on the sleeping village, killing thirty-four people and destroying many houses. All my petty aches and pains dissolved as I reflected on the drama of that night.

I soon located our B&B, and the landlady showed me to a comfortable ensuite at the top of the house, with the unusual feature of a sloping bathroom floor. Whether a quirky design fault or a sign of severe subsidence, I didn't know. Whatever the reason, the alarming tilt certainly added a frisson of danger to my bathroom visits. I unpacked and risked a shower, bracing myself to stop from sliding into the back wall of the cubicle, then fed Jess and went out for something to eat. At a hotel near the river, I ordered a ploughman's and a pint, and sat at a table outside. As soon as I relaxed my body began to complain; every bone from my hips downwards ached and my leg muscles stung as if they'd been whipped. It dawned on me that there was a world of difference between walking a dog every day and walking with a dog all day.

I peered down at Jess and wondered if she felt as sore as me. As an apology, when my food arrived I shared the wedge of cheese with her. Then I limped back to our room, towing Jess behind me, and, although early, I tucked her in and then climbed into my own bed, falling into a restless sleep.

18.1 miles • 46,076 steps • Grading: Moderate/Strenuous

DAY 3 – LYNMOUTH TO COMBE MARTIN

The next morning, I hauled myself out of bed feeling a hundred years old, swallowed a couple of painkillers, drank a cup of tea and staggered into the dining room. Two people dressed in similar attire to me sat at separate tables, and I chatted with them while devouring a full English breakfast. Both walkers had left Minehead on the same day as us and were taking on a chunk of the Coast Path. Jess flirted with Kipper, a scruffy terrier, while his owner Kelly and I discussed the route. Although early days, we agreed the unrelenting ups and downs were exhausting. I took comfort in the fact that other people were struggling. As I rose to leave, Kelly asked if I hoped to ride the cliff railway to Lynton, and I replied confidently that I thought I'd walk; I knew from the guide book the railway didn't open until ten and I wanted to make an early start. I took two bananas from the communal fruit bowl, said goodbye and ventured forth.

When I say ventured forth, I mean limped forth. I weaved along the pavement like a geriatric tortoise, ignoring the entrance to the cliff railway, and heading for the alternative option of a steeply zigzagged path. Left then right, I inched upwards. After my substantial breakfast, I felt uncomfortably full, and used this as an excuse to pause on every bend. But, with time and patience Jess and I reached the top. My amazement at completing the first challenge of the day quickly turned to frustration when I found myself outwitted by a gate. I couldn't work out how to operate the over-engineered latch. Luckily for me, no one witnessed my feeble attempts to pull, push and wiggle the lever until the gate swung open with a condescending creak. I gave it a hearty kick and staggered on.

On the other side of the gate, a flat tarmac path wound through the Valley of Rocks: monstrous boulders, dominated by Castle Rock, which soared hundreds of feet above the sea, with a configuration on top that resembled a man-made ruin. Those craving drama could clamber to the summit and see for themselves. However, I felt more than happy to take in the view from the safety of the footpath.

While I sketched, Jess loped ahead. When I caught up with her she was focusing intently on a wild billy goat blocking her way. I shot forward, grabbed her collar, and put her lead on, but she stayed rooted to the spot, beguiled. I could see the attraction: he was a splendid specimen, with thick horns that swept back from a heavy brow, a fringe, and ears like wing-mirrors. Not the least bit concerned by us, he scrambled up a rocky bank next to the path and climbed high over our heads, hooves scratching on the stone. As I followed his progress, other goats popped up from behind the rocks and looked down on us with their otherworldly eyes. These were the wild goats that for centuries had inhabited the valley, becoming as famous as the rocks themselves. They stared, unblinking, as Jess and I moved away. Their gaze made the hairs on my chin stand up. Something about those eyes.

We continued along a road that cut through the valley and passed the Devil's Cheese Ring – not a hellish kitchen gadget but another formation of rocks. Although impressive, I found it difficult to immerse myself fully in the grandeur of the landscape while keeping an eye out for cars. On the upside, using the road enabled Jess and I to make such good time that when we came across the Lee Abbey Tea Cottage, we took a break. I ordered a pot of tea and carried it outside to a table under the bough of an apple tree, decorated with a glass of wildflowers. Sipping from an elegant china cup, I listened to the sound of birds chirping in the branches above my head, and Jess snuffling in the grass for cake crumbs.

After draining the pot of tea I felt a rush of energy, and in a moment of madness I decided to take a voluntary detour around Crock Point. This involved a plod around three fields, a hike to the end of a stunted headland and a scramble up a wooded slope. And what did I gain after lumbering from the trees? A mere two hundred yards. I reined in my swearing in time to see my breakfast companions – Kelly and her terrier, Kipper – marching up the road. Sensibly, when she left the B&B she had ridden the cliff railway and ignored the detour, so easily caught up with us. I welcomed her company. She matched my gait exactly, due to the fact that she carried a backpack the size of a nine-year-old child, containing everything required to be self-sufficient, including Kipper's food. Her strategy relied on camping whenever possible and only using B&Bs when there were no campsites. Mightily impressed, I resolved to pull myself together – at least I took a hot shower, slept in a comfy bed and ogled *MasterChef* every night.

We strolled up the road and ducked into an oak wood, then jumped a stream beneath a waterfall at Hollow Brook. In seconds, the mist that had been hovering on the periphery of my vision all morning engulfed everything. The sudden loss of visibility and the unfamiliar landscape made me anxious, but Kelly brushed off my concerns. Clearly, unlike me, she felt at home hiking in all weather conditions. But she wasn't infallible, and after a while we became disorientated in the fog and, without realising, strayed away from the cliffs. After tramping through fields we found ourselves at the side of a deserted country road. Our maps were no help because we couldn't see any landmarks, but by keeping to the margins of the fields we backtracked and soon found our way to the right path.

With eyes peeled, we approached the steep slopes of Heddon's Mouth. On our descent, the mist drew back to reveal the valley walls smothered in ferns and, far below, a shingle beach and dilapidated lime kiln. At the bottom, the milky white vale swirled around us once more as we moved inland, crossed the valley floor and turned back to the sea. With no reference points, the ground beneath our feet provided the only clue as to where we were. This gradually changed from the hard packet stone of the cliffs to the heather and scree of Trentishoe Down. Afraid to wander, we kept to a deeply furrowed path scraped into the earth as if by the claws of a monstrous bear. Kelly stayed in front and I followed closely behind, fighting the urge to cling to the straps of her backpack.

We fumbled through the fog to Great Hangman, the highest point on the whole Coast Path at one thousand and forty-three feet. At Sherrycombe, to prepare for our hike to the summit, we took off our rucksacks and had a drink and a snack beside a brook. When it was time to go, I gallantly gestured for Kelly to lead the way. She politely declined. My mouth went dry. "Right, off we go then."

The track ran beside a scrubby wood and up rough steps carved into the earth. In no time, my thighs and calves burned. I could hear Kelly behind me, and tried to breathe through my nose to lessen the noise as I inhaled buckets of air. My ploy only made things worse and soon I was snorting like a congested cow. Kelly called out, "Are you all right?"

"I'm … absolutely … fine … thank you … couldn't … be better."

We hiked upwards over a sheer slope of gorse until the gradient lessened and we found ourselves, quite suddenly, on the summit. Endorphins rushed around my body, I laughed like a maniac, and Kelly and I shook hands, thrilled to have conquered one more obstacle.

After the initial euphoria of reaching the top, the summit was a let down, not helped by the fog obscuring the supposedly splendid views of Lundy Island and the coast of South Wales. Desolate and cold, the only point of interest was a stone cairn: no bunting, no sign with *Congratulations, you did it!* We snapped a few photos of each other posing in front of the cairn, and buggered off.

A plateau of heather covered the clifftops on the way to Combe Martin. In the distance, a break in the fog revealed the peak of Little Hangman. "My God, we don't have to climb that do we?" I blurted. "Check your map," Kelly instructed. With shaking hands I unfolded my map and located our position. "No, we can go around." With dusk nipping at our heels, a detour would have been a bad idea. Neither of us had packed a torch, and as the light faded, we sped up, eager to leave the cliffs. On the outskirts of the village I rang my B&B to assure them I hadn't fallen off a cliff. Kelly rang a local campsite, next to the SWCP, to book a pitch.

Before going our separate ways, we arranged to meet the next morning and walk to Woolacombe together. I thanked Kelly for her company, waved goodbye and watched as she lumbered up the hill, a backpack on legs. I walked the short distance to my B&B, grateful I wouldn't be spending the evening wrestling with tent poles and rehydrating Pot Noodles.

A ruddy-faced man with haystack hair opened the door of the B&B. "You must be Sasha and Jess. I'm Mac. We were worried about you."

"We got lost in the fog and then ..."

He put his hand up. "I know. It's a tough old walk. You should see the state of some of our guests after coming down from the Hangman. Now, can I offer you a drink? Tea, coffee ... a beer?" He opened the door to a communal sitting room with a built-in bar. "Wow, I'd love a beer, thank you." I shrugged off my rucksack and let it fall at my feet then clambered onto a barstool. Mac slid a glass of beer towards me, condensation dripping down the sides. I took a sip. "Perfect." A wave of exhaustion broke over me. I didn't ever want to move from that spot and I couldn't envision going back out for something to eat. As if reading my mind, Mac leant on the bar and asked if I wanted to have supper in the B&B. I replied, "Yes. Yes, please."

"Have a seat over there." He indicated a sofa with a low table in front of it. I collapsed into the soft cushions and Jess curled up under the table. A young geologist staying at the B&B came in and plonked himself next to me. "Wait until you taste his food," he whispered. "I don't ever want to go home."

Mac carried in a tray of delights. He placed bowls of refried beans, shredded chicken, rice, lettuce and guacamole in front of us, then returned with more bowls of grated cheese and sour cream. Finally he set a stack of steaming tortillas in the middle of the table. "Enjoy." I ate until my stomach ached. Barely able to keep my eyes open, I thanked Mac and he showed Jess and I to our room.

I fed a ravenous Jess then lay on the bed and reflected on our day. We'd racked up seventeen miles, including the highest point of the whole Coast Path. A fantastic achievement, but one which forced me to re-evaluate my expectations of this South West Coast Path adventure. The dichotomy between reality and the rosy-glowed jaunt of my imagination was becoming more evident. My naïve intention to pootle about, pausing here and there to paint, fish and even read, turned out to be bonkers. In truth, I'd wake up, swallow a couple of painkillers, eat breakfast, pack, trudge for hours, take two more painkillers, collapse into bed and sleep. Three days in, I realised I'd underestimated the toll the intense exercise would take on my body.

I needed to set realistic goals, which didn't include skipping along clifftops in a floaty nighty with the wind in my hair, a book of poetry in one hand and a pasty in the other. Time to get real. I resolved to concentrate solely on getting from A to B, immersing myself in the physical challenge. I knew the inspiration I sought would come naturally from the experience. The rest didn't matter. With my mind made up, I tipped the contents of my rucksack onto the bed, removed my watercolours, brushes and water pot, the novel and my five-piece fishing rod, and put them in my suitcase, leaving me with my essentials and a sketchbook.

Free, metaphorically and physically, from those self-imposed extracurricular activities, I went to bed full of expectation.

17.2 miles • 40,583 steps • Grading: Strenuous

DAY 4 – COMBE MARTIN TO WOOLACOMBE

Jess was welcome in the dining room the next morning and she dozed at my feet while I ate breakfast. Later, I thanked Mac for supper, packed, and ambled down to the beach to wait for Kelly and Kipper. A brisk easterly wind whipped off the sea, but the cloudless sky promised a fine day.

I hung around for half an hour, but the pair failed to turn up. Assuming they were running late, Jess and I set off to find them. The Coast Path went right through the campsite, above Sandy Cove, and I scanned the field for our missing companions. A handful of campers wandered around like pyjama-clad toothbrush-wielding zombies, but no sign of Kelly or Kipper. Torn between wanting to find her and the need to get going, I concluded she'd changed her mind about joining us. For all I knew she and Kipper might be hiding in a nearby bush waiting for us to push off. With no option, we left for Woolacombe, but I held out hope I'd bump into her later with a hilarious explanation.

From the campsite, we headed for Watermouth Harbour, protected by a verdant peninsula. A high tide covered the usual route over rocks, and we tramped along a road before re-joining the Coast Path. At Widmouth Head, I scrambled up a grass bank to look back at the harbour from the mouth of the inlet. In the distance, Little Hangman and Great Hangman soared above the cliffs like gigantic green limpets. I took a few photos, clambered down, and put my camera away. All of a sudden I heard a high pitched "Oooweeee!" and spun around to see Wind-Up Woman, poles akimbo, racing towards us.

"Shall we walk together?" she said.

To my dismay, I heard myself reply, "Why not?"

She sped off, spouting a stream of prattle.

An hour of high-speed walking later, Jess came up with an idea. She simply lay down.

I took the opportunity to have a drink and racked my brains for a way out of the situation. I tried pleading, "We can't keep up, just go on without us." This worked at first. She pulled out in front of us and out of sight, but later I found her lurking, like a drill sergeant, at the top of a flight of steps. To my mortification she watched me drag myself up, one painful step at a time, and when I got to the top, she commenced her monologue. A cold realisation hit me: short of breaking my leg and being airlifted off the cliffs, I would not escape her.

At Rillage Point I paused to give my shaky legs a rest. In the distance, Ilfracombe peeped out from behind the humpbacked Beacon Point. If I wanted to enjoy the town at my leisure, with no distractions, I needed to ditch my chatty companion. Fortunately, a chance meeting with a couple in a car park gave me the opportunity. The couple owned a ridgeback puppy, and on meeting Jess, they asked to introduce them. While we cooed over the dogs, Wind-Up Woman began rolling her eyes and tapping her watch. I turned on her and through gritted teeth said, "If you have somewhere you need to be then just go on without us." Maybe my barely suppressed anger finally made a dent in her shell; she turned on her heel and strode away.

I continued stroking the puppy and talking to the proud parents, waiting for my heart to stop hammering in my chest, then set off down the hill to Hele Bay. From there, Jess and I climbed to Beacon Point then ambled across a common into Ilfracombe. In no rush, we made our way to the harbour through St James' Park, beneath a row of imposing townhouses. At a fishmonger on the quay, Jess and I investigated a stack of freshly cooked lobsters cooling on a table outside. Jess couldn't resist a sniff, and I did a quick sketch. We pottered around the quay, and I sketched the chapel of St Nicholas on top of a grass-covered cliff above the harbour. Dating from the 14th century, the building's purpose has changed many times over the years, from a family home to a reading room, a laundry and a working lighthouse.

Ilfracombe

On our way through the town, I saw an ice cream van and bought us each a lolly. We crossed a park and then kept to a road above low cliffs. Below us was the famous Tunnels Beaches, a rocky cove with a tidal pool accessed through tunnels carved into the rock by Welsh miners in 1820. The tunnels were a clever idea to encourage more tourists to visit the town during the Victorian era. With easy access to beaches from the town centre, Ilfracombe then flourished from a fishing port to a holiday destination.

From the road, we climbed a switchback path onto cliffs above the town. "How lovely," I remarked to Jess. Before us, pea green fields gently rose and fell, stretching into the distance. A flock of black-faced sheep raised their faces for a second, saw we posed no threat, and continued munching. As I prepared to stride into this picture of perfection, I noticed a figure on a bench at the side of the path. My heart sank. Wind-Up Woman.

In a fluster, I cantered past her with a quick "Hi", hoping to create ample distance between us while she finished her lunch. When I risked a glance back, she was stuffing her sandwich in her mouth and preparing to leave. I yelled, "My God, Jess, run." We hurtled up and over a hill and were headed for a ridge when I became aware of a prickling sensation on the back of my neck and turned to see Wind-Up Woman racing up the slope towards us.

Once again she launched into a discourse about herself, with the addition of a fart like an exclamation mark at the end of each sentence. Her words melted into the background as I concentrated on breathing and watching my feet. But then I became aware that she was saying something of value. Hidden in the drivel were three pieces of advice, which shone like gold nuggets in a mound of coal. Number one: remember to look back – often the view behind is better than the one in front and can easily be missed. Number two: plan to be in a specific place by midday – a town, village or headland – as this splits a drawn-out day into two manageable chunks. Number three: when you are on a flat or boring stretch of path, speed up, then you can take your time and enjoy the scenic sections.

I'd never given a moment's thought to the logistics of a long-distance walk, and assumed you kept going until you reached your destination. These three rules would provide some welcome structure. She added one more, which explained her frenetic tempo: whatever happens, keep going, for you never know when the weather conditions might change for the worse.

After the revelation of the rules, she reverted back to speaking twaddle. I tuned out.

In my semi-conscious state, I trailed behind her through the tiny hamlet of Lee Bay. The low tide exposed a network of rock pools. Kids with prawn nets scrambled around the shore and dogs splashed in the shallows.

On the other side of the bay, we tramped up a road shaded by trees. Back on the cliffs, we clambered in and out of gorges and up stone stairways. The heat from the sun increased, sapping my remaining energy. Jess and I plodded in slow motion, heads bowed, until finally we ground to a halt on a grassy plateau above a beach. Below us, more kids and dogs played in the surf while adults lazed about on brightly coloured towels. A different world. These people were not marching like crazy automatons; they relaxed in the sun with no worries about time or random weather patterns.

The water looked so inviting. I announced in a loud voice that Jess and I wanted to cool off and have a paddle. Wind-Up Woman, some way ahead, stalked back to us and reminded me of the possibility of a dramatic change in conditions. Too exhausted to put up a fight, I wilted under her disapproval. She stomped off, and Jess and I meekly followed. I felt my face grow hot. Why did I allow myself to be dictated to by a stranger? I knew the reason. Although I was embarrassed to admit it, I didn't trust my abilities. Out of my comfort zone, I'd begun to rely on others, especially those I perceived as seasoned hikers. But they had their own agenda. When would I get it? The only person I could rely on was me.

For now, I concentrated on the one task of getting to Woolacombe and as far away as possible from Wind-Up Woman. Thankfully, we reached the town in plenty of time, without encountering anything wilder than a gentle breeze. The locals were enjoying the unusually warm September sun, many wearing flip-flops and shorts. But the jolly atmosphere did little to lift my spirits. I wanted only to find my B&B and sleep.

Dumping Wind-Up Woman outside her hotel, Jess and I went in search of our own B&B. My map showed it was on the outskirts of the town. We set off up a congested main road with no pavement, and Jess, rattled by the fumes and noise, played up. I fought back the tears while dragging her behind me shouting, "Come on, Jess, come on." On the brow of the hill, a handwritten sign pointed down an overgrown bridleway. Desperate to get off the road, I pushed through the bushes. At the end of the track, I saw a farmhouse. Three feisty dogs raced at us as we approached. A woman called them back while I shouted over their barks for directions. She answered, "You're not far, love. Turn right at the end of the lane."

Sure enough, the B&B was nearby, and it was worth all the effort. Up above the town, the views were spectacular, sweeping over Morte Bay to Baggy Point. Even better, the room came with a conservatory and private veranda. Faced with such luxury, I cancelled any thoughts of going back into the town for supper. After I'd unpacked and fed Jess, I asked the owner if she would mind making me a cheese and tomato sandwich, which I carried out to the veranda with my book. Later, as the sun set, I took a cup of tea outside and drank it as I watched the sky turn red, a cow's mournful bellow drifting across the fields.

When the temperature dropped, I went inside and noticed the ensuite was fitted with a heated towel rail. I washed my pants, socks and trousers, leaving them to drip dry in the shower before folding them over the warm rail. Although early, I didn't have the energy to watch TV or even read, so I went to bed. As I closed my eyes, I remembered Kelly and Kipper. With everything else that happened, I'd forgotten about them. I could only hope they were safe and well. However, the unresolved mystery did nothing to help my state of mind. Needless to say, sleep came slowly.

16.3 miles • 38,459 steps • Grading: Moderate

DAY 5 – WOOLACOMBE TO BRAUNTON

I woke after a broken night, partly spent pondering the possible fates of Kelly and Kipper, and partly spent berating myself for being weak-willed and easily led by Wind-Up Woman. On autopilot, I fumbled through my morning routine.

Over breakfast, the B&B owner drew me a map showing a shortcut to the coast through farmland. After a pleasant stroll through fields, we emerged above Woolacombe Beach, then walked through a car park and dropped down onto the sand. Jess ran in the shallows and cavorted about, spinning and then stopping, before launching herself into the air and spinning again. I felt like doing the same.

At the end of the beach, we walked through Putsborough Sands Caravan Park (surprisingly busy for the time of year) and onto the headland. The laid-back start to the day made a change. I usually kept a careful eye on where I put my feet, to prevent a broken ankle, but on the flat clifftop I could keep my head up. I watched an orange fishing boat chugging across the vast expanse of Morte Bay. When I lost sight of it, I took out my binoculars and scanned for seals bobbing in the water.

Something up ahead caught my attention: two people hovering next to a stile taking photos. Intrigued, I caught up and peeked over their shoulders to see a pair of fat bellied lizards soaking up the sun on a wooden post. I hadn't seen a lizard since my childhood. In my youth, my parents ran a B&B on the cliffs above Swanage Bay, with private steps to the beach, which were home to a community of lizards. When the weather warmed up I spent hours crouched, motionless, waiting for them to scurry out and sunbathe. Delighted by the rare sight, I took a couple of photos. As I put my camera away, I heard the familiar and spine-chilling "YOOHOO!" and turned to see my living nightmare gaining on us at speed.

The lizards scarpered and I prepared to plunge into the bushes after them, but left it too late. This time there were no formalities, simply an assumption we would carry on as normal. We walked, and Wind-Up Women talked, and I used the time to formulate my escape. As we approached Baggy Point, I told her I needed to make a phone call and would catch up with her later. This was true – I hoped to get a signal so I could ring Jack to give him an update. At the end of the headland, I waved her on and perched under a wooden wreck post to phone home.

Thirty minutes later, sure that by now she would be far away, I walked around the headland. To my dismay, I saw her waiting on a bench. Fortunately, she was hunched over a map and didn't notice Jess and me tiptoe behind her and sneak around the back of a hedgerow. Using the vegetation as a shield, I peered out of a gap in the leaves to see if she went by. I stayed for five minutes then, calling Jess, made a break for it.

By the time we reached Croyde Bay, I felt confident she'd gone on. Jess and I stopped at an ice cream van and I bought a couple of lollies. As I handed over my money, I felt a tap on my shoulder and heard a breathy voice say, "I've been looking for you." I swung around and stared into the wide eyes of Wind-Up Woman. Innocently, she asked if I would like to carry on walking with her, adding how much she'd enjoyed our time together. I blinked, astounded by how out of touch with reality she was. I took a deep breath, and in a voice cracking with emotion said, "Jess is exhausted, I am exhausted, I can't keep up with you, I am not fit enough, I am not enjoying myself, I HAVE DODGY KNEES. Please, PLEASE go on without us." Her face crumpled. I felt as wretched as if I'd poked a puppy in the eye. But my harsh words worked. Without saying a thing – a first – she turned, marched into the dunes and vanished from sight. I felt ecstatic. I gave Jess a hug. "We're free, Jessy, free!"

Croyde Beach

I delayed setting off, and kept to the beach rather than the dunes, to be doubly sure we wouldn't meet her again.

The beach was dissected by a shallow stream, and as I searched for a good place to ford, I met Geoff, who'd stayed in the Lynmouth B&B. He confided the Coast Path was tougher than he imagined and wanted to call it a day at Braunton. Caught up in the conversation, I naturally began to walk beside him. When would I learn? Despite my best intentions, I'd latched on to another walking companion. In his favour, he moved at my kind of speed, probably due to his age. He was in his seventies, trim in blue shorts and t-shirt, and liked the challenge of a long-distance trek, but the hot weather had sapped his energy, as had the backpack he carried, which surely weighed the same as Jess. I fared better with my handbag-sized rucksack, but it still came as a relief to round the headland and be smacked in the face by a reviving sea breeze.

From our blustery vantage point, we surveyed the expanse of Saunton Sands. The sea looked so inviting that on our way to the beach Geoff and I agreed we would paddle rather than go the official route through the dunes.

Making our way to the water's edge, we weaved through sunbathers, windbreaks, picnic blankets and parasols. Closer to the sea, dozens of surfers and bodyboarders dashed in and out of the waves. In the middle of it all, a huddle of kids dressed in wetsuits watched intently as a handsome instructor showed them how to stand on a surfboard; a lot easier to do on the beach than in the sea. Finally, at the edge of the water, I took off my boots and socks, tied them to my rucksack, and waded up to my knees in the shallows. Utter bliss. Geoff did the same, and Jess – not always a fan of water – also paddled. For an hour we sloshed through the surf, feet tingling as the salt and sand worked their magic.

At the end of the beach we trudged barefoot into the dunes at the mouth of the River Taw, put on our boots and snaffled a snack and some water. Getting ready to leave, I turned right, knowing if we stuck with the river it would lead straight to Braunton. Geoff, meanwhile, struck out into the dunes. I knew he was going the wrong way, but said nothing. As we moved further still from the river, I voiced my concern. "Um, Geoff, I don't think this is right. The river is behind us." He replied, "No, I think you will find this is the right way." My eyes burned into his back. Why couldn't I tell him to bugger off and do my own thing? What stopped me?

After an hour, we saw in the distance the same complex of cafés and surf shops we'd left two hours earlier. My knees went weak. Faced with the evidence, Geoff finally admitted, "I think we may have gone the wrong way." I chewed my lip, too frustrated to answer. He continued, "I'll double check with my GPS." He had a bloody GPS! He turned it on and sheepishly agreed we were miles from where we should be. There and then I made a vow never to walk with another person. Under. Any. Circumstances. EVER.

Before I could act on my vow, Geoff and I needed to find the correct path and get out of the dunes. Between us, we studied the map and discovered a road that would eventually lead to Braunton. We set off in silence. Geoff, shoulders hunched, led the way, while I pulled and cajoled Jess, who was on the verge of revolt.

We were a sorry threesome as we reached the outskirts of Braunton. Dehydrated and desperately needing to sit down, I staggered into the first pub we came across. Jess barely made it through the door before she collapsed in the middle of the bar like a hairy sack of spuds. Sick with guilt, I fetched her a bowl of water and a packet of pork scratchings. Geoff ordered two pints, which we downed in seconds before turning our attention to the menu. The pub did fantastic Thai food. I ordered enough for two and ate the lot. Then, after a muted goodbye, I left Geoff in the pub, and Jess and I staggered to our B&B.

That night, while brushing my teeth, I noticed a row of unsightly white blisters on my lips, no doubt caused by the sun and wind. They stood out against my sunburnt skin, but didn't hurt. I put Vaseline on them and hoped for the best.

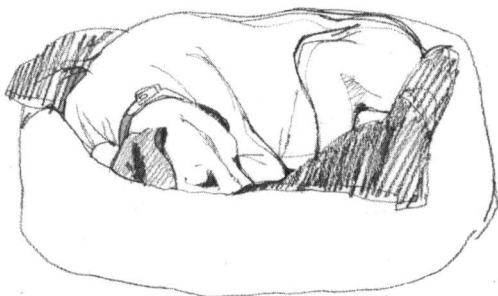

19.6 miles • 48,706 steps • Grading: Easy/Moderate

DAY 6 – BRAUNTON TO WESTWARD HO!

I woke on a low ebb after a painful night. My hips ached, and sharp pains stabbed through my big toe. The pain wasn't the only reason for the bad night. I lay awake questioning my apparent inability to do anything on my own, and the effect my bad decisions were having on Jess. I could only hope that as we both got fitter, I would become confident in my abilities and start to take control of our walk.

For the time being, Jess needed time off. So I came up with an idea. Originally, I thought we would complete a whopping twenty-four miles in one day, most of it on flat cycle tracks. Neither of us were in a state to go that far. Instead, I decided we would do the six miles to Barnstable, then hop on a bus to Appledore for a pub lunch and an afternoon of relaxation. Unfortunately, I couldn't convey this to Jess, who was in no mood to go anywhere. I buttered her up by giving her the sausage from my full English breakfast, promising more in Appledore.

After breakfast we left Braunton for the Tarka Trail on the banks of the River Taw. Initially we kept to the shade under an avenue of oak trees, but once in the open the sun felt like a hot weight pushing down on us. Jess wilted. Every time I paused to take a photo or do a sketch, she crumpled across the path, a slumbering roadblock. Her size caused a problem. We weren't the only ones using the Tarka Trail, and as the morning progressed, so did the number of cyclists. I spent much of the time either pulling Jess out of the way or apologising as cyclists swerved around her.

On our approach to RMB Chivenor, the rhythmic sound of boots crunching on gravel warned me to pull Jess to one side as a squad of soldiers, sweating testosterone, jogged past. On cue, the theme tune from *An Officer and a Gentleman* popped into my head. I hummed as I watched them disappear. What with the soldiers and cyclists, the Tarka Trail attracted a lot of people, and I could see why. Mere minutes from the busy town, we were surrounded by trees and water, totally immersed in nature. With no wind, the river was flat calm, and reflected clouds floated across the surface. The opposite bank appeared blue in the haze, with the smoky outline of trees in the distance. We passed a houseboat with bicycles and fishing rods propped up on deck next to a pile of neatly stacked firewood, the aroma of coffee escaping from an open porthole.

Further on, I saw a lizard in the middle of the path. Three in two days! As I gently placed it in the grass, away from the threat of boots and bikes, Jess ground to a halt. I crouched next to her, coaxing her on with the promise of a packet of pork scratchings when we got to Appledore. While encouraging her to get up, I saw Geoff in the distance. He gained on us fast. Jess greeted him with a slow wag of her tail and sleepy grin. He caught his breath. "I can't stop, I'm catching a train from Barnstable. I need to get home, but I'll be back to do the rest."

"Maybe go on a map reading course first," I murmured as he scurried away.

Soon after, Jess and I reached Barnstable, and in a stroke of luck found our bus idling at the terminal. We went straight to the back and Jess fell into a heap, with one paw resting on the foot of the gentleman next to me. She didn't stir for the whole journey. I felt hot and sweaty and wanted nothing more than to sit in peace and gaze out of the window. The girl in front of me swivelled around to ask, "What kind of dog is it?"

I sighed. "She's a ridgeback."

"She is asleep, look."

"Mmmmm."

"She's thinking, 'Naughty mummy for tiring me out.'"

You have no idea, I thought.

We got off the bus at Appledore and sat outside a pub in the sun, listening to the local fishermen discuss their day's catch. Later, I bought two postcards and a slice of quiche from a deli, and found a bench looking across the estuary to Instow. While I ate and watched the boats zipping up and down the estuary, Jess slept, recharging her batteries. Time slipped by and, after an amble around the cobbled backstreets, I decided to move on.

A short bus ride later we arrived in Westwood Ho! On the way into the town, I could see that the break in Appledore had worked wonders on Jess; she seemed perkier and less inclined to fall asleep at a moment's notice. We blended into the crowds bustling about the cafés near the seafront, and walked past beach shops, the gaudy buckets and spades, fishing nets and lilos spilling onto the pavement. The unusually warm weather created a laid-back atmosphere, and the outdoor seating areas in front of the bars and pubs thronged with happy drinkers getting sozzled in the sun.

I craved a different atmosphere for supper, nothing too raucous, and no loud music. We left the seafront and, on the way to our B&B, we came upon a pub tucked away from the rabble. We sat in a conservatory and I wolfed down a burger and chips and drank a glass of wine. Then, with me feeling guilty because I hadn't fed Jess, we left for the B&B.

High above the town, I hoped for a room with a sea view. But Jess and I were relegated to a side room with a view of a brick wall and a neglected garden. I'd come to realise most B&Bs had a "dog" room: not quite as well furnished as the other rooms, a bit more lived in, the carpet dotted with stains and the door scarred by scratches. Not that I really minded. By the time I collapsed into bed I felt too done in to worry about watching the waves.

Long overdue, I fed Jess, then tucked her in and put the TV on for the weather forecast.

8 miles • 20,444 steps • Grading: Easy

I awoke to find I couldn't feel my big toe. This struck me as better than stabbing pain, but worrying nonetheless. I wriggled, pinched and jabbed it, but the digit remained stubbornly numb. With no alternative, I put my socks and boots on, thinking the toe would come back to life as the day progressed. The blisters on my lips were another matter. During the night they had burst and were now raw and throbbing. Even a weak smile caused such pain it brought tears to my eyes. I applied a liberal amount of antiseptic cream and slathered on Vaseline. Despite my ailments, I was full of excitement at the prospect of meeting Jack at Clovelly later in the day. He and I often talked about visiting the village, and it just so happened my arrival there coincided with our wedding anniversary, so we were going to have a night together.

First, breakfast. With half my face peeling off, I looked a mess, so I greeted Jess's banishment from the dining room with relief. We sat on our own in the large entrance hall, the fancy candelabra above our table only serving to heighten my scruffy appearance. I nodded sheepishly at the pristine guests as they filed into the dining room. The landlady must have mentioned our adventure to one or two people, and as I carefully sipped my second cup of tea, trying to avoid the rim from burning my lips, a husband and wife approached and asked to shake my hand. They were amazed at what we were doing and wanted to say well done and good luck. This recognition from strangers gave me a real boost and I left the B&B feeling invincible.

The sun was still rubbing sleep from her eyes as Jess and I made our way out of town through a cold mist, past a line of painted wooden beach huts. I pushed through a gate that led to a tarmac path, and we were soon back on the coast. Ahead of us stretched verdant fields, but the Coast Path, as if not wanting to trespass, kept to the periphery, hugging the low cliffs. Due to the shape of the terrain and the curve of the coastline, I could see Clovelly way off in the distance, the harbour lit up in the sun at the bottom of a tree-covered valley. The village looked deceptively near, but I knew it would take eleven miles of effort to get there.

It wasn't long before the open fields turned into steep troughs and peaks along confined paths. At the same time, the early morning mist burned off and the sun, now wide awake, blazed down. In pockets of shade, the lush grass on either side of us dripped with dew and my legs became soaked through. Jess, coming up behind me, got the full brunt of it in her face. The increasing warmth did nothing to help my lips, which were an excruciating source of agony. I'd never experienced such searing pain. The merest touch of the sun caused me to wince, and I folded them together in a kind of "MMMMMM" in order to get some relief.

Up and down, down and up, the morning progressed, and my energy levels remained high as the anticipation of seeing Jack increased. Soon we entered the welcome shade of Worthygate Woods and after a time came into the tiny hamlet of Bucks Mills. An enterprising local had cut a hatchway into the side of their house from which to sell ice creams and hot drinks. I bought a vanilla ice cream for Jess and a cup of tea for myself.

The sea was visible in a gap between two cottages, and nearby I spotted access to a beach via a sloping lane. Halfway down the slope perched a tiny house with apple green windows and doors. Consisting of just two rooms, the bijou dwelling resembled a gingerbread house in a children's book, but had been an artist's studio for many years. Beyond the house, overlooking the beach, sat two ramshackle lime kilns shrouded in ivy. These were used to manufacture lime to fertilise the nearby fields.

As well as farming, the village once retained a harbour and a fishing fleet, but sadly nothing remained of either now. What did remain were wonderful views up and down the shore. To my right, the startlingly red cliffs of Peppercombe, and to the left – closer than I imagined – Clovelly Harbour. If I acquired a boat, I could sail up the coast into the harbour and be drinking a cold beer in no time. But, by foot, Clovelly was still miles away.

Leaving the beach, I located the Coast Path between two cottages, and Jess and I stepped into the cool, musty interior of Bucks Valley Woods. Giant beech trees grew from a carpet of ferns and lined the path. The canopy blocked all light, except the bright lozenges of sunlight that found a way through the gaps in the leaves and flickered on the forest floor. All was still, but as we travelled further into the trees people appeared in twos and threes. After greeting a dozen or more, I asked a perspiring middle-aged woman the reason why, and she explained they were walking the sixteen miles from Clovelly to Appledore to raise money for the Appledore Lifeboat. For over an hour, I wished "good morning" and "good luck" as a procession of bodies toddled, waddled and hobbled past.

The last stragglers, red-faced and sweaty, trudged by, and the woods fell silent once more. At a break in the trees we found ourselves in sharp sunlight at the edge of an immense wheat field. Clouds streaked through the deep blue sky and the air felt crisp after the humidity of the woods. Jess, in fine form, bounded through the wheat, her back arched, her arse in the air like a hairy porpoise.

Returning to the woods, the haphazard trail opened onto Hobby Drive, a three-mile bridleway built between 1811 and 1829 to maximise the bird's-eye view of Clovelly Harbour below. White benches dotted along the way provided an irresistible excuse to rest, and I took full advantage of them. We continued on until, at a bend in the path, a sharp cry of alarm triggered dozens of hysterical quails to burst from the trees and run hither and thither like ants around a dollop of jam. More quails burst from the bushes, a miniature Mardi Gras of feathers and commotion. I put Jess on her lead for fear she might chase them into the ravine at the side of the path, but – overwhelmed by their numbers – she stayed at my side.

Looking Down Through the Trees to Clovelly Harbour

Not long afterwards, we arrived at the outskirts of Clovelly and pushed through a gate into a car park. Nothing unusual about that, you might say, but the visitors' centre, café, souvenir shop and charge of admission to get into the village did seem out of the ordinary. The reason for the unorthodox admission fee is that Clovelly is a private village, owned by the Hamlyn family. The money raised goes into a pot, along with rent from the villagers, and is used to keep Clovelly as it has always been: stuck in time but not decaying. A living museum.

We tagged behind a group of tourists on the way into the village and stopped when they did to pet two donkeys standing, heads bowed, at the top of the cobbled hill. Cars are not allowed in the village, and the locals had the ingenious idea of using sleighs to transport everything from shopping to children up and down the hill. The donkeys helped in this endeavour, pulling the heavier loads. Placid and calm, they didn't appear fazed by the attention, and put up with the selfies and strokes.

What a lovely introduction to the village. I couldn't wait to see more. Luckily the B&B was conveniently situated at the top of the hill. I checked in, fed Jess, unpacked, and, with plenty of time to spare before Jack arrived, popped over to the pub on the other side of the street for a ploughman's.

After lunch, Jess and I set off for the harbour. I immediately noticed the contrasting expressions on people's faces, depending on whether they were going down or up the hill. I, and everyone else going down, wore the relaxed face of a person at ease with the world, thoroughly enjoying the quaint village. But those on the way up looked tortured, their faces full of regret at ever agreeing to the apparently innocent proposal of, "Shall we pop down to the harbour?" As I passed them, an uncharitable thought came into my mind: "What a bunch of unfit lard-arses. It's only a bloody hill."

I would learn the truth soon enough. For now I enjoyed a pleasant stroll down the cobbled high street, pausing to peer in the window of the village post office. Urchins and starfish, conch shells and even pufferfish were on display with boxes of fudge and painted wooden boats. Nearby stood a red phone box, in keeping with the old-world feel of the village. I couldn't help wondering if it worked or was merely a prop. Further down, a front garden overflowed with butter yellow evening primrose, pink anemones and roses, filling the air with their perfume.

At the bottom of the hill we walked to the end of the harbour wall, around the neatly stacked lobster pots, tangles of rope and sun-bleached buoys. I gazed back at the village. A tumble of houses clung for dear life to the valley walls, like mussels on a rock. A terrace of houses, each with a different veranda, and a lifeboat station with bright red double doors, sat atop a slipway. The smart Red Lion pub, painted a pristine cream, dominated the harbour itself.

The tide was out, and Jess and I wandered in between the resting fishing boats, jumping the ropes that tethered them to the shore. Standing at the water's edge, I squinted my eyes against the bright baubles of light dancing on the surface of the sea, and scanned the horizon. In the haze, the sky and sea melted together; a boat moored off shore appeared to be floating on air. We moseyed further along the beach and I skimmed stones and threw a stick for Jess. My phone rang. "Hey, it's Jack, I'm not far now." I called Jess: "Let's go."

Not long into my journey up the hill, I regretted my blasé comments on the questionable fitness of my fellow visitors. At the top of a flight of steps leading out of the harbour, I began to wheeze, my chest heaving. I paused for a minute and set off again. The gradient slowly got worse. "I'll just … stop here … and … admire this … blackboard," I said for the benefit of anyone listening, and pretended to read a tea room menu, waiting to get my breath under control. Near the top I ground to a halt once more to take a photo of an interesting plant, taking more time than necessary, and finally made it back to the B&B.

Ensconced in our room, I ran a quick bath, brushed my hair, and applied some mascara and a bit of blusher. My blistered lips were beyond repair, but I slathered on a glob of Vaseline and prayed Jack wasn't wearing his glasses. Perched on the edge of the bed, I waited for the knock. Minutes later, Jack turned up with a big smile and a hug. Jess, surprised to see him, wagged her tail so enthusiastically she sent my pot of Vaseline flying across the room. The seven days away from home felt like a lifetime and I couldn't wait to tell Jack everything. We made two cups of tea, took off our shoes, sat back on the bed and I recounted my adventure: windy Wind-Up Woman and her three golden rules, my ongoing low stamina, Kelly and Kipper's mysterious disappearance, overdosing on scampi and chips, and on and on.

Later, we ambled down to the Red Lion for a celebratory drink and were surprised to meet two friends from home. After much merriment at the odds of bumping into each other, we agreed to hook up later for a drink before going our separate ways. Jack,

Jess and I entered the bar. Three locals sat around a table. One of them was an alarming shade of pink and quaffed her pint as if it was water. My trained eye deduced she'd recently walked at speed for many miles. Either that or she had an unfortunate skin condition and suffered from alcoholism. After Jess broke the ice by going over to see if she had any crisps, I found out my hunch was right. The exhausted woman had won the RNLI Station to Station Sponsored Walk, completing it in the same time as Jess and I took to finish eleven miles. I bought her a drink to celebrate, and Jack and I pulled up a couple of chairs. Later our friends turned up and joined the party.

Before I started seeing double, I decided to call it a night. Jack wanted to stay for a nightcap or two so I put Jess on her lead, wished everyone "good night" in a raised voice, and left the pub. As the door closed behind us, Jess caught sight of a cat and shot off with me in tow. Surprised, but sober enough to realise this could work to my advantage, I encouraged her to pull me with her. The first cat fled into a garden, but she soon spied another and set off once more. In this unconventional but highly effective manner I returned to the B&B in record time and without breaking a sweat. Once there, I tucked Jess in, drank a pint of water and flopped into bed.

11 miles • 28,115 steps • Grading: Strenuous

The next morning, after a much-needed breakfast that included two paracetamol, Jack and I drove to Hartland Quay. I wanted him to get an idea of the magnificent coastline Jess and I had experienced, and I wasn't ready to say goodbye. Leaving Clovelly, we drove along the coast to Hartland Point, a remote location and a dramatic change from the previous day's low cliffs and woods. Standing on the edge of a scree-smothered slope, I peered down at the lighthouse, which remained partially hidden by a bulbous rocky promontory. The low tide revealed the twisted, rusted metal of a shipwreck, lying like a broken toy at the foot of the cliffs. The sight of it served to accentuate the real dangers of the coast and added to the bleak atmosphere. It became clear why Hartland Quay to Bude held the reputation of being the toughest sixteen miles of the whole SWCP. The more I saw, the more I worried I might not be up for the challenge, but for the time being I kept my doubts to myself and made the most of being with Jack.

We carried on up the coast, driving for a while and walking here and there. At Morwenstow we happened upon the National Trust's smallest property, the famous Hawker's Hut, a wooden construction on the side of the cliff, built from old ship's timbers. Lowering my head, I ducked inside and sat on the slatted bench that hung from the walls. In the gloom, I squinted at a hundred years of graffiti, carved or scribbled over every available surface. Far from being an eyesore, the graffiti added to the feeling of history. For all its wonky construction, the hut was beautiful, and a fitting memorial to the eccentric vicar, Robert Steven Hawker, who built it. When not smoking opium and writing poetry, he made sure any shipwrecked souls stranded on the treacherous rocks below were given a proper Christian burial in his churchyard a mile inland.

From Morwenstow, we followed the coast road, pulling in every now and then to get out of the car and savour a view. At Bude, Jack declared he'd endured ample exercise and wanted to go home. So, we drove back to Harland Quay, not far from my B&B for the night, and said goodbye. I watched the car disappear from view. Now what? I stared out to sea. Jess leaned on my thigh and nudged my hand. I scratched her ears, then, with nothing pressing to do and no commitments, we did the only thing we could – we went for a walk.

Hidden from view at the end of the headland was a full car park, a busy hotel and a museum. Scowling, I called Jess and lumbered towards the pointy carbuncle of St Catherine's Tor. Onwards we continued past Speke's Mill Mouth, its waterfall crashing onto toothy rocks below. Neither landmark registered as interesting to me; I stuffed my hands in my pockets and kept my head down. The ground began to rise slightly, and, not willing to expend any energy at all, I gave up and turned back.

I returned to the quay and we went into the hotel. The bar thrummed with people and reeked of roast potatoes and wet fur. I bought a shandy for me and a packet of pork scratchings for Jess and went back outside, where the wind whipped around the tables, blowing my hair into my eyes and mouth. This wouldn't do. I jumped up and stalked back into the bar. In the corner, a table for one looked free so I pulled up a chair and hunched over my shandy, resenting every laugh, every loud voice. As soon as I'd finished my drink, we left.

The B&B was a mile or so up the road. I wrapped my arms around myself to keep out the cold wind and, with Jess at my side, set off. On the brow of the hill I knocked on the door of an attractive cottage. The door swung open and Jess and I were ushered in by a petite woman with a friendly smile. "You must be Sasha and Jess, call me Helen," she said, and took us up to our room. Much to my relief the ensuite included a bath. I fed and watered Jess, and, as she slept, I rang Jack. "Hey, just checking you got home okay."

"I've just got in. What did you do after I left?"

"I moped around. I miss you."

"That's what I like to hear!"

"I'm all right now, the B&B has got a bath."

"God, you're easily pleased."

"Night, Jack."

I ran the taps. There is something magical about hot water, and it soothed and calmed me. As I wallowed, my thoughts turned to the dreaded next day's walk and I began to formulate an alternative strategy. If I could have changed any part of the whole walk, I would have split the famously difficult sixteen-mile stretch from Hartland to Bude into two separate days. Too late now, but I decided I would do half the next day and return to do the other half in the spring. Having made the decision, I lay back in the bath and dozed, listening to the wind outside.

Later I sat on the bed, wrapped in warm towels, and watched as the sky darkened dramatically and began to pour with rain. I quickly scrapped my idea of going back to the hotel for supper; a second cup of tea and a good book would be nourishment enough.

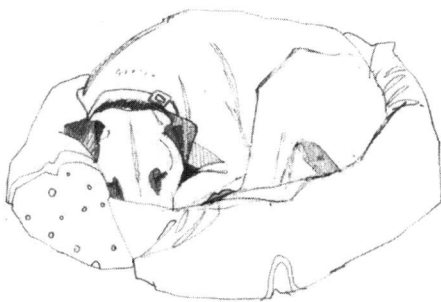

After a wonderful night's sleep, I endured breakfast with the dullest man I had ever met. He'd walked the stretch of coast I planned to embark on and took great delight in telling me how difficult it was. Then he told me about his failed marriage, rubbish job and yearly walking excursions. I was polite, but as soon as I'd finished my last sausage I fled to my room to pack.

When I told Helen about my change of plan she kindly offered to drive us to Morwenstow. Jess and I climbed into the back of her grubby Land Rover and, after a quick detour to drop off her little girl at school, we got out at the aforementioned Robert Steven Hawker's church.

I waved Helen goodbye, and we began the eight-mile trek to Bude. We headed though fields to Sharpnose Point then tramped over craggy clifftops. Below us, white rollers lined up and raced towards the cliffs, crashing onto the grey shingle shore. Jagged black rocks jutted out into the foaming sea like the spines on a mythical sea dragon: a wild, untamed landscape.

At Stanbury Mouth we carefully made our way into a deep valley, through gorse and scrub, then scrambled up the other side. From there we walked across a heath to Lower Sharpnose Point, the site of a radar station. I played Kate Bush on my MP3 player, lip-syncing to *Hounds of Love* to distract myself from the ugly wire fences, satellite dishes and oversized golf-ball-like constructions that dominated the skyline. A little further on, the Coast Path curved towards the end of a pointy peninsular. At the very tip, it turned back and we descended to Duckpool, a sheltered cove split by a river. A fine, salty mist filled the air, and spray from the

Sketches Along the Way

pounding waves blew about the shore. Wincing, I licked the salt off my lips, which were still tender, although beginning to heal.

On the other side of the river, a monstrous hill reared up from the valley floor. I pulled the straps of my rucksack tight around my middle, popped some chewing gum in my mouth and strode towards it. Jess ran circles around me as I began my slow-motion ascent. "It's all right for you, you've got four legs," I grumbled. She bounded up the hill, leaving me to focus on putting one foot in front of the other. Every time I glanced up, to check on my progress, the brow of the hill seemed further away. On and on I plodded, my knees trembling with each step, my breath coming in gasps. If I'd been in any doubt, I now knew I'd made the right decision to half the day's walk. I simply wasn't fit enough.

In a stroke of luck, I'd picked the less taxing stretch of the sixteen miles, and on reaching the clifftop, the terrain appeared to flatten off. We soon came to Sandymouth Beach and I ordered a cup of tea and a muffin at a café next to a car park. Outside, the picnic benches were full of people wrapped in hats and scarfs, hands cradling cups of tea, braving the cold to get a bit of sea air in their lungs.

When I finished, Jess and I pushed on towards Bude. In sight of the town I passed a woman wearing the same sturdy footwear and self-wicking apparel as me, just as it started to rain. In a synchronised dance she and I fished around in our rucksacks for coats, while squirrelling away our maps and guide books. We undid the zips at the side of our waterproof trousers before trying to get them over our boots, hopping on one foot and then the other, and adjusted the toggles on our hoods, pulling them tight. And then … the rain stopped. We looked at each other and laughed. "Every time," she said. "Well, I suppose it's good training," I replied, and we went our separate ways, dressed head to toe in sweltering Gore-Tex.

Bude felt like the quintessential out-of-season tourist town. Dog walkers roamed the windswept beaches and the local surfers claimed the waves as their own. The beach shops and cafés looked tatty and tired after a busy summer. We passed a tidal swimming pool, as inviting as an ice bath in a snow storm, then strolled through a deserted car park with a boarded-up café, heading for the centre of town. We'd finished the eight-mile walk in good time, allowing me to contemplate the exciting prospect of a late lunch.

Sketches Along the Way

On the lookout for a pub or hotel, we crossed the River Neet over Nanny Moore's Bridge, named after a 19th century bathing machine attendant. With no luck, we walked along a road spanning Bude Canal and I spotted a smart hotel surrounded by trees. Perfect. Feeling a bit overdressed, I got out of my wet weather gear before going inside and then made myself comfortable at a single table. I ordered steamed fish and new potatoes, the healthiest food I had eaten in days. It tasted wonderful and left me feeling completely rejuvenated. In no hurry to leave, I ordered a coffee and read the paper before setting off for our B&B.

We retraced our steps and tramped over a common to find the B&B on the edge of a golf course. After a friendly welcome, we were shown to our room, where I unpacked and fed Jess before settling down to some serious television watching.

9.3 miles • 23,489 steps • Grading: Severe.

DAY 10 – BUDE TO CRACKINGTON HAVEN

After a good night's sleep and the usual full English breakfast, Jess and I set off early for Crackington Haven. A chilly wind blew off the sea as we left the town for Compass Point. From there, the next few miles never strayed far from roads, and we made good time. At Widemouth Sands, I let Jess off her lead and she loped up and down the beach, letting off steam. The wind picked up and we moved into the dunes to escape the sand flying in our faces. A little further on, we came to a cove at Millook Haven. On a grass plateau, next to a stream, were a cottage and a net shed. It was a beautiful spot and I stayed for a while and sketched an old rowing boat surrounded by oxeye daisies. When I finished, I shared a drink with Jess and munched on a handful of nuts. A road led us away from the cove through a series of hairpin bends, and back onto the cliffs. From there, the path strayed inland between fields and sandy slopes smothered in thick vegetation.

Soon we reached Chipman Point, towering above the deepest, steepest valley on the whole Cornwall coast. Critically, I eyed the thin trail, which wriggled and squirmed like a varicose vein to the foot of the valley. Then, knees trembling, I skidded and stumbled to the bottom. Once there, I gaped at the vertical steps disappearing into the clouds on the other side. In places, the path was mere inches from the edge of the cliff and completely exposed to the buffeting wind. In a panic, I went inland to see if an alternative route existed for people who shouldn't be on the Coast Path, and instead should be at home with a rug on their knees, a good book and a soothing cup of camomile tea. But the only option was to go over the top.

In those distant, euphoric, pre-walk days, I'd googled *How do you take on a very steep hill?* Now, following the advice the search threw up, I began the climb, taking it slowly and straightening my knee on each step. The method worked; I hardly got out of breath at all, but it did take me three times longer than a person walking normally.

At the top, I found a stile with a broken step. It took more effort than usual, but I scrambled over and then called to Jess. She stared at me wide-eyed from the other side. Without the step, she simply couldn't get over. In the past I'd encouraged her to squeeze under or around an obstacle such as this, but there were no gaps. She started crying. "It's all right, Jess, I'll get you over," I soothed. Then I came up with an idea. Using the broken step lying nearby, I gouged a hole in the hard-packed earth under the stile. Realising what I intended to do, Jess helped by scratching the earth from her side until she could flatten herself and crawl under. Reunited, I gave her a drink and we followed the path away from the cliffs.

After going through fields, we turned back towards the coast and stood at the bottom of a sheer-sided ridge pointing straight out to sea. Along the top, a skinny track climbed to an apex and then faded from view. I swallowed. It seemed precarious, and I was in no mood for any more knife-edge moments. But as we got nearer, the spine of the ridge turned out to be wider than it had seemed, and was protected on both sides by hawthorn and gorse hedges. At the end, before tumbling into the sea, the path nosed down the flank of the ridge, through a thick covering of heather to a stream. The path was narrow, and loose stones underfoot made each step tricky. Halfway down my knee buckled and I slipped onto my arse. I got up, embarrassed but not hurt, and carefully hobbled to the bottom.

We crossed the stream, and as I looked back at the zigzag path slashed into the side of the ridge, I congratulated myself on overcoming yet another hurdle.

A woman materialised at the top of the ridge and skipped effortlessly down the same track that had proved such a challenge to me. As she got closer, I saw she was much older than me, but exuded vigour. Was I destined to be the most unfit person on the SWCP? I couldn't imagine a time when I didn't make a meal out of every ascent and descent. Confirming my suspicions, the elderly woman raced past us with a hearty "Hello!" and cantered up the other side of the valley.

As if to rub deep heat into my wounds and test my endurance, the last two miles were as never-ending as the washing up after a dinner party. Every time I thought I'd reached the finish line there was more. Then, when we finally got to Pencarrow Point and swung inland to Crackington Haven, I realised it hadn't been worth the effort. Bleak and desolate, the stony beach, car park and cluster of houses bore no resemblance to the "geology student party town" I'd conjured up in my head. There was absolutely no sign of anyone under twenty, but I knew from reading my guide book that Crackington Haven is a mecca for young people who enjoy ogling rocks. The reason? The local cliffs are made up of visible, folded, sedimentary rock formations. All this was lost on me but something else did catch my eye – a pub, overlooking the beach. The Coombe Barton Inn was our home for the night, and Jess and I eagerly escaped the cold and settled down at a cosy table in the bar. I ordered a ploughman's and a pint and we spent an hour unwinding before retiring to our room.

12.9 miles • 32,309 steps • Grading: Easy/Strenuous

The sky was still dark when I woke, and I crept about my room, very aware – having heard my next-door neighbours' conversation during the night – that the walls were paper thin. I'd made the decision to leave before breakfast, in order to get a good start on what I knew would be a strenuous day. With that in mind, before going to bed I'd asked the pub manager if he could provide me with a packed breakfast. He'd rooted around in the kitchen and produced a deeply uninspiring bag of fruit, which I took up to my room. Dipping into the bag, I pulled out and ate a banana, an apple and a nut bar, then shouldered my rucksack and tiptoed out of the pub.

The cold, grey morning presented me with no reason to revise my previous day's assessment of the town. I sighed and zipped my waterproof coat up to my chin, wishing I was snuggled in bed watching the weather rather than experiencing it. We crossed the road, and soon all thoughts of comfort were scrubbed from my mind as we marched towards Cambeak, an extremely high, pointy hill. At the summit, I felt shaky and out of sorts, but put it down to the early start and my general poor stamina.

On the descent, we negotiated a barren landscape dotted with gorse and rabbit holes. As I continued, the shakes got worse until, while scrambling up a slope, I became disorientated and confused. Adrenaline pulsed through my veins and I began to sweat. I sat down with a thump on the side of the path and scrabbled in my rucksack for something to eat. I drew out a bag of Mini Cheddars, prised them open with trembling hands, and shoved a handful into my mouth. But my tongue felt sandpit dry and, unable to swallow, I spat them out.

Still shaking, I drank some water, then rummaged for a more appropriate snack. Nuts. I poured a mound of mixed nuts and raisins into my mouth with a swig of water, and instantly noticed a change. I could feel my body absorbing the sugar, sucking it up like blotting paper. Mightily relieved, I stood up and slowly tottered on, grazing on the rest of the nuts and raisins until I felt back to normal.

It was a sobering lesson: I could not afford to miss breakfast again. For the first time in my life, I required food for fuel, and I needed lots of it. The full English might not be the healthiest of breakfasts, but it was essential if I didn't want to become a gibbering wreck. I also learnt that although I loved the cheesy goodness of Mini Cheddars, they were not the go-to snack in a crisis. This didn't stop me snaffling a packet once the nuts ran out, just to make sure.

Feeling steadier on my feet, I wound my way in and out of bracken and gorse covering a landslide at Rusey Cliff. Jess suddenly pushed past me, on high alert. I couldn't see anything and presumed she'd spied a rabbit or bird. Ears up, she ran full pelt towards the cliff edge, flushing out a herd of moth-eaten wild goats. I yelled at her to stop, terrified she might fall to her death. The sound of alarm in my voice stopped her dead and she dropped on her haunches, panting heavily. "Stay there!" I ordered, and ran up to her, heart hammering in my chest. I fumbled around my neck for her lead, but it was gone. I must have lost it when I went through my sugar meltdown. Improvising with my pencil-thin camera strap, I pulled her away from the cliff edge in time to see the goats fleeing over a ridge.

With Jess safe at my side, I followed the Coast Path in and out of a steep-sided inlet, then struck out for Penally Hill, which curves like a protective arm around the entrance to Boscastle Harbour. Without realising it, I missed the official route and instead took the "only for people who are bonkers" way around the headland: a knee-shakingly precarious path clinging to the side of the cliff, with nothing to stop a person toppling to their death. Nerves jangling like a prison guard's keys at a jailhouse disco, I repeated a mantra in my head: "One step at a time, don't look down. One step at a time, don't look down." Of course, the more I told myself not to look down, the more compelled I was to do just that; I've never liked being told what to do. However, I kept my eyes on my feet long enough to find the official path on the other side of the headland, and as the path widened and moved inland I saw the comforting sight of Boscastle's harbour.

Although now a picture of calm, it had been a different story eight years before when, on the sixteenth of August, after an afternoon of torrential rain, a wall of water rushed into the village, sweeping away cars and houses. The local news that night showed dramatic images of people being winched by helicopter from rooftops, and cars being swept out to sea like children's toys. Unlike the Lynmouth disaster, which, coincidently, happened on the same date fifty-two years earlier, there were no fatalities, but Boscastle had been left in tatters.

Eight years on, the rebuilding complete, the village bustled with holidaymakers and coach parties. On our way to the other side of the harbour the heavens opened and everyone ran for shelter. I found a seat outside a café with an oversized umbrella above the tables. Unfortunately, it couldn't cover all the seating and we were forced to get cosy with our fellow diners. Everyone crammed under the dry bit and lamented the soggy summer. I disagreed. When I thought back, Jess and I had been extremely lucky with the weather until this point. We'd experienced the odd shower and a bit of wind (especially in the company of Wind-Up Woman) but no persistent rain.

I ordered a prawn sandwich and a pot of tea, and while waiting talked to the couple next to me. When my lunch arrived, rather than allowing me some time to eat, they continued the conversation. Every time I raised my sandwich to take a bite, they asked a question. Not wanting to appear rude, I lowered the sandwich to answer. Over and over I lifted and lowered my sandwich, until, defeated, I gave up. Under the pretence of going to the loo, I discreetly asked the waitress for a doggy bag, made my excuses and left.

During my failed attempt to eat lunch, the rain had stopped, but as soon as we left the refuge of the café it began once more. Hastily squirrelling away my sandwich, I pulled out Jess's raincoat. Once she was dressed, I struggled into my own wet weather gear, then, swaddled in Gore-Tex, we left the harbour for the cliffs.

With our heads down, we pushed into a wall of rain. Fat drops fell from my hood, pinged off my nose and ricocheted off my knees, leaving my coat and trousers sodden. Jess, wretched, slumped behind me, her fur two shades darker. My heart went out to her, but there was nothing to do except keep moving. In a bid to outrun the weather, I opened up the throttle and, at a half-jog, half-stumble, encouraged Jess on. I kept my eyes down and saw nothing of the coast, only the stony path beneath my feet.

A few miserable miles later, we scrambled down into a gorge at Rocky Valley. As we clambered up the other side, the sun burst out of the clouds and all around us the vegetation steamed as the colours of the landscape transformed from grey to a vibrant green. I peeled off my coat, feeling the warmth on my damp shoulders, and then did the same for Jess. She shook, then ran in loops, as thrilled as me to be dry.

While Jess played, I got my bearings, after hours hidden behind my hood like a blinkered horse. On the far side of Rocky Valley the clifftop was smothered in row after row of caravans, gleaming in the sun. Out at sea the retreating mist revealed Long Island, a sea stack rising hundreds of feet out of the water and resembling a badly chewed shark's fin. Below me, waves pulled in and out of charcoal black caves, crashing against the walls. Inaccessible coves, islands and sea stacks all appeared, one after another, as we approached Tintagel.

As we drew nearer, Tintagel Island came into view, a ruined medieval fortification amongst the rocks and close-cropped grass covering the peninsula. It is said to be the birthplace of King Arthur. What a place to be born, an isolated castle atop a rugged island on the beautiful north coast of Cornwall. I'd visited the castle many years ago with Jack, so didn't feel the need to take the tour, but I appeared to be the only one of this opinion – dozens of tourists filed past us, eager to get onto the island.

I found a bench a short distance from the crowds and peeled off my waterproof trousers. While putting them away, I rediscovered – to my delight – the two, now squashed, prawn sandwiches. Suddenly ravenous, and mindful of warding off another blood sugar crash, I snaffled them and awarded a patiently waiting Jess with the crusts. We then merged with the steady stream of people hiking up the hill to Tintagel Village. At the top, the tourists melted into the town looking for cream teas and souvenir tea towels, while I scoured the streets for a pub.

After a pint and a packet of crisps I strolled out of town through a residential street to the B&B, where another warm welcome awaited us. I fed Jess and pottered about the room, unpacking and writing my notes. After ten days of walking, I'd begun to feel a host of positive effects. I'd stopped automatically taking two painkillers at the end of the day. My weary muscles and restless thoughts were replaced with a deep feeling of calm. Despite my questionable fitness, numb toe and blistered lips, I'd never felt more content.

14.6 miles • 36,221 steps • Grading: Moderate/Strenuous

DAY 12 – TINTAGEL TO PORT ISAAC

Another side effect of all the exercise was better sleep, and I woke the next morning feeling well rested. Jess and I were the only patrons of the B&B and we had the informal dining room to ourselves. The owners were grieving for a lost dog and pressed me to let Jess off her lead, perhaps pining for the familiar feel of a wet nose. She trotted into the kitchen and drooled by the oven as they cooked my breakfast. All her pitiful "my owner doesn't feed me" looks worked, and they popped two sausages in a bowl for her. I tucked into a full English breakfast, then packed, and after saying goodbye, Jess and I stepped into a beautiful morning.

As we ambled down the road to Trebarwith Strand on the coast, I glanced at the guide book. The ten miles between Tintagel and Port Issac were described by the author as *severe*, with one arduous valley after another. But, I told myself brightly, we had all day and absolutely nothing else to do. This uncharacteristically relaxed attitude vanished moments later when I was confronted by a flight of hundreds of stone steps rising towards the clifftop. "And so it begins," I remarked darkly to Jess.

I made a start, using my tried and tested method of straightening my knee on each rise but, despite a big breakfast, I felt lethargic. I never knew from day to day how I might perform. There didn't seem to be a reason why I would be low on stamina on this particular morning, with a full belly, a great night's sleep and ten days of training behind me. But only twenty minutes after setting off, I felt as if I'd run miles with a backpack full of lead. Drained, I staggered up the last few steps and caught my breath, watching seagulls wheel above the dome-shaped Gull Rock out at sea. When I'd recovered I had a drink and Jess and I pushed on. The Coast Path followed the contours of a freshly mowed field towards Dennis Point. From there, we descended left and right down the slopes of a rugged valley to Backways Cove.

On the other side of the valley, the path writhed through butter-yellow gorse, glowing in the sun: an ideal adder habitat. I made Jess stay behind me, just in case. Ahead of us, two people were cutting back the overgrown scrub, red-faced and sweating. As I squeezed by with a "Lovely day!" I realised they were the only people I'd seen all morning. Jess and I had the clifftops to ourselves apart from the meadow pipits trilling above the gorse, and perhaps an adder or two. Most tourists flocked to the bookends of Tintagel and Port Isaac without considering the miles of stunning scenery between the two. They surely missed the best bit.

Over Treligga Cliff the ground stayed level, but not for long. Another energy-sapping valley down to Tregardock Beach chipped away at my depleted reserves. I chewed on two glucose tablets and finished my bottle of water. Once again the cliffs flattened off, giving me time to prepare myself for the next ravine. At Jacket's Point a monstrous cliff towered over us, with a gouge hacked out of it. Steps snaked along the rim of the gouge, perilously close to the edge. A shiver ran through me; how on earth was I going to get to the summit without fainting in fear?

If ever there was a time for walking poles, this was it. Mine had been lashed to the back of my rucksack for 154 miles, patiently waiting for their moment, and here it was. In some excitement, I untied them, adjusted their length, put on the Velcroed hand straps and slipped the hoops into the corresponding notch on the handles with a satisfying click. Instantly I felt empowered. Bionic. As if I'd sprouted an extra pair of legs.

What a difference. Even with my rusty technique, I immediately felt the benefits. Using the sticks to haul myself up each step gave my knees and thighs a much-needed break. Not for the first time, I thought back with a twisted fondness at my experience in Wind-Up Woman's company. She knew the secrets of the walking pole, and now I, her unwilling apprentice, did too. Armed with my new abilities, I made short work of the remaining valleys and soon came in sight of Port Isaac. One final push onto Tresungers Point revealed a fantastic view across Port Isaac Bay, taking in headland after headland all the way back to Tintagel. Leaning casually on my sticks, I surveyed the miles Jess and I had walked, and felt heroic. We left the cliffs and wandered into the tiny harbour at Port Gaverne.

Port Gaverne and Port Isaac are as close as siblings, with only a hill between them. Where one is well known and popular, the other appeared, on first impressions, quieter, less brash, and all the better for it. The harbour, once a busy hub that exported slate from the local Delabole Quarry, had a laid-back atmosphere. The kind of atmosphere that inspired a person to stop for a while outside a pub with a pint and a packet of pork scratchings.

Jess and I walked into a nearby pub and I ordered a pint and a packet of pork scratchings. Outside, I sidled up to a group of people chatting near the door and self-consciously propped my sticks against a table. With such paraphernalia, there was no disguising the fact I was someone who seriously liked to walk. The other drinkers were enthralled by the idea of tackling the whole SWCP, and were full of questions. How many miles a day did we walk? What were my favourite parts? And, from the women: Aren't you brave? Don't you get lonely walking on your own? Clearly Jess didn't count.

The more I talked to people, the clearer it became that the SWCP was beloved by both locals and tourists alike. Most people who lived on the coast had a favourite stretch for a Sunday stroll or everyday dog walk, while others clocked up hundreds of miles by doing the odd weekend over many years. I left the pub with a renewed sense of good fortune, full of anticipation for what would come next.

Over the years, I had visited – and even painted – most of the coastal towns and villages in Cornwall, but I had never been to Port Isaac. I knew it had become very popular thanks to a TV series about a jug-eared doctor, and a group of singing fishermen, but I wasn't prepared for the crowds. Leaving the chilled-out vibe of Port Gaverne and arriving in Port Isaac felt like falling asleep during a yoga practice and waking up in a Zumba class. Overwhelmed, I decided to find the B&B before braving the streets, and ten minutes later I sat sharing a cup of tea with the B&B owner in her homely kitchen. After unpacking, I fed Jess and, wanting something to eat myself, left the B&B for the harbour.

It was easy enough to find. We simply drifted with everyone else, past cafés and gift shops, galleries and restaurants to the Platt at the bottom of the hill. The smell of diesel and seaweed wafted about the slipway, as evocative as the aroma of freshly baked pasties. The pungent whiff reminded me of Jack, who, when we first met, owned a fishing boat.

Net bins, bongos, fish boxes and dahns were all neatly stacked by the sea wall, ready for the next tide. Facing away from the harbour, a smart blue-doored building housed a fishmonger selling the local catch, and although I couldn't buy anything, I relished the chance to inspect the freshly caught fish. Big-eyed pollack and silver bass, red mullet and hake lay on ice, next to bags of mussels and piles of scallops, all glistening, fresh and smelling of ozone. I pictured a bowl of moules in a fragrant broth and pan-fried scallops with pancetta and a squeeze of lemon. Hit by a sudden fierce hunger, I left in search of food. The pub opposite boasted a large seating area outside, but a rowdy group of locals holding court at one of the tables put me off. Instead, I returned to a pasty shop I'd passed earlier, and ate one while walking back to the B&B. It wasn't the gourmet meal I'd envisioned, but it filled me up.

My room in the B&B didn't have a TV, so, later that evening, Jess and I wandered into the communal sitting room to watch the weather forecast. Three people lounged on the sofa, and I asked if they would mind if I put the TV on. To my intense humiliation, I couldn't find the on button. Their sniggers may have had nothing to do with my ineptitude, but certainly didn't help. I ran my hands all over the box, and peered underneath and behind it. As their sniggers became guffaws, Jess, sensing my growing unease, intervened. She broke wind. An inspired move. The three friends gagged, held their noses, and staggered from the room. Jess, the picture of innocence, stretched out and fell asleep. My girl. Dignity once more intact, I found the elusive button on the remote control and settled down to watch the weather.

Later, we returned to our room and I wrote up my notes and read before turning in early. Big mistake. It soon became clear that the shared bathroom adjacent to my room was the only one in the entire house, and possibly the street. For three hours, dozens of people slammed the door, flushed the loo, ran the taps, ran baths, took showers, sang in the shower, flushed the loo … The walls were tissue thin. When the bathroom wasn't being used, I could hear people walking up and down the stairs and in and out of rooms, laughing and shouting; it was like being back at boarding school. And then, to top it all, the landlady decided ten o'clock at night was the perfect time of day to fry mackerel, the stench of which seeped into our room, waking Jess, who then cried at the door because she wanted to be let out to help eat the mackerel.

Needless to say, I didn't sleep particularly well, but I evened the score at six o'clock the next morning when I regaled the house with fifteen minutes of Dolly Parton's greatest hits while in the shower.

9.8 miles • 24,436 steps • Grading: Severe

DAY 13 – PORT ISAAC TO PADSTOW

Over an early breakfast, the B&B landlady told me about a well-known shortcut through farmland that would enable us to bypass a particularly horrendous valley and would take us straight to Port Quin. It goes without saying that Wind-Up Woman would have parped in horror at such cheating, but I had no such qualms, and left the B&B clutching the directions on a piece of paper.

The shortcut may have been less strenuous, but it didn't lack danger. In the first field, we were approached by a herd of curious young bulls, and we had to leap over a low wall to escape death-by-trampling. On the other side of the wall I landed in a quagmire and nearly lost a boot trying to extricate myself. Later, a torrential downpour had us running to take shelter under a hawthorn tree in the lea of a stone wall. With so much early morning action, it was a relief to reach the sleepy hamlet of Port Quin in one piece.

Perched at the end of a rocky inlet, Port Quin took three seconds to walk through, and we were soon tramping up the road on the other side. To the right, I spotted the acorn sign and a stile, which on close inspection was fiendishly designed to be impossible for Jess (or any big dog) to get over, under, or around. But another sign nearby showed a diversion. So, keeping our eyes peeled, we set off in that direction. After hiking up a road, I saw a way through farmland, and we struck out over fields of skittish sheep. Frustratingly, I could see the Coast Path, almost touch it, but couldn't get to it through the miles of wire fencing. All the time I'd saved by getting up early and taking the shortcut was wasted. I turned and retraced my steps, releasing some tension by shouting "bugger" over and over again. Finally, we stood once more in front of the offending stile. This time, glancing left, I saw – only a few yards up the road – another turning and acorn sign, which allowed us to bypass the stile.

Now on the right path, and determined to make up the lost time, I walked as fast as I could, using my sticks to propel me forward. Around Doyden Point, I flew past a faux castle. Built around 1827 by Samuel Symons as a place to entertain friends with gambling and drinking, it is now a holiday home owned by the National Trust. From the castle, we rounded a stubby headland and I peered down on two beaches separated by a short promontory. White rollers rushed at the shore and then pulled back, tumbling seaweed and stones. Beyond the breakers, the sea was dark blue, with little white waves scudding over its surface.

On the other side of the bay, I stood behind a low wall and studied a slender rock arch. The wall was so minimal it presented more of a trip hazard than a safety barrier, and I wisely kept well back while taking the obligatory photo. Onwards, sticks pumping and legs a blur, I approached The Rumps. Sheep grazed in amongst the rock-strewn grass, but one (there's always one) balanced on top of a tall rock rising out of the sea. Clearly an adrenaline junkie, she didn't seem the least concerned by her circumstances and happily chomped on what little grass grew from cracks in the stone. The puzzle was that the rock didn't appear to be attached to the mainland. I wasn't sure of the right protocol when faced with a sheep on a rock in the sea. Should I ring the RSPCA? The coastguard? The farmer? She seemed content enough, so I took a photo and hoped she'd find her way back.

From The Rumps, we rounded Pentire Point and I stood slack-jawed at the view. I could see right across Padstow Bay to Stepper Point, at the mouth of the Camel Estuary, and beyond; miles and miles of coast to Harlyn Bay. And on my side of the estuary, tucked to one side, Hayle Bay and the town of Polzeath.
On the outskirts of Polzeath, I developed a sudden craving for a cool, refreshing ginger beer. I found a snack van on the beach selling ginger beer, but it was hot. Hot ginger beer? Next, they'll be selling cold coffee. Oh, wait … In a reckless and totally out of character move, I asked for one. It tasted delicious. I bought Jess a less controversial vanilla ice cream.

We pushed on, past surf shops, surf schools, surf hire and actual surfers – there is a definite theme to Polzeath. However, a caravan park on the outskirts revealed the family holiday destination side of the town, all sand castles and sun. On the other side of the caravan park, a flat, wide path swept around the headland. With no need for my sticks – they would have been excessive, like using a chainsaw to cut bread – I reverted to legs-only propulsion, and Jess and I fell in with the dozens of other casual walkers mooching along the path between Hayle Bay and Daymer Bay.

By the time we reached Daymer Bay, the tide was right out, making it possible, if not essential, to walk on the beach all the way to Rock. This avoided Brea Hill and the sand dunes under Cassock Hill but, more importantly, it meant we could paddle. As I sloshed through the shallows with my boots tied to my rucksack and my trousers rolled up to my knees, I kept an eye on the bright yellow ferry pottering to and fro between Padstow and Rock. In an extraordinary piece of precision timing, we arrived at the ferry stop at exactly the same time as its ramp touched the sand. I fist bumped the air, and thought I detected a few admiring glances as I waltzed onto the ferry with Jess bringing up my rear. This was her first experience on a boat, and I watched carefully to see her reaction. I needn't have worried. She shimmied up the ramp, pushed her nose into the groin of everyone sitting on board – an unexpected but friendly gesture – lay down and fell fast asleep. My girl.

Padstow Ferry

Padstow was packed. People sauntered about, eating, drinking and peering in shop windows. All the pubs and restaurants were full, with people sitting outside, eating and drinking. All the seagulls were eating and drinking. Jess and I were booked into a in a pub bang in the middle of the harbour; I walked in and ordered something to eat and drink.

Replete, after a supper of burger and chips served on a wooden board, I happily nursed my dry white wine. From my position at a table outside the pub, I had a ringside view of the comings and goings of the street and couldn't help noticing the extraordinary number of dogs and variety of breeds on show.

Jess struck up a flirtation with a spotty Great Dane and they rolled around between the tables. To start with, everyone laughed at their antics but, with their combined size and weight, their play quickly stopped being endearing when glasses started to fly. I pulled her away, apologising, and left to have a wander around the town.

I know Padstow well. For years I sold my work in a gallery on the harbour, and visited often to get inspiration and ideas. In that time, Padstow changed from a working harbour to a tourist trap. A lot of this was down to Rick Stein. His restaurant, hotels and celebrity TV chef persona drew people – and dogs, it seemed – from far and wide. Nicknamed "Padstein" (not as catchy as "Rickstow" in my opinion) the town and the man are now as inseparable as me and my walking sticks.

I like Padstow, but the real lure is the surrounding coast. The walks are fantastic. This is the reason, I think, so many people bring their dogs. For those who like to ride bikes, the nearby Camel Trail runs all the way to Wadebridge, along the banks of the picturesque Camel Estuary.

Well, Jess and I would have our fill of the beautiful coastline tomorrow. For now, I dawdled, happy to go with the tide of people milling around the harbour. As the shops and galleries closed and the crowds melted away. I returned to the pub for a glass of wine and then climbed the stairs to my garret room. With Jess tucked in, I took a shower, watched a bit of telly and turned in.

15.6 miles • 38,860 steps • Grading: Strenuous/Easy

DAY 14 – PADSTOW TO PORTHCOTHAN

After breakfast the next morning, I texted my friend Fran to confirm we were meeting later in the day. She was one of the few people I had been in contact with while doing the walk, and she'd been a great support when I felt particularly feeble. Walking the Coast Path was on Fran's bucket list, but with two tiny children, skipping off for seven whole weeks simply wasn't an option. Thinking of Fran reminded me what a privilege it was to be able to do this. Fired up with the thought of seeing her, I downed the last of my coffee and ran upstairs to pack.

The harbour was deserted, a stage set waiting for the actors. From the wings, two seagulls squabbled over a discarded pasty crust, until they saw Jess and took off in a flurry of feathers. They flew over the head of a fisherman who stood on the edge of the harbour wall, slowly flicking a fly rod back and forth. At his feet, grey mullet cruised like mini-submarines, inches below the surface, rising every now and then for a morsel. Intent on his quarry, the man paid no more attention to Jess and me than the fish paid to his fly. Leaving him to it, we ambled up a tarmac path lined with benches to a WWI memorial.

In no time we were back on the coast. The tide was out, so at Gun Point we scrambled down the rocks onto Harbour Cove. Keeping to the wet sand, I watched as black-backed gulls swooped over the shallows, looking like B52s in comparison to the delicate sanderlings dashing up and down the shore. Across the estuary, the creamy sand of Daymer Bay shone in the sun, with the turtle shell hump of Brea Hill behind. Perfect.

In no hurry, Jess and I pottered along the tideline until we reached the end of the beach, where the sand merged into marshland. We made our way over a boardwalk then turned right towards Stepper Point. A little further on, at Hawker's Cove, a row of coastguard cottages overlooked an old lifeboat station tucked into the side of a tiny inlet. It was the perfect place to stop and look across the estuary to Trebetherick Point, towards the coast Jess and I walked the day before. I never grew tired of seeing how far we had come, knowing we had achieved it all on foot – or paw. On the other hand, looking ahead was usually a bit daunting. However, when we reached Stepper Point, the view to Trevose Head was so stunning that far from being put off by the miles of curving coastline interspersed by beaches and coves, I couldn't wait to set foot on it.

Everything felt right, from the weather and spectacular views to the easy-going terrain. It made such a change not to be clambering in and out of precipitous gorges or hauling myself up steps, face purple with the effort. This was good, old-fashioned, one foot in front of the other perambulation.

Onwards we walked, past Pepper Hole – a hole scooped out of the clifftop – and Butter Hole – not a hole, but a little cove – and through fields of laid-back cows, cuddly in their brown jumpers and overgrown fringes. The entire way to Harlyn Bay, I walked in a state of low-level euphoria, as if I'd drunk one too many cups of camomile tea.

At the beach, I had the chance at last to tell everybody what a delightful day I was having. In my enthusiasm, I boomed at the first man I saw, "ISN'T IT A BEAUTIFUL DAY?" Startled, he bobbed his head and moved quickly away, dragging his dog behind him. I terrorised the shoreline, informing everyone of what a beautiful day I thought it was, and didn't they agree? Most people did agree, but whether to placate the loud woman or because they genuinely felt as I did, I couldn't tell. So preoccupied with spreading the word, I forgot to keep an eye on the tide, and at the far end of the beach I had to take off my boots and scramble over rocks to avoid drowning.

Next to Harlyn Bay was Mother Ivey's Bay, dominated by an expansive holiday park. The high tide left only a ribbon of sand, so we stayed on the Coast Path in front of rows of caravans. On the other side of the bay, a baby blue lifeboat station perched on a leggy slipway. Behind it, a line of pointy rocks created a natural barrier, protecting the seemingly fragile construction from the worst of the weather. From there we pushed on to the snub-nosed Trevose Head, and looked down on the lighthouse, a reminder that however benign it might appear, the coast can be treacherous.

And not just because of the sea. Turning the corner, we came across a massive hole. A hole, in the middle of the clifftop, with no barriers. Nothing to stop you flinging yourself in. I told Jess to stay put and inched nearer. About a metre from the edge, I peered in, feeling sick but at the same time thrilled to be doing something scary. Far below, the sea swirled and frothed like boiling milk in a saucepan. I quickly stepped back and returned to Jess, having had more than enough thrills for one day.

The afternoon floated by, and as we approached Porthcothan my thoughts turned to Fran. I hadn't seen anyone I knew since Jack in Clovelly, and I couldn't wait to catch up with her. I sped up as I anticipated our meeting, and in my haste trod on a slow worm – a misnomer for what is actually a legless lizard, and not – in my experience – slow. I deduced this one was either cold or dozing when I trod on it. Either way, it appeared to be all right, despite the faint impression of my sole on its back, as it slid into the undergrowth.

If seeing the slow worm was the icing on the cake to a perfect day, then Fran was the plastic figurine on the top. On reaching Porthcothan, I waded over a shallow stream, scanned the beach and, finding no sign of her, sat at the base of the sand dunes to wait. It wasn't long before she came scrambling down the dunes, a wisp of a baby in one arm and her curly-haired boy in tow. We hugged, and Fran unfurled a blanket and set up camp. Once settled, she pulled from her bag all sorts of snacks, knowing I would be hungry. I diligently worked my way through them as we talked.

While recalling my adventures, it became clear I remained clueless when it came to the practicalities of a lengthy walk. Fran told me of the humble oatcake, essential for staving off low blood sugar, and the use of zinc lip salve to stop sunburnt lips – something I wish I'd known weeks before. After I'd eaten everything and we'd talked ourselves dry, we took a cursory look around the village. It had an odd character, mirrored by the attitude of the local shopkeeper. The moment we entered his shop, he regarded us with distaste and didn't take his eyes off us as we checked the freezer for ice lollies. Under his disapproving gaze I felt like an intruder who'd broken into his house and was rummaging around in his pants drawer. We grabbed four lollies, paid and left.

Determined to find something to like about the village, we gave the pub a try. As it was the middle of the afternoon, the bar lacked atmosphere, but children and dogs were welcome. We ordered drinks and, while Fran's little boy ran around, discussed the next day.

I planned on walking to Newquay then on to Fran's house above Fistral Beach. From there, Jack would pick me up, and for the next two weeks Jess and I would stay at home. There was no sense in paying for B&Bs when I lived in nearby Penryn. Every morning, my brother-in-law and I would drive in convoy to the end of the walk, where I would leave my car. He would then drop me off at the beginning of the day's trek. The logistics felt like a real palaver, but I thought it would work well once we got into the swing of things.

With everything fixed, Fran decided to make a move. I happily waved her off, knowing that tomorrow I would see her again … and Jack … and my home.

Jess and I walked the short distance to the B&B and were let in by the owner's daughter. I went through the usual routine of unpacking and showering but, unlike Jess, who fell asleep almost as soon as I fed her, I couldn't relax. Although loath to wake her, I needed to eat and wanted to give the pub another go. So we tramped back up the hill.

In the few hours since Fran and I left, the bar had transformed and was crammed with people. Taking this for a good sign, I found a table and ordered my usual scampi and chips and a glass of wine. When the food arrived, it tasted fantastic. The perfect end to one of the best walks ever.

After supper, we returned to the B&B and I tucked Jess in and clambered, exhausted, into bed, only to realise the sheets and duvet were damp. With a sigh, I put on my boots and left the room in search of someone at whom to direct my complaint. After checking the sitting room, I went into the kitchen, and while looking out of the window into the back garden I heard – coming from behind a door – a low, throaty growl. I froze, then slowly, carefully, backtracked out and bolted for my room. I re-evaluated my situation. There was no need to complain; damp sheets were in fact good for you, like cold baths and enemas, I reasoned. Lucky me, I insisted on telling myself, as I pulled on wool socks and a jumper, before peeling back the sheets, getting in and curling into a foetal position.

14.1 miles • 35,188 steps • Grading: Easy

I woke with a raging appetite, having expended all my energy using my body heat to dry the sheets, only to find there was a wait for breakfast. The dining room, the landlady informed me, could only fit four people in it at any one time, and I was booked in after an American couple. From my room, on the other side of the hall, I could see the diners and I furtively peeped through my keyhole to keep an eye on the American couple's progress. They ate in comfortable silence, as if they had simply run out of things to say. I expect they'd been married forever and there was nothing left to discuss. Luckily, this meant they could get on with eating, and they flew through their eggs and bacon and were out in no time.

The table occupied a sunny bay window overlooking the front garden. I ordered scrambled eggs and bacon, and when I finished felt inclined to linger over another pot of tea. Unfortunately, when the B&B owner appeared she informed me that she was going for a swim and promptly stalked out of the front door. For a moment I waited to see if anyone else would take my order, but no, the house, it appeared, was empty. Having learnt my lesson the night before, I gave up on the idea of searching in the kitchen for anyone to assist me and instead wandered back to my room.

I packed, helped myself to a packet of biscuits from the drinks tray, and left for Newquay. Ah, Newquay. The name conjured up images of women with L-plates, naked men sellotaped to lamp posts, and psychotic seagulls. In my youth I had experienced the party town, but as I got older I unearthed all sorts of other attractions: the harbour, the aquarium, the wonderfully old-fashioned Headland Hotel. And, of course, the beaches. All of which could be enjoyed without excessive alcohol – or sellotape.

We walked out of Porthcothan along a residential road parallel to the beach, and onto the cliffs. At Park Head I took the rash decision to go all the way to the end of the headland, rather than take a shortcut. My impulse was rewarded with a spectacular view of Bedruthan Steps, Watergate Bay, Lusty Glaze Beach and, finally, Newquay, which sprawled like a grey birthmark for miles up the coast before merging with the much smaller Porth and spilling inland to St Columb Minor.

On the way to Bedruthan Steps, a man with a sheep dog asked if I had seen the choughs. I said no, but now that he mentioned it, I might have heard the call of one the day before. Choughs – black birds with distinctive-looking red beaks and feet – had returned to Cornwall of their own will after an absence of twenty-eight years. A symbol of the county, they feature on the Cornish coat of arms, along with fishing and tin mining. I had only seen a handful over the years and they always delighted me.

Eyes peeled for the elusive corvids, I scanned the cliffs above Pentire Steps beach. Five stacks of rock rose from the sand below me – the famous Bedruthan Steps, named after a giant who, legend has it, used the stacks as stepping stones. Each stack is named: Queen Bess, Samaritan Island, Redcove Island, Pendarves Island and Carnewas Island.

Although early, a few people had already hiked down the hundreds of steps onto the beach. If I'd taken the same demented decision I might have missed seeing my first ever adder. At my approach, the snake, sunbathing in the path, slowly unwound itself and slid into the undergrowth, giving me a moment to marvel at the distinctive diamonds on its back. Absolutely beautiful. Luckily, Jess sloped far behind me, unaware of its presence, but I put her on her lead to be safe.

From Mawgan Porth we rounded Beryl's Point and looked down on Beacon Cove, a mere sandpit compared to its next door neighbour, Watergate Bay. With two miles of sand pounded by Atlantic waves, and only thirty minutes from the town centre, no wonder this surfers' favourite is so popular. A jet ski competition was kicking off at the water's edge, and high up on the cliff I occupied a ringside seat. I watched for a while as they zipped around buoys and tore through the surf, then we pressed on to Porth.

Cut deep into the land, Porth is a child-friendly, family-orientated beach. At low tide there are plenty of rock pools for children to play in, and it is considered a safe place to swim, unlike some of the north coast beaches. Unfortunately for Jess and me, dogs were banned until the end of September, so we walked along the road.

It wasn't long before birdsong and the sound of waves were replaced by the drone of traffic, the green cliffs replaced by bricks and concrete. Along pavements, we mingled with a mass of people migrating to the town centre. A carnival of colour and noise, the air was full of clashing perfumes and aftershaves with a splash of morning-after beer breath. Garish shorts and tiny skirts were the norm, and I stood out like a teetotaller at a cider farm. But I wasn't a stranger to Newquay, and every now and then I would see a nightclub or café that reminded me of my youth. Those days felt an age away as I travelled through the town, weather beaten and sunburnt, dog in tow.

We soon reached Fistral Beach and heard the excited whoops of spectators watching a surfing competition. A loud tannoy whistled and crackled over the heads of the throng, the words indecipherable. On our own private mission, Jess and I skirted around the hubbub. On the headland, behind the revellers, stood the stately hundred-year-old Headland Hotel. I couldn't resist doing a sketch of the intricate facade, with its red brick details and rows of windows. While I drew, Fran texted me to say she could see us through her binoculars. Mortified, I gave a self-conscious wave and a thumbs up in her general direction. She sent another text saying she'd put the kettle on.

The Headland Hotel

That was all the encouragement I needed and I quickly put my sketchbook away. As I shouldered my rucksack, a commotion over my head revealed a low flying helicopter, which landed two hundred yards away on the wet sand near a group of lifeguards. The unfolding drama attracted onlookers from both ends of the beach. Jess and I purposefully went in the opposite direction, towards a flight of wooden steps that led to the clifftops. From there, a short walk around the headland ended at Fran's flat.

Ever the pragmatist, Fran handed me a plate of beans on toast and a cup of tea as soon as I got through the door, then placed a bowl of water down for Jess. I greedily tucked into my food, while recounting the walk from Porthcothan. A short while later, Jack knocked on the door and Jess went wild, wagging her whole body and grinning from ear to ear.

I offered to drive us home, eager to be behind the wheel after two weeks without a car. The forty-minute journey gave me time to reacclimatise; I had been living in a bubble with nothing to do but walk, and nothing to think about but reaching the next B&B. Now, whether I liked it or not, I would be embroiled in the little things: food shopping, bills and cleaning the house, all while completing a fourteen-mile walk every day. Still, it was a wonderful feeling to go through the front door and be surrounded by familiar things.

A bath and glass of wine later, I flopped down on the sofa ready for my daily dose of weather. Jess snuggled up in her bed and fell asleep, blissfully unaware we still had four hundred and thirty miles to go.

12 miles • 31,671 steps • Grading: Moderate

DAY 16 – NEWQUAY TO PERRANPORTH

That first night at home I had such a good night's sleep it took all my willpower to get up. Putting off the decision, I burrowed under the covers and went over the day's walk in my head. The ten-mile stretch was one of my favourite walks in Cornwall. It consisted of four beaches, sandwiched between exposed headlands. There were no hikes in and out of bottomless valleys, and no relentless flights of steps, just beaches and headlands.

I ate a healthier-than-usual breakfast of porridge, then packed my rucksack while listening to the local radio for the weather forecast. While I bustled about, I kept an eye on Jess, wondering if, with the choice to stay at home, she would still opt to come with me. I found out soon enough. At the door, I experimentally called her name. She yawned, hauled herself out of bed, stretched, scratched, then staggered to the car and clambered in. Such zeal. It reassured me to know she came of her own free will and not, as I feared at the beginning, under duress.

As planned, Andrew turned up at seven, and we drove in convoy to Perranporth to leave my car. I felt out of sorts driving to the start of the walk after two weeks of going everywhere on foot. But there were benefits of travelling by car, and I skipped a dreary walk around the Gannel Estuary by asking Andrew to drop us off at the National Trust car park behind Crantock Beach on the other side.

I thanked Andrew for the lift, and Jess and I got going, walking beside a little stream and onto the sand. The tide was beginning to push up the Gannel, covering the exposed depressions and pools. At high water the river almost touches the steps of the Fern Pit Café on the other side of the estuary, and would cut it off were it not for the little ferry that runs from the beach to a pontoon on the other side.

Standing on the shore and looking at the café brought back a wonderful memory. A close friend lived in Crantock and had once invited me for lunch on a sticky June afternoon. She and I had ambled barefoot to the beach from her house and hopped on the ferry. The owners of the café caught and cooked their own lobsters and crabs, and we reverently picked out a lobster, still warm from the pot. Then we returned to her house and prepared a simple lunch: new potatoes with mint and butter, a salad with a homemade French dressing, and the freshest lobster I had ever eaten. A meal I will never forget.

With my head full of memories, I'd reached the end of Crantock Beach before I knew it. We scrambled up a sheer sand dune and onto an overgrown track snaking along the cliff side. Over low bushes, I took in the fantastic views across the bay to Pentire Point East and, beyond the headland, an island called The Goose, which looked nothing like its namesake. They never do. The path gently rose and fell making its way to Pentire Point West. As we approached the end of the headland, we abandoned the confined path for wide open clifftops. Optimistic that I might catch sight of a seal, I kept to the edge, scrutinising the rocks below.

Rounding the headland, we turned back on ourselves and were soon looking down on the skinny strip of sand at Porth Joke, the second in a string of four beaches, and a hidden gem. Tricky access and no amenities means the beach is often only visited by locals. At the back of the beach, a little stream flows from a valley, running the length of the sand to the sea. I was about to jump across when the sky turned an ominous grey and it started to pour with rain. We took cover in one of the many caves cut into the steep-sided cliffs, but within minutes it stopped. A freak shower. We made our way onto the low cliffs on the other side of the beach and soon reached Kelsey Head. In early summer, sea pinks smother the headland – a sight to see – and when they die back the ground becomes a joy to walk on: a spongy, springy carpet of close-cropped grass. Again, I kept a sharp eye out for seals but saw only cormorants and gulls bobbing about on the dark blue water below us.

It wasn't long before we reached the third beach – Holywell – bigger than Porth Joke, but still a baby in comparison to Perran. During the winter months, fishermen visit Holywell to fish for bass; I'd spent many a blustery day attempting to cast into the crashing waves in the hope of outwitting a monster. For now, the waves were mere ripples and the bass would be in deeper water, terrorising the reefs and shipwrecks.

The benign weather might not have been good for fishing, but suited walking perfectly. Jess and I made short work of the next mile, keeping to the firm sand at the water's edge. At the far end, we crossed a stream and climbed onto the next headland. Immediately I noticed a change in the landscape, with the springy grass and open clifftops being replaced by dusty shale tracks and gorse. Wild ponies, straggly manes obscuring their eyes, grazed in amongst the sparse vegetation, unconcerned by Jess and me.

Despite the presence of the ponies, most of the clifftop between Holywell and Perran is MoD land. This became obvious when we were corralled into a wire-enclosed pathway shielding us from blocks of unsightly concrete barracks and other army paraphernalia. Not the most beautiful section of the Coast Path, but the best was yet to come.

First, we negotiated a ribbon-thin path, so close to the edge of the cliff that a puff of wind could send us tumbling to our inevitable death. I kept my eyes down, watching every step until the danger passed. When at last I did look up, I took in the jaw-dropping view of Perran Beach, its majesty enhanced by the low tide, which exposed miles of extra sand, making for a fantastic dog walk. When I lived in Truro, I went there almost every day with my dog, Poppy. She had been difficult to tire out until I devised the game of "whacking a ball with a baseball bat up the sand dunes". Up and down, all the way along the beach she would keep going until my swinging arm went numb. In comparison, Jess was a doddle to walk, never requiring me to throw – or do – anything.

Halfway along the beach, the dunes rose up to cover the back of a monstrous cliff that threw dark shadows over the sand. The temperature dropped in the shade and I moved into the sun. From a distance, the wall of rock towered above the beach, a brooding presence that dwarfed the figures walking beneath it. Seagulls, mere specks, swooped in and out of the shade and squawked from nests hidden in deep recesses. Beneath the raucous gulls, rock pools brimmed with turquoise water, and behind them coal-black caves burrowed into the base of the cliff. It's no wonder I've been compelled to paint so many pictures of those cliffs over the years.

Less inspiring is Perranporth town, a typical seaside resort. Beach shops, surf shops, cafés and chippies line the high street. Whereas St Ives is all about artists, Newlyn about fishing and Padstow about food, Perranporth caters for tourists. The town lacks the romance and charm of some of the other famous Cornish hot spots, but none of that matters to the thousands of people who visit every summer, cramming onto the beach and filling the cafés and pubs. I took advantage of the shops and bought a hoard of oatcakes and nuts, and even found a surf shop that sold zinc lip balm.

When I got home, I opened my computer and trawled through two weeks' worth of emails. Most were spam or work related, but one came as an unexpected surprise: a message from Kelly, the woman who'd evaporated from the face of the earth after spending the day with me (gulp). Intrigued, I read the email. After saying goodbye, she'd found the campsite, put up her tent, eaten a Pot Noodle (probably) and gone to bed. All well and good. However, that night her dog, Kipper, became violently ill, and Kelly took him by train to her parents' house so he could be treated and nursed back to health. When she knew he would survive, she left him with her parents and returned to the Coast Path. He'd been suffering from exhaustion and dehydration, but made a full recovery. I thought back to his little legs and the fact that he'd needed Kelly to carry him at the end of the walk, and it all made sense, poor chap. So, mystery solved. No murder or foul play, merely a dehydrated Kipper.

12.1 miles • 30,250 steps • Grading: Moderate

DAY 17 – PERRANPORTH TO PORTREATH

I rose early, ready for another day on the Coast Path. Once again, Jess wanted to come, and after a quick breakfast, we made a move. I drove to Portreath, parked my car and got into Andrew's car, and he ferried Jess and me back to Perranporth. The car journeys at the beginning and end of the day affected the overall feel of the walk. Rather than arriving and leaving on foot, the smooth momentum was broken by the need to find free parking, change cars and consult maps. Despite the disruption, I tried to keep in mind that at least I got to see Jack every evening, and was able to sleep in my own bed.

So, another drop-off, a wave goodbye, and Jess and I were on our way. We left the car park beside the beach and walked up the hill to Droskyn Point. Near the end of the headland was a youth hostel with views that a boutique hotel would charge crazy money for. Before setting off, I peered down on the beach, transformed from the day before. Spray, foam and booming waves swamped the shore, leaving only a thin piece of sand. Dog walkers, confined to the strip, tramped, heads down against the belligerent onshore wind. High on the exposed headland, Jess and I also took a battering. My hair danced about my face, blinding me, as I fought to get it into a ponytail. Once I'd tied it back, I only had a moment to look about before a gust impatiently shoved me from behind, urging me to move on.

We set off along a path etched into heathland. There were no trees or shrubs, nothing to temper the bullying wind. As we left the youth hostel far behind and struck out over the cliffs, I felt skittish, compelled every few minutes to look over my shoulder. I didn't know if my disquiet was due to the desolate landscape, the fact we were alone, or the wind, but for the first time even Jess's reassuring presence wasn't enough to make me feel safe.

I resolved to walk faster and with the help of the wind I made good progress. Near Cligga Head we came upon a scruffy clearing in the heather, scattered with the crumbling remains of industrial buildings. I hesitated; if something awful were to happen, it would be here. Playing for time, I opened my guide book and learned that the ruins were the remains of a wolframite and tin mine and the site of an ammunition factory. This information did little to allay my anxiety, but it did provide a possible explanation for my unease. Maybe the heath was haunted by a man who'd worked in the factory. One fateful day, he lit a fag while mixing something dangerous with something volatile. And voila! My jitters were caused by a restless (and probably limbless) spirit.

There was nothing for it but to sprint through the ruins and keep running. As a compromise, I half trotted, half stumbled, until I was well clear of the area. The short spurt of energy got me to the edge of Perranporth Airfield, where I noticed a shift in the atmosphere. Whatever had bothered me – be it the isolation or the torso of a spirit miner – evaporated. My mood improved further when we reached the village of St Agnes and at last saw signs of life. As Jess and I mingled with the dog walkers at Trevaunance Cove, I felt relaxed for the first time since setting off, back on familiar territory.

Over the years, the Coast Path from St Agnes to Portreath has been one of my favourite walks, elevated by a café at Chapel Porth and a bar at Porthtowan, both of which I hoped to visit. First stop, St Agnes Head to take in the view: headland after headland all the way to Godrevy Lighthouse. From there, the path split in two. Without thinking, I chose the lower one, which wriggled along the cliff edge towards the iconic and much photographed Towanroath Engine House. On the way, I remembered to pick up a couple of stones and put them in my pocket for later …

We continued along the rough track, banks of heather on one side and a vertical drop to the sea on the other; a wild, wind-battered environment. There were mine shafts all over the cliffs, capped off with metal pyramids called "Clwyd Caps". And, of course, engine houses. Built to contain a living, breathing, steam engine, their robust design held up against all the storms the Atlantic could throw at them. In fact, Towanroath Engine House, with its red brick window arches and thick granite walls, resembled a new build waiting for a roof, rather than a hundred-year-old ruin.

There are plenty of engine houses scattered all over Cornwall, but Towanroath occupies one of the best locations. Built on a cliff edge, surrounded by heather, with surf beaches and rocky headlands as a backdrop, the building and the landscape encompass all the rugged romance of Cornwall's north coast in one spot. I wanted to sketch it, so I made myself comfortable on a wall and began to draw. I concentrated on the gable end of the engine house and the arched windows. There were three, one above the other, each with a different coloured view: grey brick, purple heather and blue sky – like stained glass in an ancient chapel.

I made notes on the colours then put everything away, ready to make a move, but before I left there was something else I wanted to do. A few feet from the ruin, a metal grid covered a mine shaft with a six-hundred-foot drop. Six hundred feet! You could lower the BT Tower into it and have room to spare. The ground around the grid was picked clean of anything small enough to fit through the holes. But I came prepared. I conjured up the stones I'd acquired earlier, dropping one after the other into the shaft, and waited. When at last I heard the echoing splash, I felt oddly satisfied, hoping the offering would bring me and Jess luck.

Sure enough, the wind dropped on our way to Chapel Porth, and when we arrived, the café was serving my favourite: hot chocolate. I ordered a mug and found a packet of oatcakes in my rucksack to share with Jess. Then we sat near the beach and watched the waves while my drink cooled enough for me to slurp.

We didn't linger; there were miles to go, starting with a tedious tramp inland then a sharp right turn, towards the sea on a steady incline. Then a stroll over the clifftop, weaving around patches of heather and spoil heaps, an ugly legacy of the tin mining years. Before long, we peered down on the beach at Porthtowan. Surfers sat astride their boards, bobbing about in the still water behind the waves, dogs frolicked in the shallows and kids rooted about in the rock pools.

Behind the dunes was The Blue Bar, yet another haunt from my youth. As if hijacked by muscle memory, I skipped through the door and found myself standing at the bar before I had time to think. Nothing had changed, not the wooden floor covered in sand, nor the smell of chips and sun cream, nor the music, a little too loud. Raising my voice, I ordered a beer and grabbed a table. While I sipped my drink, the bar began to fill up, and soon rowdy punters pushed in on us from all sides. Jess started to cry, and when someone asked for a chair, I offered them the table, taking it as a sign to leave. We turned our backs on the noise and bustle and returned to the blessedly peaceful cliffs.

The strip of coast between Porthtowan and Portreath is owned by the good old MoD and is the site of an air defence radar station operated by the RAF. A chain-link fence running parallel with the Coast Path was decorated with signs warning us of the possibility of blundering off crumbling cliffs and falling into bottomless mine shafts. I put Jess on her lead to keep her near me, but, despite the dire warnings, the path remained level and stayed well back from the cliff edge, making for a pleasant walk. And then we came to a flight of wooden steps disappearing into the abyss of a sheer-sided valley. I untied my walking poles from the back of my rucksack, took a deep breath, and lowered myself, step by knee-knackering step, to the bottom. Then, after a short pause, I hauled myself up the other side.

No sooner had I recovered than I found myself at the top of another flight of steps into another valley. Once again, leaning on my poles with every step, I lumbered all the way down and hauled myself all the way up. When my breathing returned to normal, I staggered on until halted by a diversion. This steered around a sizeable landslip, on the exact spot where – years before – I had set up my travel easel and spent an afternoon painting. To my surprise, the cliffs I'd captured on canvas that day were gone. All that remained was a pile of mud and rubble dissolving into the sea. The erosion was so extensive that the diverted Coast Path kept away from the cliffs altogether, and we finished the walk by missing out the final headland and ambling down a hairpin road into Portreath Harbour.

With my car parked nearby, Jess jumped in and I drove us home.

12.4 miles • 33,113 steps • Grading: Moderate/Strenuous

While ploughing through a bowl of porridge, I mulled over the impending eighteen-mile walk. The guide book described the terrain as *moderate to easy*, consisting mostly of beaches, including a tedious schlepp around the Hayle Estuary. The extra miles, through industrial areas and along main roads, would add nothing to the experience, so ruthlessly I cut them out. Instead, I opted to leave my car in Hayle, drive around the estuary and continue the walk to St Ives. This plan also gave me the choice (if I felt tired when I got to Hayle) of driving home and doing the last few miles the next day.

Shaving a bit of distance off the walk improved my motivation and, in high spirits, I packed and called Jess. She appeared as eager as me and clambered into the boot of the car with barely any encouragement and only a light shove.

After the usual hoo-ha of finding somewhere to park and changing cars, Andrew drove Jess and me from Hayle to Portreath. We left the car park and followed Battery Road onto the cliffs. After two steep valleys, the ground levelled off and we walked between furrows at the edge of a thin field, the prickly remains of the harvested crop scrunching under my boots. Jess, obviously enjoying the same sensation, pounded up and down the field as the stems snapped and crackled beneath her paws. By the time we reached the stile at the other end of the field, she was panting with exertion. I felt her hot breath on the back of my legs as we walked along a road and through a string of car parks.

Where there are cars, of course, there are people, and within a few metres the peaceful clifftop transformed into a bustling thoroughfare. I could see why. Owned by the National Trust, the North Cliffs are easily accessible and almost flat, perfect for a gentle stroll, dog walk or spot of seal watching. The many sheltered coves and caves on the way to Navax Point attract large numbers of seals at certain times of the year, and to spot them takes no more effort than walking from a parked car to the cliff edge. Unfortunately, the proximity of the cliffs attracts people looking for something other than wildlife. Hell's Mouth, a little further along the coast, lures souls searching for oblivion.

On the other side of the road from Hell's Mouth I spotted a café of the same name. Somehow, this didn't sit well with me. Betty's Tea Rooms, Katy's Cake Emporium or Sally's Sandwich Bar sound like places of comfort and cheer, but Hell's Mouth Café brought to mind images of fire and brimstone better suited to a Meatloaf album cover. Needless to say, I didn't cross over but continued on to Godrevy Point.

We walked through fields of gorse and heather, home to a herd of Shetland ponies. They seemed docile, but after a previous encounter, I knew they could stick up for themselves. A well-aimed kick from one of the little steeds forever solved my first dog's compulsion to chase horses. She never approached a horse again, no matter what size, preferring to run very fast in the opposite direction.

As we got closer to Navax Point, I kept a sharp eye out for packs of humans standing, necks strained, at the cliff edge: a sure giveaway seals were nearby. It wasn't long before the sound of snapping cameras alerted me to a likely group. Careful not to startle the engrossed photographers, I tagged on to the end of the line and followed their gaze. Far below, dotted about the low water mark, jostled a harem of whiskery blobs: grey seals. They played up to the paparazzi above, fighting and bickering like actors in a soap opera as we watched, enthralled. The human group swelled to a dozen or more as others came to watch the seals, and I left them to it, confident I would see plenty more in the weeks ahead.

We took a shortcut through fields, missing out the tip of Godrevy Point and the accompanying crowds. The attractions of the offshore lighthouse, a great surf beach, café and loos, all make Godrevy a popular destination, even out of season. For the time being, the summer dog ban still applied on the beach so we continued over low cliffs and through a National Trust car park. On the other side of the car park, behind the beach, a scruffy nature reserve served as an alternative route. Despite the air of neglect, the waymarks (slabs of granite with the acorn chiselled into them) worked a treat and looked very smart.

On the other side, we had two choices: either go through the sprawling warren of Gwithian dunes (with its risk of adders) or make our way along Hayle beach, which was dog-friendly from this point. I chose the beach: no adders and no distractions. If we stayed on the sand at the water's edge, we could make good time. I checked my watch; there'd be plenty of daylight to get us to St Ives, as long as we didn't dawdle. With this in mind, I kept my boots on rather than following my usual habit of taking them off and paddling. I regretted the decision for the next three miles.

Godrevy Lighthouse

Repeatedly, I asked myself why, while absolutely refusing to stop and take them off.

Three miles later, feet throbbing in burning hot socks, I reached the River Hayle. At low tide the water looked benign, a cinch to cross on foot, but it was deceptive. When the tide turned, the currents and swells in the river would become treacherous. Even standing on the bank, I could feel the power of the surge.

Not surprisingly, all the nutrients and other tasty morsels that swept into the river encouraged bass, mullet and flounder, which in turn encouraged lots of fishermen. The brave few wore waders and went in up to their waists while the water swirled around them. Ever cautious, on my own excursions to the river, I would fish from the quay, perched in my car boot, with a flask of tea to hand.

But not today. To the left of the river, Jess and I walked through a landscape in turmoil. The acrid smell of hot tarmac filled the air. Half-finished buildings, encased in scaffolding, loomed beside an unfinished road. Tiny figures in hi-vis vests manoeuvred diggers and tippers that belched clouds of brown smoke. And everywhere, the din of men asking each other things in loud voices.

Hurrying through the building site, we crossed a bridge into the town. On the way to my car, I bought a hot pasty, and, while we walked, tore off chunks for Jess and chunks for me. In the time it took to find the car, throw in my rucksack, help Jess into the back, and plonk myself with a sigh into the comfy driver's seat, the pasty had worked its deadly magic. Moments after the last mouthful, the delicious alchemy of potato, turnip, beef and onion with a light seasoning of salt and pepper, all wrapped in pastry, put me into a stupor. Unwilling to give up when we were so close, I turned the air-con on full and aimed the vents at my face. The blast of freezing air woke me up, and I quickly regained my faculties. Another lesson learnt: never, eat a pasty for lunch when you've got important things to do in the afternoon.

With the windows down and Dolly Parton at full I-will-always-love-you volume, I raced around the estuary and parked on the other side. The short trip invigorated me, and I leapt out of the car with renewed fervour, unlike Jess, who, still groggy from her pasty come-down, took a while to come around. Mindful of her fragile state, I slowed right down for the last few miles.

After a short stroll past a church and over a golf course, with views right up the coast to Godrevy Lighthouse, we turned left into the dunes. Then, steering clear of the maze of sandy tracks, rabbit holes and marram grass, we followed the railway line between the dunes and the golf course. The single-track branch line that links St Erth to St Ives has a reputation as one of the most beautiful train journeys in the country. Beautiful, but brief: the trip lasts a mere fourteen minutes. Handily, the tracks were going in the same direction as us, and we walked beside them for the length of the dunes before climbing steps into a tunnel of thick vegetation.

The foliage blocked all views, forming a barrier that both protected and confined us as we picked our way in the dim light along the cliff edge to the tip of the headland. We finally squeezed between a row of gardens and emerged, blinking, onto a rocky ledge. I stood on the natural platform and savoured the spectacular view, dominated by an arc of clotted-cream-coloured sand that swept for miles up the coast.

In contrast to the virtually empty Porthkidney Sands, Carbis Bay – on the other side of the headland – teemed with people, the sheltered beach covered in blankets, parasols and windbreaks of all colours. Above the beach, the smart Carbis Bay Hotel overshadowed all the other buildings. The Coast Path went right past the front door and offered us walkers a tantalising glimpse of the luxury on offer. Soon after, we met up with the railway line once more, crossed a footbridge and walked beside the track and into the railway station at St Ives.

We were caught up in the flow of tourists getting off the train, but when they scattered into the town Jess and I lined up with a group of people waiting patiently at the bus station, both of us glad to stop and rest in the afternoon sun. The atmosphere felt congenial, everyone sated and ready to go home after a day of overindulgence and sightseeing. When the bus arrived, we clambered on and were instantly surrounded by school kids. They formed a circle around Jess, who lay asleep on the floor, and fired questions at me about her. When I told them she was bred to hunt lions, they stepped back, eyes wide, until I reassured them she loved children. Reverently, they took it in turns to stroke her as she dozed.

At our stop, the crowd of kids respectfully parted to let Jess through and waved through the window as the bus moved off.

I found our car, cranked up my Dolly CD, and drove us home.

15.2 miles • 37,758 steps • Grading: Moderate/Strenuous

DAY 19 – ST IVES TO ZENNOR

A Granite Tor

The six-mile trek from St Ives to Zennor holds the reputation of being the toughest part of the entire SWCP. A glance in the guide book confirmed it was, indeed, *severe*. Not *moderate*, or even *strenuous*, but *severe*: the hardest of all the descriptions. With some difficulty, I swallowed a mouthful of porridge and tried to focus on the bright side. There were two things in my favour: one, the walk was short, at just over six miles; and two, the landscape around Zennor was known for its wild beauty.

Back to St Ives, and this time I asked Andrew to drop Jess and me off at the opposite end of the town, near Porthmeor Beach. The first mile, in sight of the beach, was surprisingly sedate, giving me ample time to get my nerves under control. Around Clodgy Point, the flat clifftops and uninterrupted views of St Ives attracted a motley mishmash of people taking part in a morning stroll. But one by one, as the terrain began to change, they abruptly remembered an important appointment and turned back. In no time, Jess and I were on our own, which suited me fine. I wanted space and solitude for this challenge.

Beyond Clodgy Point, the path weaved between clusters of boulders. These soon multiplied, crowding the path and smothering it altogether in places. Strangely, as I scrambled over and around the obstructions, I realised I was enjoying myself. As my heart raced with exertion, I craved more. I began to jog slightly, brushing aside bracken and brambles, puffing around granite outcrops and mounds of stunted heather. Although I'd seen the moorland and weather-beaten tors between St Ives and Zennor before, I'd always been in my car. Up close, the rough-hewn landscape looked and felt like nothing I'd experienced.

We hiked around rock-strewn coves and craggy headlands, waded through bogs, leapt over streams, and climbed slopes littered with boulders. All this, and a backdrop of turquoise sea more befitting the Caribbean than the north coast of Cornwall. I fought to keep my eyes on the ground, despite the distracting landscape, and tried not to dwell on what would happen if I broke an ankle or Jess got a leg caught between the rocks. The fear only heightened the thrill.

A little further on, we were confronted by a sea of boulders with no apparent way through. Heart hammering, I heaved myself up and over the first one, and then turned to assist Jess. In this manner, we clambered up and scrambled over, scooched around and scaled each new obstruction until, legs shaking, we slid from the last boulder onto the clear ground, my elation mirrored by the look of gratification on Jess's face to have all four paws on a flat surface. I gave her an oatcake and reassured her the worst was over. From Porthzennor Cove, the cliffs levelled off, and at Zennor Head a track going inland met up with the road into the village. At the car, I opened the boot and Jess jumped in. I gave her a stroke. "Good girl, Jess. You did well." We both did well. I tentatively wondered if maybe this was it, maybe I was finally getting fitter.

6.5 miles • 16,248 steps • Grading: Severe

DAY 20 – ZENNOR TO ST JUST (CAPE CORNWALL)

Andrew dropped Jess and me off at the tiny car park in Zennor. Before he left, I gave a positive thumbs up, full of bonhomie. Then, eager to test my new abilities, I pulled on my rucksack, tightened the straps around my middle, popped a humbug in my mouth and set off …

And from there all my bravado from the day before melted away as fast as ice cream in a pizza oven. A twinge in my ankle triggered a niggle in my knee that travelled to my hips; not a good sign in the first few metres of a fourteen-mile walk, and a terrible sign at the start of a stretch described in the guide book as *moderate to severe*. Deflated, I lowered my expectations and resigned myself to a long, hard slog.

Windswept, Rugged, Beautiful

I took two paracetamol and we made our way back to the coast. I soon forgot about my dodgy joints when we picked up the path from the day before. The landscape was stunning: every headland garnished with stacks of granite ranging in size from cereal packets to small cars, the grey stone split by fissures and splattered with blobs of white lichen. Inland, fields and the occasional farmhouse were separated by ancient stone walls from the surrounding moorland. In the shelter of the walls grew twisted hawthorn trees, cowering from Atlantic storms. Windswept, rugged, beautiful. And quiet. An absolute silence surrounded us as we walked. No birdsong, or screeching seagulls, no tractors belching diesel, not even the ubiquitous sound of the waves on the shore. Only my laboured breath and Jess's panting.

Wincing and wheezing, I struggled on, past Cove Cottage – plonked on the end of a stubby promontory, as close to the sea as a house could be without being swept away. Beyond the cottage, jutting into the sea, was Gurnard's Head (I don't need to tell you it looked nothing like a gurnard's head, or any other fish's head).

Fortunately, we didn't need to investigate further, and instead cut across what was presumably meant to be the gurnard's neck. One challenge evaded. But there were plenty more hurdles, starting with the Coast Path itself, which wriggled over the ground like a snake in its death throes, often fading away altogether, as if rubbed out, particularly through marshland. As I deliberated over how to get through one such area, I became aware of voices behind me. Spooked, I turned to see, a fair distance away, a colourful gaggle of ramblers. The sight of them shocked me into movement and, calling Jess, I hurtled across the saturated ground. But as hard as I tried to stay ahead, they effortlessly gained on us, and then, to my humiliation, overtook us.

Shrugging off my rucksack, I let it drop to the ground with a deflated thump, then lowered myself onto a lump of granite and shared some oatcakes with Jess. What was wrong with me? Was I genetically incapable of walking at a respectable speed for an extended length of time, forever destined to be bringing up the rear?

I scowled from my perch as the ramblers retreated over a ridge, then heaved myself into a standing position, hauled on my rucksack, inserted a humbug into my mouth and followed. They stayed in sight for the next mile until, near Pendeen Lighthouse, a bottleneck at the top of a flight of steps gave Jess and I a chance to catch up. I peered along the line of impatiently waiting walkers and observed a doubling of their numbers. In addition to the group I'd trailed behind, there were ladies in fleeces and knitted bobble hats, and men in army-type uniforms. A motley bunch, all focused on the same objective: Pendeen Lighthouse, at the top of a steep hill. One by one, they filed down the steps and up the other side of the valley, and suddenly the race was on for the summit. By the time Jess and I showed up, most of the walkers were lounging on the grass around the lighthouse, tucking into sandwiches and airing their feet. Seizing my chance to shine, I straightened my back, and, swinging my arms, strode past the lot of them.

It occurred to me later that a rest and a bite to eat might have been a better idea. My feet felt like sandbags and my hips burned but I couldn't stop. The thought of being overtaken again was too much to bear. Fuelled solely by my own ego, I pressed on.

The clifftops on the other side of the lighthouse showed copious signs of Cornwall's industrial past, hence being known as the Tin Coast. We came to Geevor Tin Mine, which was a working mine until relatively recently, but had been converted into a museum and heritage centre. The site sprawled over acres, with the museum and mine set back and the red-soiled clifftop scarred with remnants of the mining process. Covered in dust, the ruins resembled an archaeological dig in a desert. Tourists flitted from one pile of stones to another, taking pictures and consulting guide books, while Jess and I shuffled past like ghosts.
The Tin Coast tour continued, including a brief diversion to the Levant Mine and Beam Engine, site of a disaster that killed thirty-one miners in 1919. The building now houses a restored 1840s steam engine.

At the side of the car park, I took a wrong turn, and while finding my bearings met an equally lost couple with their Border terrier. Together we consulted our maps and promptly found the right way. Retracing our steps through the car park, we realised our walking strides matched, and naturally started to chat. They introduced themselves as John and Hanna; they were interesting and funny, and in no time I forgot about my issues and began to enjoy myself. Jess revived too and frolicked with the terrier.

We walked away from Levant Mine, towards the most iconic and precariously placed of all the engine houses in Cornwall, Botallack Mine. I gawped at the two engine houses built on top of rocky outcrops at the base of the cliffs. "How on earth did they achieve it?" I wondered aloud. Hanna shook her head. "Unbelievable." While John took photos, I did a rough sketch, then we pressed on, past more ruins littering the landscape around the cliffs. In single file we descended into a little valley, keeping up the conversation by talking to each other's backpacks.

Soon we were in sight of the peaked headland of Cape Cornwall, crowned with an ornate red brick chimney. The distinctive landmark was once part of the Cape Cornwall Mine, until saved from demolition and used as a navigation aid for ships. A fitting exclamation mark at the end of the dramatic seven-mile stretch of Tin Coast.

Although the days of mining tin are over, Cape Cornwall retains a modest fishing fleet. A dozen painted boats lined up at the top of the slipway in the shelter of Priest Cove and above the high-water mark fisherman's huts were clinging to the surrounding rocks. Constructed from a mishmash of bleached planks, stone and corrugated sheets, they were not pretty, but practical – a place to store the lobster pots, buoys and net bins – and wonderful to sketch.

Above the cove sat a National Trust car park and the end of my walk. A burger van sold hot drinks and lollies, and, after ordering cups of tea for the humans and lollies for the dogs, I sat with Hanna and John at a picnic table. Although my walk had finished, they still had two miles of coast to get to their B&B. With such a head start it was unlikely we'd meet again, so I thanked them for their company, wished them luck and said goodbye.

Tired and sore, I opened the boot for Jess and slumped into the car. I had a long drive home, but at least I could sing along with Dolly and relax in a comfy seat.

13.7 miles • 34,145 steps • Grading: Strenuous

DAY 21 – ST. JUST (CAPE CORNWALL) TO PORTHCURNO

A briny breeze blew in from the sea as Jess and I clambered out of Andrew's car at Cape Cornwall. From the car park, we walked up a road beside a row of run-down cottages. After some tramping across clifftops, the path altered course and went inland above Cot Valley. My instincts rebelled; I'd become so used to the coast on my right that anything else seemed wrong. I felt tethered to the sea by an ethereal elastic band: the further I pulled away, the stronger the resistance. In time we crossed to the other side of the valley and turned back towards the sea, and I relaxed. As the valley opened out onto the coast, we came to Porth Nanven Cove. Speckled egg-shaped stones of all sizes covered the seashore. At the top of the beach, the stones were almost white, graduating to a burnt butter brown at the water's edge. Not the most comfortable spot for sunbathing, but great for fishing, or, at low tide, rock pooling.

Beyond the valley, we travelled across slopes of bracken, turning a rusty brown in the last days of summer. In amongst the vegetation, rocks peppered the ground, and tumbled from the low cliffs onto the beaches and into the sea. Despite the rocky terrain, the Coast Path remained level and well worn, a sure sign we were on a popular section. Although the area appeared isolated, there were a number of car parks within easy walking distance, and surfing hot spot Sennen was nearby. With all that in mind, Jess and I had yet to encounter a single person.

And then, while negotiating a flight of uneven steps into Nanquidno Cove, I heard a woman calling, "Sasha!" I couldn't have been more surprised if Jess had sprung onto her hind legs and danced the can-can. Raising my head, I saw my sister's friend waving to me at the bottom of the steps, with her husband and little boy. In unison, we cried, "What are you doing here?"

"This is one of our favourite beaches," she replied.

"It's great for bass fishing," her husband added, knowing what a keen fisherwoman I am. "Is that why you're here?"

"No, actually, I'm on a six-hundred-and-thirty-mile walk."

They both laughed.

"You are hilarious, Sash," she said, whispering behind her hand, "and we're on a drug smuggling mission."

"Ha ha," I responded, nonplussed. "Well, I'd better go." I waved goodbye and stomped off.

After a while, I realised that in my haste I'd chosen a path going away from the sea. I traced my steps back to the cove, where my sister's friend and her family were busy exploring the beach. They didn't see me, but I'm sure I could hear them still chuckling.

Further on we came to a sizeable granite protuberance erupting from the middle of the path. I investigated the vicinity for a way around the obstruction, but after a thorough search I resigned myself to climbing over it. Tightening the straps on my rucksack, I scrambled onto the first ledge and cajoled Jess to follow. It wasn't as precarious as I'd feared, and we soon reached the top, squeezed through a narrow cleft and emerged onto a flat rock. As I readied myself to clamber down, I noticed, stuffed into a crack, a wad of loo paper. I didn't need an imagination to know why someone put it there, but I was flummoxed by how anyone would think the exposed ledge at the top of a granite stack, visible for miles, would be a suitable place to expose their arse.

In fact, the sight of loo paper was common all over the South West Coast Path. Two other things also appeared to be indigenous to the path – glossy, liquorice-black slugs, and fat, hairy caterpillars. Loo paper, slugs and caterpillars. An unusual threesome that seemed only to coexist on the SWCP. Did one need the others to survive? It remains a mystery.

After making it to the other side, Jess and I rounded Aire Point and were rewarded with a fantastic view across Whitesand Bay to Sennen at the far end. Dogs were banned from the sand, so we took a convoluted path through the dunes. In a car park near the beach, I caught a whiff of chips coming from a snack van and suddenly felt ravenous. Instead of joining the queue, I went further along the prom to a café I knew. At the counter, I ordered a prawn salad sandwich to take away. Outside, too greedy to wait until I found a bench, I ate as I walked.

This turned into an unexpected challenge. Scraps of prawn and lettuce fell out of the soft bread every time I tried to take a bite. Jess snapped the morsels up and weaved around my legs in search of more. As I wrestled with keeping the ingredients together, negotiating a flight of steps, and avoiding my dog, the bread disintegrated entirely and landed with a splat at my feet. In a supernatural turn of speed, Jess pounced on the soggy mess and gulped it down in one go. Angry, and hungry, I ransacked my rucksack for a packet of oatcakes, consoling myself with the fact that at least one of us had benefited from a nourishing lunch.

Within sight of Land's End, the clifftop filled with people. Not the usual ramblers but ordinary, everyday people of all ages, including young kids. Up until now, the majority of people I'd encountered were either retirees – including one memorable woman in her eighties who sported immaculate hair, pink slacks and trainers – or foreign students, with unwieldy backpacks and boundless enthusiasm. I rarely saw civilians, especially on the remote sections between towns.

Sketches Along the Way

In no mood to hang around, I nonetheless thought it would be a good idea to have a photo in front of the signpost for Land's End. A crowd milled about a barrier in front of the sign while people took turns taking pictures and posing. When our turn came around, a nice woman offered to take a photo of Jess and me together, but Jess refused to cooperate. She yawned, stretched, and pretended not to know me. Through gritted teeth, I pleaded with her to stand next to me, for the nice lady. As she edged nearer, I lunged forward, gripped her collar and dragged her towards me, yelling, "Quickly, take it!" The resulting picture would not win any awards – both of us came out blurred – but the sign was sharp, at least proving we were there.

Having a photo taken in front of the iconic sign is one of dozens of things a person can do at the furthest point on the map. If I wanted, I could eat a three-course meal, snaffle a pasty, buy a necklace or a jumper, or treat myself to an ice cream or some fudge. I could even pet a ferret. In fact, at Greeb Farm, a two-hundred-year-old restored smallholding only yards from the central hub, visitors have the opportunity to fondle all sorts of furry creatures. It struck me as an odd choice of attraction to celebrate the UK's most southwesterly point. Perhaps I'm missing the obvious connection between stroking little animals and the windswept, barren landscape of one of the most famous locations in the country.

The SWCP runs through the middle of the farm, so we did pay a brief visit, during which Jess tried to instigate a game with the free-range chickens, provoking such a clamour I expected a reprimand from the farmer at any moment. Maybe their hands were full juggling ferrets, but for whatever reason, no one came, so I grasped Jess's collar and bolted out of the gate.

Leaving the farm, we struck out for Pordenack Point. Out at sea, the sun tore through a bank of dark clouds hanging over the horizon, and its rays sparkled on the grey water. Silhouetted against the glittering light, dozens of tiny figures clambered around the varied rock formations spread out over the clifftops. A brave few sat on the summits of the higher stacks, legs dangling over the edge. The clouds inched closer, blocking out the sun, and in an instant, the atmosphere darkened, as if somebody had turned a dimmer switch. Fearing a downpour, I Velcroed Jess into her raincoat then zipped myself into mine.

Before long, we reached Pordenack Point, a favourite spot for bird watchers: gannets, manx shearwaters, razorbills, fulmars and even choughs were known to hang out around the granite covered headland and local area – not one of which was in residence as Jess and I passed by. My binoculars remained at the bottom of my rucksack; it wasn't worth the effort to fish them out for the two mangy gulls bickering over a dead rabbit.

We pushed on to Nanjizal Cove, which – from the path – looked like many other secluded coves on the north coast. But I knew it hid a secret. I called Jess, and we walked towards the waves, jumping the boulders scattered over the shore. Then I turned left and was rewarded with the most beautiful sight: the Song of the Sea – otherwise known as Zawn Pyg or Zawn Peggy – a slim rock arch carved through a sloping headland. Light shone through the arch and was reflected in a tidal pool beneath the cliff. Magical.

Open moorland, designated an Area of Outstanding Natural Beauty, covered the clifftops from Nanjizal Cove to Gwennap Head, which was adorned with two brightly painted day markers. On the other side of the headland we came to Porthgwarra Cove. Two fishing boats lay at the top of a cobbled slipway, protected on both sides by lumpy promontories covered in deep wrinkles and cracks, like the dusty skin of an elephant. Tunnels had been carved through the cliffs by tin miners many years before, enabling farmers to access the shore with their horses and carts, to harvest seaweed for the fields. Now, the tunnels provided tourists with a perfect photo opportunity. I tried to persuade Jess to sit, like a good dog, at one end of the tunnel so I could take her picture from the other end, but she kept trotting back to me. My increasingly frustrated shouts of, "Stay. No, Jess, STAY. Stay there, just stay, stay, no don't come to me, Jessy. STAY!" drew a crowd of tourists, confused to see me directing instructions into a tunnel. In exasperation, I tried a different tack: "Here, Jessy, here Jess, good girl. HERE, Jessy. WILL YOU COME HERE!" She sat beautifully while I took the photo.

The last mile flew by, and soon we were weaving in and out of coach loads of tourists milling around the Minack Theatre car park. In the company of two hundred sweaty people I didn't know, I wasn't inclined to visit the famous amphitheatre carved into the clifftop. I desperately searched for a way out, and we walked through another car park and up a road to finally reach my car.

Twelve miles done.

12 miles • 30,804 steps • Grading: Moderate

Porthcurno

For the next three days, I would have the company of my youngest sister, Bess, who'd travelled down from London to join me. She, of all my sisters, relished a good long walk; the tougher, the better. Fit, optimistic, and up for a challenge, Bee possessed all the qualities I lacked, qualities I hoped would rub off on me during the three days we would spend together. She had stayed the night in Penzance with our oldest sister, Sophie, and I met her there early in the morning. Sophie then drove us to Porthcurno, the start of the eleven-mile walk to Penzance.

Months before, when Bee expressed an interest in walking with me for a few days, I took some time to choose a section of the Coast Path that captured, in my eyes, the best of Cornwall. Eventually, I'd decided on the forty-three miles between Porthcurno and The Lizard, which included a plethora of harbours, a castle on a rock, remote beaches and cows: the perfect Cornish experience. Still, for all my careful planning, I couldn't pick the perfect weather. After weeks of sun, the clouds rolled in on the day she arrived: black clouds, strong winds and rain.

Listening to the forecast on the car radio, Bee exclaimed happily that a bit of rain would surely add to the experience. I kept my mouth shut. The only thing to do was wait and see. Sometimes, even the direst of weather forecasts turned out to be damp squibs. For all the talk of howling winds and torrential rain, it had stayed dry on the drive to Porthcurno, with nothing more than a gentle breeze as we got out of the car.

As we set off, I informed Bee earnestly that the first half of the walk would be strenuous. Her reaction couldn't have been more different from my own feeling of dread. She greeted the news with a hearty smile and thumbs up. I shook my head; poor child, totally unprepared for the rigours ahead. Unconcerned and carefree, she bounded off, flighty as a young gazelle.

We ignored the track down to Porthcurno Cove and hiked up a scrubby slope between fields, set back from the cliff edge. Past Pedn Vounder Beach, we peered along the back of a jagged peninsular, looking for the famous Logan Rock. Perched on top of one of the pinnacles, the eighty-ton granite boulder rocked when gently pushed. Or at least it had, until a group of seamen decided to prove something to someone by toppling it into the sea. Unsurprisingly, there ensued such an uproar from the locals that they put it back in place, but in the process Logan Rock stopped rocking.

A little further on, we reached Penberth Cove. A dark blue fishing boat sat alone on the cobbled slipway, with neat coils of rope, oars and a bright orange life ring lying on the deck; shipshape and ready to go to sea. I lent on a boulder and did a quick sketch while Jess and Bess inspected the various net sheds and the handful of cottages that make up the hamlet. When I finished, we crossed a shallow stream at the back of the cove then walked beside a single granite house festooned with buoys: the Cornish version of window boxes and bunting.

Back on the cliffs, we pushed on to St Loy woods. Oak trees and sycamores flowed down the valley before coming to a stop yards from the sea. There, a wall of bamboo flourished near the high-water line, obscuring a cove of boulders tumbling over one another into the sea. The Coast Path faded into the mass of oversized pebbles, before reappearing under trees at the other side. Gingerly, I picked my way through, helping Jess when she needed it, while Bee leapt deftly from one boulder to another before landing with a curtsy.

Hmmm, I clearly needed to up my game. But not immediately. For the time being, slow and steady was all I could manage. Much to my shame, as I began to tire, so Bee ramped up her speed, creating a gap large enough for two buses. Watching her growing smaller, I couldn't help but be impressed; nothing riled her, and she never got out of breath. She retained a steady gait, no matter the terrain. I put it down to a combination of youth and the lungs of an ox.

The Coast Path lived up to the guide book's description of *strenuous*, and by the time we arrived at Tater Du Lighthouse, I was yearning for something to eat and a lie down. Twenty minutes later we strolled into Lamorna Cove. Most of the houses in the village line the wooded valley that leads to the cove, but there are a few cottages, a café and a car park by the water. Dogs were banned from the inner harbour, so we made ourselves comfortable on a wall near the car park and greedily ate the Welsh cakes that Sophie had baked especially for us, finishing up with lashings of ginger beer; the perfect lunch, providing a sugary hit that fizzed in my veins. Feeling a little light-headed, I swung my rucksack onto my back and tightened the straps, while Bee did some stretches. We pushed on.

The last cottage on the way out of the village stands at the bottom of a hill made from granite chippings. The waste heap is a relic of a time when the village thrived on quarrying granite, shipping it all over the world. In 1911, the quarries stopped production, and soon after, the harbour and surrounding coast became a place of inspiration for artists of the Newlyn School, in particular Samuel John Birch. He loved the village so much he changed his name to Lamorna Birch. (I wonder what he would have done if he'd fallen in love with Mousehole.)

The Coast Path meandered past a cottage and a beautifully kept rockery, sheltering all sorts of salt-loving plants. The flowers were a welcome splash of colour after days of seeing only granite and gorse. We climbed up and away from the harbour towards a stone tor. The misshapen mound of rocks protruded above the tip of the headland, forcing us to skirt around the base, perilously close to the cliff edge. On the other side, skew-whiff steps descended to low cliffs, from where we glimpsed our first view of St Michael's Mount.

Even from a distance, it looked impressive: a gothic castle perched on a lonely rock, like something from a Grimms' fairy tale. Thought to be the site of a monastery in the 11th century, and a destination for pilgrims, the island is now managed by the National Trust but home to the Aubyn family, custodians for over four hundred years. A lone fishing boat chugged towards the mount, trailing a cacophony of seagulls in its wake as it steamed for Newlyn to offload its catch. By the time we reached the fish market, the crew would doubtless be downing the first of many pints in the Swordfish Inn. Lucky boys. Meanwhile, Bee and I would make do with water and the promise of lunch when we reached Mousehole.

We continued through a pine wood – the air musty and damp, the ground sodden – then picked our way around clumps of ferns and smooth-sided boulders, before jumping over stepping stones fording a stream. Sometimes we went up, sometimes down, until we found ourselves at the edge of the sea, where flat slabs of rock pushed into the calm water. And then, the final hurdle: an unforgiving stone stairway rising up and up and up. All the sweet Welsh cakes in the world couldn't help me now. Time slowed as I battled, one step at a time, while Bee skipped nimbly away and disappeared from sight.

At the top, the path levelled off and eventually merged with a road high above Mousehole. Bee slowed down and we walked side by side down a hill beside a tall stone wall covered in honeysuckle. At the bottom, the road narrowed and wound through tightly packed cottages, compact gardens, cafés and galleries to the harbour. The tide was in, and neatly arranged boats spread out like a fan, bows facing in, filled the crescent-shaped inner harbour. Mullet glided in and out of the boats' shadows like grey ghosts.

We leaned over the railings, watching the mullet and breathing in the salty air. I'm very fond of Mousehole. My oldest childhood friend lives in the village, and I've spent a lot of time there over the years. I love the way the harbour walls curve in from two sides, like protective arms, the turquoise water clear enough to see hermit crabs scuttling over the sand. I love the narrow streets and whitewashed cottages, and the beach with its shallow tidal pool. I return time after time to sketch there, sometimes even setting up my travel easel and painting *en plein air*.

Both Bee and I wanted to stay for a while, so we decided to go to the The Old Coastguard, a favourite of mine, for lunch. We found a table in the garden with a view of St Clements Island. The food tasted fabulous: plaice and crab risotto and a glass of wine for me, something vegetarian for Bee, and the odd scrap from my plate for Jess. In the convivial surroundings, I nearly forgot we still needed to complete the three-mile walk to Penzance.

Luckily, the worst was over; the Coast Path stuck to the pavement, taking us past Newlyn's fish market and harbour, then the lido at Penzance, to Sophie's house. Rain, which had held off all day, fell half-heartedly. In between the lacklustre showers, vast rainbows straddled Mount's Bay, one after the other, the shimmering arcs of colour dwarfing the castle out at sea.

We were nearly there when I remembered how every muscle and bone had ached at the end of my first day. Concerned, I turned to Bee and asked how she felt.

"Absolutely fine," she replied. "No probs."

"Really?"

"It's the stretching I do before and after. You should try it tonight, it'll make a real difference."

"Mmm, okay."

We both knew the only thing I would be stretching when I got home would be my arm as it reached for the wine bottle.

And with that in mind, I left her and drove home.

13.8 miles • 35,373 steps • Grading: Strenuous/Easy

DAY 23 – PENZANCE TO PORTHLEVEN

The next morning, I returned to Sophie's house, collected Bess, and together we walked through the town to the seafront. Neither of us spoke much. I was preoccupied by a colossal, charcoal-black cloud above our heads, but didn't want to mention it, fully aware that my obsession with the threat of rain was growing tiring for my sister, who hungered for a good old storm to pep up the walk.

"I really don't like the look of that," I remarked at last, unable to keep quiet as the cloud bore down on us.

"It'll only be a shower," Bee answered, gleefully.

"But you'll get soaked."

She wore a thin top, a pair of leggings and Converse trainers.

"But I'll dry off."

"Well, I don't want to start the day soaking wet." I scurried off with Jess to shelter behind a lifeguard hut. Reluctantly, Bee came too, as the apocalyptic cloud raced towards us, dumped two tonnes of rain, and sped on its merry way.

"There," I declared. "Now we can continue our walk while remaining lovely and dry."

Bee didn't look convinced; I feared she craved drama, even in the form of life-threatening pneumonia.

Out in the bay, St Michael's Mount dominated the view, the castle and rock merging into one grey silhouette. I wouldn't have been surprised to see a cloud of bats pour from the eaves of the chapel and set about terrorising Penzance.

But for all the gothic atmosphere, the actual walking was easy – along cycle tracks above the beach – and in no time we reached the village of Marazion, linked to the mount by a man-made cobbled causeway. The tide was high, cutting off access on foot, but there was a passenger ferry for those who wanted to cross. I raised an eyebrow at Bee, waiting for her to insist on swimming to the island and back as a warm up for our fifteen-mile walk, but she happily trotted on.

From the causeway, we sauntered through silent streets to the other side of the village, then turned down an unkempt track to a beach. Standing on the pebbly shore, we saw a different view of the mount, captured from behind with the grey outline of Penzance in the background.

A metal staircase at the end of the beach led to low cliffs. The path then moved inland, and the three of us tramped in single file around the edges of cabbage fields, the air heady with their peppery pong. After a while, we reached Perranuthnoe Beach and I shared with my young cohort the interesting fact that the Coast Path to the left of the beach was one of the worst places in Cornwall for adders – or one of the best, depending on your view. On hearing this, Bee insisted on walking in front, and I readily agreed. As she strode off, a cheerful spring in her step, I pulled out one of my sticks as protection, put Jess on her lead and cautiously followed. Despite her bravado, Bee kept a watchful eye on the ground as we made our way along a sandy trail, past adder warning signs. Only when we began to climb away from the low cliffs, towards Cudden Point, did we let our guard down.

When we reached the headland, we made our way along its back as far as we dared, between pale granite rocks that erupted from the mossy ground. To our right stretched the whole of Mount's Bay, and to our left, miles of coastline. "That's The Lizard," I pointed out, "thirty miles away. If we don't expire in the meantime, you and I will stand on the end of that headland tomorrow."

Bee squinted. "Thirty miles. Imagine running all that way."

As she spoke, I dashed past her.

"Wow! Are you going to give it a go?"

With Jess in tow, I cantered towards a tunnel of tamarisk trees as the sky turned black. The feathered boughs above our heads created a natural umbrella as the rain fell in sheets. In no hurry, Bee ducked in beside us, her shoulders and hair already soaking wet.

"I didn't know you were capable of moving so fast," she commented.

"I … have … hidden depths," I puffed, touching my toes to get rid of the agonising stitch in my side.

The shower quickly passed and we continued through the trees, emerging onto a stunted headland overlooking Prussia Cove. The rocky inlet, once home to notorious smugglers the Carter Brothers, was a hidden gem: a tiny half-moon of sand surrounded by shelves of dark rock stretching into emerald green water. All around the cove, half hidden by vegetation, cottages of various sizes dotted the grounds of the Porth-en-Alls estate, which owned both the houses and the foreshore. All the houses are available to rent, including the impressive manor house – a favourite for weddings.

From the headland, the sea view was concealed by ivy bushes, and we traipsed along a cramped path to an open gate. Beside the gate squatted two dilapidated net stores, their roofs a mishmash of corrugated sheets and thatch held together with chicken wire, their doors barely hanging on, although fitted with robust padlocks. I peeped through a missing pane in one of the windows, wondering what of worth would be kept in such a shabby building, but saw only wooden planks and an old bucket. As I stepped back, I trod on a cabbage growing at my feet – not your usual hedgerow plant. Cabbages grow like weeds around Prussia Cove, the seeds blowing in from nearby fields. I did a sketch, while Bee used the gate as a rustic piece of gym equipment and stretched.

We pushed on through an overgrown path with views of Kenneggy Beach, then skirted around Hoe Point to Praa Sands. The sight of the café by the beach triggered a recent memory: two months before, my sisters and I had met there for lunch. The weather was awful; not a day for being out, and certainly not a day for walking. While we were waiting for our food, a man came through the door, shoulders hunched, glistening wet. A walker, there was no doubt about it: he wore all the right gear, including a backpack. I couldn't keep my eyes off him, knowing I would be in his boots in a few weeks' time. He squelched to the bar, ordered food, and sat down at a table with a sigh. After a few moments, he pulled a map out of the pocket of his backpack and unfolded it on the table, then bent over to study it, running his finger over the contours. When his pizza arrived, he methodically worked through every slice then got up, pulled on his wet coat with a grimace, put his map away, heaved on his backpack and staggered out into the rain.

The man possessed a sort of resigned determination that I couldn't understand. I know for sure that if I'd come in from the rain that day, I would have devoured the pizza then called for a taxi to take me home for a hot bath and a cup of tea.

We didn't go into the café, but sat instead at the edge of the car park to wolf down our sandwiches and homemade biscuits. Suitably refreshed, and having clocked the signs banning dogs from the beach, we walked up the road and traipsed through the dunes towards Rinsey Head. The Coast Path kept well back from the tip of the headland, which was instead occupied by a beautiful granite house. Built in the 1920s, the Arts and Crafts abode was now available to rent as a holiday home, and had featured in the TV series Jonathan Creek.

Through a car park, we walked around a smart, restored engine house owned by the National Trust. The ironically named Wheal Prosper hadn't prospered, closing in 1866. Remnants of two other engine houses clung to the cliffs a little further on, alongside warning signs for open shafts. I put Jess on her lead and warned Bee to stick to the path. She rolled her eyes, despairing at my cautious nature, then perked up on spotting a couple of climbers preparing to abseil down a granite outcrop on the edge of the cliffs. I rummaged in my rucksack and opened a packet of oatcakes while we eagerly waited for them to fling themselves from the top, but they hovered awkwardly at the edge, pulling at ropes and fiddling with their equipment.

"It's us," Bess hissed.

"What do you mean?" I adjusted the focus on my binoculars.

"We're putting them off. They've got performance anxiety."

"Oh … Sorry!" I shouted, waving at them. "We'll go, shall we?"

We left them to deal with their peculiar issues and went on our way.

One last headland and we reached Porthleven. From the Ship Inn we looked across the outer harbour entrance to a distinctive clock tower; a miracle of stone and very strong cement. Whenever a powerful Atlantic storm batters the coast, the tower – duly engulfed by waves – appears on the local news. But it stands its ground year after year, a testament to good design. Or luck.

Bess, Jess and I mooched around the inner harbour to a car park, where Sophie was waiting patiently to ferry us back to Penzance. Once at Soph's we jumped out of her car and into mine, and I drove Bee and Jess back to my house.

That evening, Bee methodically went through her stretches while I sat on the sofa and released the tension in my right elbow by lifting and lowering a full wine glass.

15.5 miles • 38,738 steps • Grading: Moderate/Strenuous

DAY 24 – PORTHLEVEN TO THE LIZARD

Bee's last day. After I parked my car at The Lizard, Andrew (now back in service) drove us to Porthleven. It rained the whole way. Andrew squinted through the spray on the windscreen. "Are you sure you want to walk in this?" Before I could reply with, "No, let's go home," Bee piped up from the back: "We've got a brolly, we'll be fine." She referred to the pink polka dot brolly that Sophie had lent us the day before, a flimsy contraption better suited to a cocktail glass than a serious hike. "You're welcome to the brolly, Bee," I said. "I'll settle for staying toasty and dry in my precision-engineered Gore-Tex jacket and trousers, thank you."

Despite my smug attitude, I worried about Bee's welfare. Considering the conditions, she came under-dressed and under-prepared. Even Jess wore a coat. Bess, on the other hand, wore a hooded top (without a vest from what I could see), thin leggings and those flimsy Converse trainers. Not surprisingly, her choice of footwear had resulted in a blister. When she reluctantly admitted that her toe hurt, I foraged in my rucksack, produced my first-aid box and offered her a range of plasters and antiseptic concoctions, but she wanted nothing to do with my nursey administrations.

We stayed in the car for five minutes while a deluge raced overhead. Setting off from the car park, a short walk led to Loe Bar, where a shingle beach separates the largest freshwater lake in Cornwall from the sea. The stones proved hard to walk on, and we climbed onto the low cliffs behind the beach as soon as we could. Moments later, a torrential rain shower forced us to seek shelter behind a granite memorial. Bess unfurled the brolly and hunkered under it with Jess. I zipped my jacket to my chin and pulled the peak of my hat over my eyes. While we waited for the rain to ease, I read out the plaque at the base of the memorial: in memory of one hundred and twenty men who lost their lives when their naval frigate went down only yards from the beach. Reading how close to shore they'd been, I was reminded of something a friend had told me about the dangers of fishing at Loe Bar due to the steep drop-off. He said that "if your feet get wet, you are as good as drowned." Those deadpan words were the reason I never fished there.

The rain stopped, but the sky remained heavy with clouds clamouring to release their cargo. As we trampled along the unprotected dunes, the wind whipped sand in our faces. Bee developed a spring in her step, revelling in the inclement conditions, while Jess and I trailed behind her like stroppy teenagers who'd been coerced into a family walk. After a tiring slog, we pushed through a kissing gate then were struck by a sharp shower. This time, when Bee unfurled the brolly, the spotty fabric looked jaded, some of its bright perkiness already fading with the stress of being used. I could only wonder about the state the material would be in by the time we returned it to Sophie. I hoped it wasn't a favourite.

On the other side of Gunwalloe Beach, the Coast Path merged with a road then branched off through fields towards Church Cove. Protected by a wall of tamarisk trees, the medieval church of St Wynwallow is tucked into the side of the beach. Although unbearably picturesque, the location does have a downside: sand dunes in the graveyard, along with winter gales, have taken their toll, giving rise to the nickname "The Church of the Storms".

We crossed a bridge over a reed bed and clambered onto the next headland. When I got my breath back, I told Bee about the advice handed down to me by Wind-Up Woman. The rules impressed her, particularly the one about being sure to look behind. The perfect illustration of this came moments later when we took a breather above Poldhu Cove; when we turned our faces away from the wind and looked back, the waves were churning and frothing against the cliffs, while further out to sea slashes of turquoise ripped across the surface of the water. The sky was saturated with clouds that threatened to smother the headlands beneath them.

Surfers were the only people bonkers enough to venture into the sea at Poldhu Cove, and we were the only people bonkers enough to be watching them. While the beach at least offered some shelter from the wind, the headlands were as exposed as a nude posing on an iceberg. At Poldhu Point we walked past a prominent care home mere metres from the cliff edge. Nearby was the Marconi Centre, an unassuming wooden shed that marked the site of the first transatlantic radio signal.

Onwards, we soon reached Mullion Cove, where the Coast Path entered the harbour beside a café. We ordered a cup of takeaway tea and hunkered on a bench, beneath a net loft, to scoff our sandwiches. Jess gave up begging for a crust as it began to spit with rain. She slunk under a nearby boat, tail between her legs. We ate in silence, saving our energy for shivering. When we finished, I offered Bee my waterproof trousers to help keep her warm, but she adamantly refused. At that moment, a gaggle of older walkers tramped into the harbour wearing shorts, t-shirts and cheerful smiles. "You see," Bee said. "It's only you who feels the need to dress up in Gore-Tex. I'm beginning to think you might have a fetish."

We left the sanctuary of the harbour for the windswept Mullion Cliff. High above the sea, I trained my binoculars on Mullion Island, a safe habitat for nesting great black-backed gulls, guillemots and oystercatchers. We squelched over the saturated heathland of Predannack Cliff, which is part of the Lizard National Nature Reserve, and a haven for flora and fauna. Soay sheep and Shetland ponies crop the gorse and heather, keeping the growth under control and allowing other plants to flourish.

As we pushed on, we were accompanied by increasing numbers of black-faced sheep, and I put Jess on her lead. Moments later, two red-cheeked farmers came running towards us, arms outstretched. "Farmers, how lovely," I remarked to Bee, thinking they were coming to greet us. "They're after the sheep," she replied. Evidently, unlike the Soay, the black-faced sheep were not free-range, and Bee jumped out of the way as the flock fled past, followed by the men. We gave them some space, not wanting to scupper the operation, and watched as the farmers expertly herded their wayward charges into a nearby field.

In sight of Kynance Cove, we came upon more livestock, this time a herd of Dexter cattle tearing at mouthfuls of sedge. Sharp, grey horns garnished their bony heads and gave them a fierce countenance, but their eyes remained soft. Still, we moved slowly around them, not wanting to cause a stampede. In fact, we had no choice but to take our time. The ground became pitted with depressions – made no doubt by the cows' hooves – in amongst hummocks of spiky grasses, and large areas were completely flooded. We leapt from one tuft of grass to another until we came to higher ground.

At Rill Point, the wind blew strong enough to lean into. We moved as close to the cliff edge as we dared, arms outstretched, clothes billowing like sails. Cheeks stinging, we continued to be buffeted by gusts as we approached Kynance Cove. Below us, waves swamped the superbly named Asparagus Island, the spray flying high into the air. Two other sea stacks rose from the churning sea around the island – Devil's Bellows and Gull Rock – their dark flanks splattered in yellow lichen.

The Coast Path went past a busy café overlooking the cove, with picnic benches full of people outside. We paused for a moment; should we rest or keep going? For me, the problem with stopping was the difficulty in starting again; even ten minutes' sitting would be enough time for my joints to seize up. Invariably, I preferred simply to carry on even if I was tired. We decided to avoid the queues and the crowds by refuelling on the go; I gave Jess a drink then shared a packet of oatcakes with Bee while we climbed an arduous hill, heading away from the cove.

Halfway up, we slowed to a crawl, exhausted. Bee winced with each step. She didn't say anything, but I knew the blister on her toe was causing her pain. I, meanwhile, happily explained the source of my own misery. "It's the soles of my feet. They're stinging with every step. I'm in agony." If I hoped for sympathy, I howled at the wrong moon. Bee, in a stern voice, made it clear we would get to The Lizard even if we crawled on bleeding hands and knees. I shut up and concentrated on my ailments.

Onwards, and we spied a signpost pointing inland for Lizard Village and, nearby, a plaque set on top of a stone with the words "The Lizard" written on it. At last. Bee and I took photos of each other sitting on the stone. We'd made it.

Or had we?

We examined the map from every angle, but couldn't locate the road to the village. I thought for a moment. Didn't The Lizard have a café? And a shop selling serpentine? And a car park? As my addled brain began to work correctly, a cold realisation seeped in: we were not, in fact, at The Lizard. We stood in a place where someone had screwed a plaque onto a stone telling you about the Lizard National Nature Reserve. The realisation proved too much for me to bear. In my head, I'd finished the walk and driven home to a hot bath and a cup of tea. I glanced at Bess, hoping for comfort, and saw, with a stab of horror, a determined glint in her eyes. She would see The Lizard if it killed me.

"Come on, it can't be far." She frog-marched onwards.

I limped behind her; what choice did I have? Every step hurt and my hips, knees and ankles throbbed. Then we rounded one last headland and climbed one final rise – and we were there. Now our surroundings made sense, the Polpeor Café, the shop that sold serpentine, and the car park. And, as expected, lots of people taking photos. Our arrival felt a bit of an anticlimax after the effort we expended to get there, but at least I could tick off another landmark, and – best of all – Bee had reached The Lizard.

All that remained was a trudge up the road to the car park. Bee dithered over whether to buy an ice cream when we got to the village. While she hummed and hawed I began to feel shaky. "I need nuts," I blurted, and staggered for the car and my emergency stash of snacks in the glove compartment. Once there I shoved Jess into the boot, collapsed onto the seat, crammed a handful of nuts and raisins into my mouth and gratefully chewed. Relief flooded through my body as the shakes lessened. In her own sweet time Bee rocked up, licking a mint choc chip ice cream, and settled into the passenger seat. "Are you all right?"

"I am now."

We sat for a while, digesting our snacks and congratulating ourselves on the day's walk. Sixteen miles: the furthest Bee had ever walked.

I drove us back to Penzance. At Sophie's house, we relaxed around her kitchen table, drank tea and gossiped, laughing over the frightful state of her polka dot brolly. As I handed it back I conceded that a more robust umbrella could be a useful addition to my walking kit and decided to buy one of my own. Bee discussed flat hunting and a new film she wanted to see when she got back to London. Sophie planned to visit the Tate in St Ives and catch up with a mutual friend. And me? While Bee returned to the real world and Sophie got on with her busy life, I'd be walking every day, all day, just walking. On the way home, after saying goodbye, the challenge felt too much, and I wondered if I had it in me to make it to the end.

15.5 miles • 38,603 steps • Grading: Strenuous

DAY 25 – THE LIZARD TO COVERACK

I woke in a better mood, the melancholy of the previous evening gone. Jess, however, refused to get out of her bed. Evidently, I would be both Bess- and Jess-less for the day.

I set off alone from Polpeor Café on Lizard Point in a reflective mood, unsettled without my sidekick. I missed the sight of her arse in front of me as she sashayed along in her unhurried manner, coming to a halt every few yards to eat or sniff something disgusting. On very narrow stretches of Coast Path, her habit of stopping to inspect the slightest thing caused me much frustration. I would be forced to squeeze past, or shove her from behind shouting, "MOVE JESS, MOVE." One thing was certain: I'd make better time without her.

I missed Bee too. Having a human being to share the ups and downs (quite literally) of the walk had been a treat, helped by the fact that I knew and liked her, unlike some of my previous walking companions.

A man and his terrier dog appeared up ahead, and, suddenly craving company, I increased my pace so I could pretend the dog was mine. We walked in single file – the man oblivious to my hijacking of his four-legged friend, who I christened Colin – towards the Lizard Lighthouse Heritage Centre. This imposing building consists of two towers on either end of a row of cottages, with six tall, black chimneys. Originally, both towers were designed to hold a lantern, but over a hundred years ago the western tower was decommissioned and the remaining light became automated in 1998. I continued to follow Colin and his owner along the coast and around Housel Bay until they dropped down onto the beach. Alone once more, I texted Jack: *How's Jess?* I got an answer straight away: *She's asleep, are you ok?*

Yeah.

You old softie, you'll see her when you get home xxx

I looked across the turquoise water of the bay to Bumble Rock, the black chimneys of the lighthouse poking above the headland. The sky was an empty deep blue, unlike the day before when there hadn't seemed enough room in the heavens for all the clouds. I pushed on, and as I got into my stride, all my worries about not being able to continue the walk seemed melodramatic, most likely caused by dehydration and the need of a hearty meal than by any real fear.

I set my sights on a bright white building up ahead with LLOYD'S SIGNAL STATION written in four-foot-high letters on the side of it. This, I deduced, with startling insight, must be Lloyd's Signal Station. Designed in the Art Deco style, for years the handsome building was used to send and receive messages to and from passing ships with signal flags, but it was now a private home.

With no one to sit by and share water or a packet of oatcakes with, I carried on around Bass Point to the less ostentatious National Coastwatch Institution Lookout. This was still in use, having reopened in 1994 after the loss of a Cadgwith fishing boat and crew in the patch of sea the – then derelict – station should have safeguarded. Boats aren't the only things the coastguards keep an eye on: climbers, fishermen and even SWCP walkers all come under the protection of the men and women who work at the station. I managed to go by without inflicting an injury on myself. Nevertheless, I liked the thought that a guardian angel, in the form of the coastguard, had my back. Without Jess and Bee's company, I felt less confident and more aware of how isolated the cliffs were.

However, I let my guard down and relaxed as I drew nearer to the tiny fishing village of Cadgwith. On the outskirts, I stopped to sketch the Devil's Frying Pan, a collapsed sea cave. Imagine Satan flipping pancakes in a frying pan, and then dismiss the image and replace it with that of a rock arch between two other rocks, and you'd have a fair idea of the picture before me.

A lane led out of the frying pan into the village. Out of season, Cadgwith was nigh on empty. Two fishermen, rollups hanging from their moustaches, were preparing to launch their boat by hooking it up to a tractor. When the tide rose, they'd push it down the slipway into the sea, but for now their friendly banter echoed around the cove, mixing with the sound of waves collapsing onto the shingle shore.

I left the village for the cliffs, via a row of whitewashed cottages above the harbour. As I made my way along a track above a rocky cove, I glanced down and saw the head of a seal bobbing out of the water. Charmed, I waited for it to do something. The seal remained very still. Probably watching me, I thought, still thrilled. After two minutes I began to worry that it was dead. I fished out my binoculars and, as I fiddled with the focus, I realised to my utter mortification that the seal was a rock. Some moments are better not shared; just then I was glad to be alone.

More hedgerow-flanked paths led to Kennack Sands, a great fishing mark for plaice. With time to spare, I decided to have lunch at a café on the beach. I ordered a ham and cheese panini and sat at a picnic table with a mug of tea, enjoying the rare luxury of being able to rest for a while and enjoy the view.

After lunch, I located the Coast Path behind the beach and tracked it over a boardwalk onto the Eastern Cliff. From there, it wasn't long before I reached Downas Cove. Serpentine boulders, shot through with veins of red and white, covered the shore. An arduous climb out to Black Head gave my lungs the first proper workout of the day, and as I regained my breath at the end of the headland, I felt the familiar rush of endorphins. In high spirits, I carried on along a confined path, hemmed in by overgrown gorse and bracken. At a particularly narrow section, the vegetation to the side of me started to sway and shake, and a furry brown cow lumbered onto the path. In looks and manner, the cow reminded me very much of Jess; it stood blocking my way forward in the same way she so often did. I wasn't going to knee it up the arse and shout as I would with Jess – the cow had horns after all, and we weren't acquainted – so instead shuffled behind until it careered off into the bushes, leaving a trail of destruction.

On the outskirts of Coverack, I walked past a row of holiday homes, complete with gingham curtains, wooden boats in the windows, and agapanthus in the well-tended gardens. A ginger cat stretched out on the path, meowing for a tickle, which I happily provided – another consequence of walking *sans* seven-stone dog. When I reached the village, I bought a bottle of lemonade and drank it while leaning over the railings above the harbour. Below, fishing boats gently rocked on their moorings. Seagulls hopped about the decks and pecked at scraps of seaweed and fishy detritus. Like Cadgwith, the village was hushed, the atmosphere that of calm after a storm. A few people sat outside cafés, drinking wine or sipping coffee while soaking up the late-September sun; others strolled along the prom with their dogs. I ambled to the car park on the other side of the bay, soaking up the laid-back vibe, then climbed into the Volvo and drove home.

11.6 miles • 29,055 steps • Grading: Moderate

Jess jumped out of bed, full of beans after her day off and more than happy to accompany me. Andrew drove us to Coverack once I'd left my car in a lay-by near Gillan Creek. The official end of the day's walk was on the other side of the creek, by the Helford River, but the tides were wrong and there was no ferry service, so I'd pre-emptively cut out the last mile. I waved Andrew off, and Jess and I made our way along the seafront and onto a stunted headland. Misshapen boulders littered the ground, some sunk deep into the boggy earth, some resting on the surface, as if felled. Using my sticks for balance, I lurched from rock to rock, trying to dodge the mire that had been churned up by cows into a stinking soup of dung and mud. Jess mirrored my every move and together we made slow progress, back-tracking many times when the route vanished under water.

There was nothing enjoyable about the experience, and no reason on earth why anyone would want to partake in the walk unless, like me, they were fulfilling a dream to tackle the SWCP while at the same time finding inspiration. With this in mind, I was baffled to see a couple, dressed for the office, scrambling over the rocks nearby. The woman wore strappy sandals, a thin blouse and a flowery pleated skirt. The man wore a blue suit and smart shoes. I kept my distance, wondering what they were doing and when they would stop doing it and turn back; but they kept going. I admired their tenacity. The man – as men are wont to do – led the way, reaching back for the woman with instructions on where to put her feet. Arms flailing, the woman squealed as she slipped towards him. Lunging for his hand, she tottered for a moment then landed, one sandalled foot in – and one out of – the dung-infused mud. I suppressed a smile and picked my way around them as she turned, crimson-faced, on her companion. "For Christ's sake, Barry, this is NOT what I had in mind when you invited me for a romantic stroll along the prom!"

Poor Barry. I could still hear his beloved as I approached Dean Quarry. By straining to catch the unfolding argument I'd diverted my attention, and instead of going through the quarry, I drifted inland through fields and ended up in the pretty square at the centre of St Keverne Village. Having no idea which way to go, I asked a couple of old boys sitting on a bench for directions. No sooner did they stop talking than I promptly forgot every single word they'd uttered. I tried again in the post office, and this time wrote everything the woman said in my notebook. Following my scrawled instructions, Jess and I left the square via a graveyard, then tramped through a succession of fields and were soon standing on the shore at Porthoustock.

A mile or so out, beyond the dull, grey sand and ugly remnants of quarrying, lay The Manacles, a reef famous for its shipwrecks. The lethal rocks attract plenty of fishermen and divers, and when the shoals of mackerel arrive in late spring Porthoustock invariably plays host to the first catches from the shore.

The Coast Path led away from the beach, and we pushed through farmland and back roads, into and out of hamlets, surrounded by green and rarely catching sight of the sea. In places, the paths were choked with new growth – all that summer rain – and my trousers and boots were soon soaked through.

Cold and wet, I was not in the best of moods as we encountered a group of people with chainsaws and shears hacking away the verdant foliage. Unfortunately, their efforts came too late to help our progress, but watching them work made me appreciate the extraordinary effort it takes to keep the six hundred and thirty miles of Coast Path open and passable. I thanked them heartily as they turned off their saws to let us pass. Coming up behind me, Jess pressed her nose into their crotches as her own form of appreciation.

Our cross-country hike ended at Porthallow Beach. From there, the last mile through fields more than made up for the rest of the walk, and I revelled in the panoramic views across Falmouth Bay. Half a dozen tankers lay at anchor in the dark blue waters offshore. In the distance, I could see Pendennis Point and St Anthony's Lighthouse on the far side of the River Fal, landmarks as familiar to me as my favourite paintbrush.

Skirting round Nare Point, we passed a coastguard hut then tramped through yet more fields to reach Gillan Creek and my car.

12.9 miles • 32,311 steps • Grading: Moderate

DAY 27 – THE HELFORD TO FALMOUTH

I wouldn't need to pack a guide book for this walk; Jess and I knew it by heart, having completed the route numerous times when attempting to get fit before taking on the SWCP. To Falmouth and back was twelve miles – a reasonable distance – but it was a relatively gentle walk, with few ups and downs, and it had done little to prepare me for the shock of the north coast of Cornwall.

Looking Across the River, Through Pine Trees

After I parked my car on the seafront in Falmouth, Andrew dropped us off outside the Ferry Boat Inn on the Helford River. From there, we turned left through a gate and into fields that fringed the estuary. Gorse grew at the edges, obscuring the river, but now and then I glimpsed a view to the other side. The sun glittered on the surface of the water and cormorants fished the shallows, disappearing and then popping up yards away. I hopped over stepping stones through a tunnel behind a private beach that belongs to Trebah Gardens. There's no access to the beach from the path; a wire fence blocks the riffraff from getting in. But, if you buy a ticket, you can get to the beach via a gorgeous tropical garden that spills down the valley to the seashore. Bamboos the size of your thigh, gigantic gunnera, magnolias and rhododendrons all thrive in the subtropical conditions.

Jess and I carried on through fields until we reached the tiny hamlet of Durgan, which boasts a permanent population of ten. The majority of the cottages built around the pebbly beach are owned by the National Trust, and are rented out to tenants or let as holiday homes. In two seconds flat, we'd seen all there was to see and were out the other side. We hiked up a road, clambered over a stile, and stood on the edge of a meadow at the bottom of a terraced garden. A flight of stone stairs led to Bosloe House, an imposing Arts and Crafts manor house, also acquired by the National Trust and available to rent.

An open gate on the other side of the garden revealed rolling fields, sandwiched between the river on one side and farmland on the other. Jess bounded towards an oak tree on a hill in the distance, stretching her legs. Ten seconds later, she reappeared, hurtling towards me at full pelt. I braced myself: "Careful, Jess!" Just when I thought she would surely barrel into me, she splayed her toes on the soft ground and came to a stop inches from my legs, her chest heaving. In the distance, a brown smudge materialised into a miniature dachshund, which raced towards us. I heard a shout. "Peanut, where are you? PEANUT!"

"She's here," I called. A woman jogged towards us. "I'm so sorry, she is a pickle." She turned to Peanut and scolded, "You are a pickle, Pea."

Peanut barked in response, then waddled off with her owner, and Jess and I continued on our way. We pushed through a kissing gate at the corner of the field, down to a cove with a slipway and boathouse, then back into fields. A flight of steps led into a wood with a floor carpeted in crackly leaves. To one side of us, a steep slope bristled in pine trees and fell away to the platforms of rock that made up the river bank, and bright glimpses of the river flashed through the gaps in the trees.

Back out into the sunlight, we pushed on to Rosemullion Head at the mouth of the estuary. This bulbous peninsula gives fantastic views across Falmouth Bay to St Mawes and St Anthony's Lighthouse. Sitting at the end of the peninsula, our backs to a clump of gorse, Jess and I munched on a packet of oatcakes washed down with water, then pushed on.

In no time we were looking down on the sheltered Maenporth Beach, one of my favourite kayak-launching spots. One memorable July morning, I'd set my alarm for four o'clock, squeezed into my wetsuit and driven to the beach, kayak in tow. The tide was low, and I dragged my kayak across the expanse of cold sand to the water's edge, setting off. The sea was so still that each stroke felt like dipping my paddle into oil. On the horizon, the sky blazed red, and by the time I reached the wreck of the

Ben Asdale at the entrance to the bay, the sun was up. With the sun came a breeze, chopping up the surface of the water, creating waves that broke over the kayak's bow. From the shore, the two-toned trill of curlews pierced the air. I paddled to the mouth of the Helford, making my way up river to the Ferry Boat Inn, fishing as I went. Hours later, I returned to Maenporth with enough mackerel to justify lighting the barbecue.

I snapped back to the reality of a packed beach. Families were out in force, making the most of the mild weather, building sandcastles and playing cricket. Jess and I went to the café and I bought us both an ice cream before returning to the cliffs for the final mile to Falmouth.

On the way, in the gaps between hedges of hawthorn and honeysuckle, I caught glimpses of hidden coves. The sea was a deep blue in places, iridescent green closer to the shore, and so clear I could see submerged rocks, seaweed, and glittering shoals of sand eels: lunch for the cormorants, who were drying their wings on the rocks nearby.

Dropping into this peaceful tableau – like a brick into a bowl of custard – came a yell and a thwack. Falmouth's golf course presides over the cliffs between Maenporth and Swanpool, parallel with the SWCP. The location couldn't be better, with the unbroken views of Falmouth Bay. However, anyone inclined to walk could enjoy the same view without paying an annual fee to hit a white ball with a stick for four hours every Saturday. The thwacks came thick and fast, as did the yells, until we left the cliffs for the blessedly calm Swanpool Beach.

From there, the Coast Path curved around a short headland to Gyllyngvase Beach, the biggest of the three local beaches, minutes from Falmouth's town centre. We ambled along the seafront to my car, and I drove us home.

7 miles • 17,533 steps • Grading: Moderate

DAY 28 – PORTLOE TO ST ANTHONY'S LIGHTHOUSE

The official way to start the walk from Falmouth to Portloe is to board a ferry from Falmouth, crossing the River Fal to St Mawes, and then take another, smaller boat from St Mawes to Place. However, it was easier to drive around the estuary. There was very little free parking at Portloe, so Andrew and I decided to leave my car at the National Trust car park at St Anthony's Lighthouse so that Jess and I could set off from Portloe. For the first time, we'd walk clockwise, with the sea on our left.

From the car park, we strolled past The Lugger Hotel to the beach, a rocky, naturally protected inlet, shielded from the worst of the weather by a harbour wall. We hiked up to Jacka Point, the route choked with bramble bushes. Majestic pine trees loomed over the cliff edge. After crossing farmland scattered with sheep, we reached a deep valley, hauled ourselves down one side and up the other and started the lengthy climb onto Nare Head. The summit was studded with irregular lumps of granite, which in turn were decorated with splotches of white and yellow lichen. The tip of the headland turned away from Portloe to point across the broad sweep of Gerrans Bay, all the way to Killigerran Head, eight miles away.

Gerrans Bay and the beaches of Carne and Pendower were go-to places for Jack and me to moor our boat. One summer, we dropped anchor in the bay to put the kettle on and throw out a few fishing lines. I fancied a swim and, having forgotten my costume, improvised by wearing my pants and bra. After snorkelling around the boat, I waded out of the sea to poke around in the rock pools. A mother and young daughter were paddling in the shallows and glanced up at my approach. In reply to my jovial "good morning" the mother grabbed her child by the hand and marched away from me, up the beach. I stared after her, perplexed, and soon became aware of Jack laughing from the boat. Ignoring my husband, and the bizarre behaviour of the mother, I pottered up and down the shore searching for mermaid's purses. When the sun went behind a cloud, I swam back to the boat, and it was only once aboard that Jack let me know that my wet underwear was completely see-through.

There was no danger of me flashing anyone on this particular day. The weather was too cold for a swim, but ideal for a Sunday stroll, and lots of people were using the Coast Path, including two men posing for photos at the end of Nare Head. While I waited for my turn to take a picture, we struck up a conversation. They were also hiking the whole six hundred and thirty miles, but not in one go. So far, they'd taken eight years, doing the odd weekend when they could. I took a few snaps, and we walked back along the cliffs in single file. The men made short work of all the ups and downs, throwing questions over their shoulders at me, while I floundered in their wake, rushing to catch up and answer when I got my breath back. At Carne Beach they detoured for a cup of coffee at the Nare Hotel, inviting Jess and me along. Not wanting to outstay my welcome, I made an excuse about having to be somewhere at a certain time, wished them luck and waved goodbye.

It was often awkward, when meeting people on the Coast Path, to know when and how to leave their company. Should one speed up, or stop? The go-faster method would involve a vague excuse such as, "Bugger, I'm late!" and a sudden increase in speed. The only problem would be keeping up enough pace to stay ahead. With my unreliable fitness, going faster wasn't an option for any length of time. Instead, I relied on the stop method, using one of three excuses: "You go on, I need to: a) replace my shoelace; b) darn my sock; or c) eat a packet of oatcakes." Knowing my own issues with unwanted walking companions, I was acutely aware that I might equally be perceived as a pain in someone's arse. And so I left the two men to enjoy their coffee in peace.

In sight of Porthscatho, we came across The Hidden Hut café overlooking Porthcurnick Beach. Oversized tables and benches were chock-full of contented punters slurping from bowls and shovelling cake into their mouths. Those who couldn't find a space around the tables spilled onto the grass banks to the side of the hut and used their coats as blankets. The menu was straightforward, but inspired; you could choose between slabs of homemade cake and steaming bowls of soup – sweet or savoury, or both. Ideal comfort foods, and perfect for alfresco dining. I opted for a sticky square of chocolate cake and a cup of tea, squeezed into a gap at a table, and soon launched into a chat with the couple sitting next to me, while Jess lay with their dog at our feet.

The tea and cake worked wonders on my energy levels, and I skipped into the village of Porthscatho, more than ready to take on the last few miles. We strolled through the terraced streets, past galleries, cafés and pubs, to the harbour. A fishing fleet sat on a square of sand, sheltered by the harbour wall. Most were day boats, designed to pootle around the coves and inshore reefs for lobsters and crabs. Beyond the harbour, Nare Head and the little islet of Gull Rock stretched out into the sea, and behind them loomed the grey outline of Dodman Point, the halfway marker of the next day's walk.

Leaving the harbour behind, Jess and I pushed on. We kept to the margins of arable fields then tramped through pastures and around a herd of nut-brown cows who were cropping leaves from the bushes. At the bottom of the cliffs, the rocky shoreline softened to the white sand of Porthbeor Beach, little known and loved by the locals for that very reason. Out of season, the shore resembled virgin snow, with no sign of footprints on the pristine sand; with our destination almost in sight, we left it that way. Around Zone Point, we at last reached St Anthony's Head at the very tip of the Roseland Peninsula.

Standing on the foundations of a battery that defended the Fal Estuary during both world wars, I could see across Falmouth Bay for miles in all directions: Pendennis Castle at the entrance to the harbour; Carrick Roads, not a road but an estuary and opening to a number of tidal rivers; and, in the distance, Porthoustock. With time to spare, I took the unusual decision to take a detour down to St Anthony's Lighthouse, tucked into the cliffs below the battery. After a long walk down, we found the lighthouse was closed. Despite this, I appreciated seeing the building up close after years of passing under the light in our boat.

Mission accomplished, I hauled myself back up to the car park, clambered into the car and drove home for what would be the last time during this trip.

12 miles • 31,789 steps • Grading: Strenuous/Moderate

I woke, got dressed, packed my suitcase and did the same for
Jess. After two weeks at home, she and I were embarking on the
last three weeks, on our own. Far from feeling apprehensive,
I couldn't wait to get going: no more household chores or
answering emails or phones. Nothing to do but walk. After
loading the car, I called Jess. In the pause that followed I
wondered if she had, understandably, suffered enough exercise
thank you very much. Then she sloped out of the house, tail
swishing back and forth, in no rush as ever, and scrambled
into the boot. My girl. As Jack started the engine, I suddenly
remembered an important new addition to my walking gear.
"Wait!" I shouted and ran back into the house. I re-emerged with
a spanking new, built to last, understated, black brolly. I strapped
it to my rucksack and told Jack to put his foot down.

Jack drove Jess and I the forty miles to Mevagissey to drop off
our suitcases at the B&B, then back to Portloe. Not needing to
concentrate on the road, I let my mind wander, recalling the
start of the walk. My pristine clothes. My boots, barely broken in,
still shiny and smelling of polish. Now, my walking gear felt like
a second skin. My boots were cracked, stained with mud, and
looked hundreds of years old, but were so comfortable I barely
sensed them. I knew every nook and cranny of my rucksack,
from the grubby guide book in the side pocket to the squashed
energy bar at the bottom that I couldn't bring myself to eat. The
hand straps that slotted into the handles of my Nordic walking
poles were such a part of me that I bore white stripes on the
back of my hands where they shielded my skin from the sun.
Everything fit.

Jack took my silence for nerves. "Only three more weeks, then
you'll be home again." I nodded, not wanting to admit to him
that three weeks wasn't enough.

After parking the car, we hugged, and I reassured him that Jess
would look after me and I would ring him every night so he
knew we were safe. "Now, do you know which way you are going?
Remember, keep the sea on your right," he joked.

"Don't worry about me; this is what I do."

This is what I do … Half an hour later I blushed to recall the
cocky statement. I might look the part in my battered attire and
aged boots, but I still possessed the athletic prowess of a six-year-
old in a sack race.

A brutal first hour consisted of a series of laborious hikes up scrubby slopes and flights of steps. Young sycamore trees, their leaves beginning to darken and curl, lined the paths, along with gorse, brambles and the skeletal remains of cow parsnip. The air felt damp and smelt of decay; the first touch of autumn.

We soon reached West Portholland, a tiny hamlet of half a dozen houses at one end of a kidney-shaped beach. At the opposite end, a terrace of drab cottages behind a concrete sea wall made up East Portholland. A bike leaning against a picnic bench, and a pair of boots on a door step, were the only signs of habitation.

Leaving the ghost town, we sauntered through a tunnel of trees between fields, where Jess, running in front, scared up a flurry of pheasants. They flew into the air, followed by two sharp cracks that exploded above our heads. Jess galloped back to me, ears flat on her head, as I shouted, "WE ARE HERE." In reply, another volley of shots rang out, yards in front of us. Fearing we might have inadvertently blundered into a shoot, I jogged towards a stile and, with Jess at my heels, scrambled over it into a field. Protected by a thick hedge, I crept beside the boundary to the far corner, from where I could see the fields above us. A group of six people stood there, cradling guns, hidden from the path we had been on by tall hedgerows. Surely they must have seen us by now. After all, I was wearing a bright red jacket. Yet they didn't acknowledge us with a wave, nor a shouted "SORRY!" Shaken, I put as much distance as possible between them and us, tensing for the sound of more shots.

I only let my guard down when the Coast Path turned onto a road, reasoning that a pheasant shoot – even one with a casual attitude to health and safety – would not encroach on a populated area. The pavement ran alongside a high stone wall that led to a twin-towered, castellated gatehouse. Behind the gate sprawled the 140-acre Caerhays Estate, home to the National Collection of Magnolias. Both the manor house – designed by John Nash – and the magnolias were obscured from view, and with nothing to see I crossed over the road towards Caerhays Beach, then clambered over a stile into a vast field. Watched by wary sheep, Jess and I tramped around the periphery searching for the way out, but found none: no stile or gate, just an unbroken hedge all the way around. Baffled, I improvised by climbing over a padlocked gate – first making sure Jess could squeeze under it – then through a copse of trees and over a barbed wire fence. Back on the proper path, we set off for the imposing Dodman Point.

On the way, we came upon a man and woman, identically dressed, sitting on a bench nibbling sandwiches. Both wore dark blue trousers with matching t-shirts and a white cap. The caps came with flaps on the back, presumably to protect their necks from the savage autumn heat. Jess, smelling food, sashayed up to them, on the lookout for stray crumbs. But as she got nearer, the woman screamed and flung her leg out as if warding off a rabid wolf. Jess, unperturbed, wagged her tail furiously and dived under the bench for a titbit. The woman, still waving her legs like a topsy-turvy beetle, ordered me to "restrain that dog", ignoring my reassurances that Jess was friendly. While protesting, I hauled Jess from under the bench, clipped on her lead and stepped back. This gave the woman time to roll up her t-shirt sleeve to reveal a bite scar. As if on cue, her previously silent partner pulled up his trousers to brandish his very own blemish. Was this the time to show off my appendix scar I wondered for a thrilling second? Instead, I retaliated with, "Not all dogs bite." To this, she snapped that she didn't like their wet noses. A fair point: a cold, wet dog nose isn't for everyone. I offered an apology and pulled Jess away.

One of the problems with owning a large dog is other people's preconceptions. Jess provokes two reactions in strangers: they either fawn over her or cross the road to avoid her. Yet, in my experience, most big dogs are too laid-back or lazy to cause any harm. Certainly, that was true of my accomplice. I gave her an oatcake as compensation for missing out on the titbit, and we pushed on.

It wasn't long before we stood at the end of the Dodman under a tall, granite cross. The monument, built in 1896, served to warn ships of their proximity to the peninsula also known as Deadman's Point. From the Dodman we made good time, marching across low cliffs smothered in copper bracken. Through the harbour of Gorran Haven, we then walked past Chapel Point, the narrow peninsula dominated by Chapel Point House. From there, we strolled along a lane then followed a quiet road into Portmellon Cove, a suburb of Mevagissey. Turquoise water filled the harbour, drowning the stone slipway and half-moon of sand. I leant on the railings and focused on the water, hoping for the sight of a mullet in the shallows. No fish, but there were lots of crabs scuttling in and out of the emerald green seaweed that wafted in the waves.

A road linked Portmellon to Mevagissey. We walked along the pavement to Stuckumb Point, overlooking Mevagissey's outer harbour. Through a tiny park and around the back of the aquarium, we soon reached the inner harbour. I love Mevagissey. When I lived in Truro, I would often spend time sketching the fishing boats and visiting galleries. Favoured by ice-cream-eating northerners, Mevagissey has its fair share of tourist shops and attractions, but the harbour retains a fishing fleet and an air of authenticity. The reek of diesel and net bins in need of a hose down intermingled with the smells of pasties and stale beer – a proper working harbour.

I fancied an early supper, so after a brief visit to the B&B to drop off my rucksack, I searched for a pub. While I waited for my scampi and chips in one of the harbour's many drinking establishments, I sipped a vinegary white wine. Every time I picked the glass up from the table, it resisted, due to the stickiness of the wooden surface. I rolled down my sleeves, afraid the residue would strip the hairs from my arms if I leant on it. Surely in this day and age there is a product that can degrease a pub table? Hot water and washing up liquid? Despite my reservations, the food, when it arrived, was just what I needed. I left happy and full – after prising my notebook from the table.

Back at the B&B, I took a moment to take in my surroundings. Whoever had decorated my room must have laughed in the face of convention and the strict rule that all B&Bs within ten miles of the sea must use stripy or gingham soft furnishings, have wooden boats or seagulls in the windows, seashells in the bathroom and anchors on the towels. The theme for my room seemed to be "1980s hair salon with a tattoo-parlour twist". Purple walls with accents of black, silk bedding, and a purple light shade that bathed everything in a sickening hue. I perched on the edge of the bed, slid off, and decided to sit on the chair instead, not sure if I could spend an extended amount of time in the room without getting ill.

While I debated how to make an eye-mask out of a sock, a knock at my door revealed the male B&B owner. He asked if I needed anything. A tin of white paint, I thought. When I assured him everything was absolutely perfect, thank you, he launched into a ramble about his recent divorce and subsequent life as a single man looking for love. The single man aspect at least explained the design of my room. I stood in the doorway and sympathised with him and his situation, and this may have been the trigger that led him to ask, "Would you like to share a bottle of wine with me later?" I was so shocked I immediately said "yes", and before I could take it back, he said, "Great, see you later!" and left. I closed the door and sat on the bed, slid off, and sat on the chair. Bloody hell, what did I just agree to? Apart from the unexpected request, he hadn't given me a time. For two hours, I lay on the bed with a sock over my eyes, waiting for his knock.

When the knock finally came, at 9pm, I slid off the bed and tentatively opened the door. Marinated in aftershave, the owner brandished a bottle of wine in one hand and two glasses in the other, which, with a coy smile, he chinked together.

"Ready," he purred.

"Ummmmm," I floundered. "The thing is, I'm exhausted. It's been quite a day. Do you mind if we …"

He lowered the wine bottle. "Oh … That's fine. I'm tired too. I'll see you in the morning?"

Relief flooded through me. "Yes. Night then. See you for breakfast."

I closed the door and let out a sigh.

14.6 miles • 36,378 steps • Grading: Strenuous

Low Tide, Mevagissey Harbour

The next morning, I sat near a German couple in the dining room and tucked into one of the best full English breakfasts of the whole walk. Neither I nor the resident lothario mentioned the aborted date, much to my relief. Instead, he bustled about the dining room, topped up teapots, and brought extra toast and marmalade and, as a surprise, two sausages in a bowl for Jess. As I watched her devour the meaty treats, I couldn't help thinking that this act of kindness was a good sign. A man who loved animals and could cook wouldn't stay single for too long.

After breakfast, I said goodbye to the hopefully soon-to-be-snapped-up B&B owner, and returned to the harbour. The streets were empty of both foot and road traffic, so I let Jess off her lead and gave her the freedom to sniff at every single lamp post and shop doorway. From the harbour, we walked in front of a terrace of houses and across a common towards Penare Point. The sound of young children playing drifted over the fields from a nearby school, their shrieks mixing with the delicate chirps of birdsong. In the bay, a blue fishing boat puttered from buoy to buoy, trailed by an expectant seagull.

Soon, the sound of children faded away, replaced by the boom of waves crashing against the cliffs. The path dipped and rose then snaked inland, behind Pentewan Sands Holiday Park. From there, a lengthy slog ended at Black Head, a humpbacked headland with the remains of an Iron Age cliff castle. From what I could see, the only sign of a man-made structure came in the form of a memorial to the Cornish writer A. L. Rowse. Carved into a rectangular stone slab facing the sea were the poignant words: *This was the land of my content.* I wholeheartedly agreed.

Jess and I rested for a while with a packet of oatcakes between us, and I took in the views across Mevagissey Bay to our right and St Austell Bay to our left. We pushed on, and soon the path plunged into a tree-lined valley – Ropehaven Cliffs Nature Reserve, owned by the Cornwall Wildlife Trust. While picking my way through the trees, I became aware that I was wading through a covering of leaves, and for the first time I noticed the branches above us were bare. We had walked out of one season and into another. The days of blistered lips, bleached hair and drinking litres of water to stay hydrated now seemed an age away.

We left the trees and tackled a series of valleys. Below us, visible through thickets of bramble and ivy, remote coves and dark reefs dotted the coast. From a flotilla of bright orange kayaks out in the bay, children's laughter floated over the water. More children ran about on the beach at Porthpean, dressed in wetsuits and lifejackets, no doubt taking part in some essential team-building exercise for the under-tens.

Glad to leave the frenetic energy of the young scamps, Jess and I departed the beach for a tree-lined footpath that cut along the back of a bluff. On the other side, we came to another beach, this one privately owned by the adjacent Duporth Holiday Village. Jess and I kept to the path and soon found ourselves on the outskirts of Charlestown.

A pink ice cream van was parked on the harbourside and I bought us a lolly each. Jess ate hers there and then, and we investigated the two tall ships moored in the harbour. Charlestown is famous for the square rigger ships that use the port as a base. Their presence, and the unspoilt look of the Georgian buildings, means the town is often used as a backdrop in historical films. There's no escaping the fact that without the tall ships, Charlestown is not the most exciting of places, and after walking once around the lozenge-shaped inner harbour, I felt I'd seen the highlights.

Leaving Charlestown, we followed the Coast Path through fields into a housing estate. For a while, we traipsed through a dark tunnel created by a tall, wooden fence on one side and bushes on the other. This opened out onto a common, which we crossed to reach a car park above Carlyon Bay. Behind wire fencing, a sprawling building site swamped the beach. Ominously quiet, the scarred landscape remained frozen in time, neither progressing nor being dismantled: an ambitious project of redevelopment stuck in a mire of opposition and planning regulations. The beach is a favourite of mine and a great fishing mark, and it saddened me to see the state of it.

Above the beach stretched the pristine Carlyon Bay golf course, with the Coast Path running beside the edge of the fairway. I stayed close to the bushes and kept Jess on a short lead, wary of projectiles. From the look of the brightly dressed figures teeing off and marching towards the next hole, today was ladies' day. I hoped the fairer sex would be mindful of where they hit their balls.

As we passed the first hole, the lush green of the fairway darkened and a black cloud crept ever closer to the golfers. Jess and I were also in the firing line, but I wanted to see what the ladies would do: seek shelter or play on? I didn't have to wait. As the first few spots fell, I unstrapped my new brolly and Jess and I hunkered underneath. From the side of the fairway we had a great view of the players. The ladies continued thwacking their balls as the sky turned black then released sheets of water onto their heads. One or two put jackets on, but most simply carried on, raising their voices slightly against the din. I caught snippets of shouted conversation: "Daphne, could you be a love and attend the flag?" and, "Are you going to use your pitching niblick Carol?" and, "Watch out for the worm-burner!" The deluge stopped as suddenly as it started, and I sheepishly shook out the umbrella, ashamed by my lack of fortitude. Yet glad to be dry.

The last mile consisted of a deeply uninspiring schlepp along roads and railway lines into Par. Our B&B for the night was out of town, and I'd arranged to call the owner for a lift when I reached the end of my walk. It was only two o'clock, and I didn't want to call it a day, so, hoping for a late lunch, I found a pub. The barman informed me the kitchen was closed, but as a consolation offered an extensive range of crisps and nuts. Never one to say no to a packet of crisps, I bought two packs and a pint of local beer and pulled up a stool. Jess slept while I talked to the locals, wondering, as I always did, what the characters around the bar did for a living that enabled them to spend hours in a pub in the middle of the day. No doubt they pondered the same thing about me.

Outside, the sky darkened, and it began to rain. The barman nipped out and returned with an armful of logs, then lit the fire. Jess hauled herself from the floor at my feet, lay on the hearth, inches from the flames, and fell fast asleep. Sighing, I ordered another pint, moved to a table nearby and watched the fire crackle and hiss. The cosy heat and numbing effect of the alcohol dampened any urgency to leave, and I spent an hour writing in my notebook and working my way through my drink.

The weather worsened. Gusts of wind threw buckets of water at the windows, causing the glass to rattle. I poked my head out of the front door, shivering as I left the heat of the fire. Rain fell from the overloaded gutters above the porch. A waterfall of water poured onto the pavement and ran down the street. If I didn't leave soon, I'd either be too drunk to move, or stranded by a flood. I rang the B&B owner and asked for a lift, apologising for making her come out in such awful conditions.

A while later, a squeaky car horn heralded her arrival. Waking Jess, I thanked the barman for his hospitality and, with a goodbye to my fellow afternoon drinkers, wobbled out of the pub. After introducing myself, I hustled Jess onto the back seat of the tiny car, along with my rucksack, and climbed in front. The woman beamed at me and did a fantastic job of ignoring the fact it was four o'clock in the afternoon and I reeked of beer and cheese and onion crisps. "Call me Sally," she said, adjusting the windscreen wipers to full pelt and pulling away. Rosy-cheeked and ample of bosom, Sally looked to be in her sixties. She exuded the homely but no-nonsense air of a farmer's wife, as proficient at reviving a premature lamb in an Aga as using the same Aga to create a hearty lamb stew. I liked her at once.

A skinny, wire-haired dog greeted us enthusiastically when we stepped into Sally's warm kitchen after a short drive. Her husband hunched over the table reading the paper while keeping an eye on two grandchildren who ran around in their school uniforms. The air was suffused with the savoury smells of cooking, the windows steamed up from the pots and pans rattling on the stove. Jess and I were absorbed into the mayhem as if family. Sally showed us to our room, shadowed by the kids, who asked questions about Jess and showed me all the things I needed to know, including where to find my separate bathroom. I poked my head around the door to find a blessed bath. That was my afternoon sorted.

Sally bustled the children out of my room, and I unpacked, made a cup of tea and ran the bath. Jess cried when I left, so I dragged her bed into the bathroom and, while she slept, I lay back and listened to the rain and wind, thinking how fortunate I was. Later, while I lay on my bed watching the weather forecast, Sally knocked on my door and asked if I would like to join them for supper. I gladly accepted, having eaten nothing since breakfast except two packets of crisps. Failing to learn from the previous night's experience, I neglected to ask for a time, so I spent the next hour peeking out of my room trying to judge when to make my move, going by the sounds and smells coming from the kitchen.

At last, I left my room with Jess in tow and headed for their dining room, to be confronted by a table heaving with food. Sally popped up behind me. "There you are, have a seat." I pulled up a chair next to her husband, expecting to see places laid for the grandchildren, but they had gone home. In their place sat Sally's daughter and son-in-law. After introductions, Sally piled my plate with food. There were seven different kinds of veg – "all from the garden" as her husband proudly informed me. Mashed swede glistening with butter, thinly sliced green beans, sticky red cabbage, peas, parsnips, broccoli and crispy roast potatoes. Thick slabs of turkey took up the remaining half of the plate, drowned in glossy gravy. I took a deep breath and began eating.

Twenty minutes in and I'd barely made a dent. I felt as if I'd inhaled an elephant, tusks and all. Around me, husband, wife, daughter and son-in-law sat in front of pristine plates wearing expressions that made it clear they were ready for more. With apologies to Sally, I put my knife and fork down and admitted defeat. She frowned, then announced, "Pudding!" She scurried into the kitchen and produced bowls of ice cream slathered in raspberry sauce, with four wafers around the edge. I tucked in, not wanting to upset my host, and was barely able to vacate my chair at the end of the meal. Having said my thank-yous, I lurched to my room, beached myself on the double bed and slept.

11.4 miles • 28,421 steps • Grading: Strenuous/Easy

I woke early, made a cup of tea and returned to the warm bed. From the bedside radio, the weather forecaster was predicting a dry morning with the risk of heavy showers after lunch. This information caused me to spring out of bed, all thoughts of a relaxing lie-in shoved to one side. The earlier we left, the less likely we'd encounter the aforementioned heavy showers. I dressed, packed, roused Jess and went in search of Sally. I found her in the kitchen, bent over the stove, a cup of tea in one hand and a frying pan in the other. With a grin, and a tip of her head towards the conservatory, she enquired, "Full fry?" I obediently went through and sat at a table laid for one.

Closing my eyes, I took three deep breaths to ready myself for the culinary onslaught. As the smells of fried food coming from the kitchen reached a crescendo, Sally swept into the room. She held before her, like an offering, a plate heaped with two sausages, two pieces of bacon, mushrooms, beans, tomatoes, one egg and two rounds of toast. I gave her a wan smile and, unbuckling my belt, got to work. While I concentrated on the veg and egg, Jess helped take down the sausages and bacon. Half an hour later, I pushed my plate away and burped behind my hand. Sally popped her head around the door and asked if I wanted a packed lunch. My god. "Yes please." In a flash she returned and handed me a turkey sandwich as thick as an encyclopaedia, and two chocolate bars wrapped in greaseproof paper. As an afterthought, she added an apple and a banana from the fruit bowl, "In case you get peckish before lunch."

After breakfast, Jess and I climbed into Sally's car and she drove us to Par Beach. We hugged in the car park, and I thanked her for her generosity and excellent cooking. Over her shoulder, dark clouds began to form above Gribbin Head, the first headland of the day. "I don't like the look of that," I said, and went through the rigmarole of putting on my jacket and trousers and getting Jess into her coat. "You take care," Sally said, pressing a toffee into my hand, then she drove away with a beep of her horn. I pulled my shoulders back, adjusted my walking sticks, and Jess and I set off towards the village of Polkerris.

Such was its diminutive size, Polkerris took only thirty seconds to walk through. From what I could make out, it consisted of a pub, a house or two, a watersports centre (by which I mean shed), a beach and a harbour wall. It took longer to get out than to get through – the path snaked left and right through a wood

Polkerris Harbour

that fringed the bay and led through a gate into a soggy field. Mud built up on my boots, doubling their size and weight and making it difficult to get any traction. Using my walking sticks like ski poles, I slipped and slid towards Gribbin Head, which was crowned by a red-and-white-striped day marker.

From the headland we continued across fields until we reached St Catherine's Castle on the outskirts of Fowey. The castle was built around 1538 – along with a twin on the opposite side of the estuary – to defend the harbour. I didn't stop to look around; the threat of rain kept me moving.

Past the fortification, a steep flight of metal steps led down to Readymoney Cove. I skipped down them with ease, but when I glanced around I saw Jess frozen at the top, crying. The treads were see-through, and she would not walk on them. No matter how hard I called to her, she would not budge. I did the only thing I could and shouted, "Bye then, Jessy," striding purposefully away. As I left the beach, I heard her sprinting towards me. Reunited, I gave her a handful of treats for being so brave, clipped on her lead and headed into Fowey.

Initially, I'd planned to pop into a gallery that sold my paintings on my way through the town, but after giving it some thought, I decided to stay incognito. I didn't want to re-join the real world and wasn't ready to think about work. Instead, we made our way to the ferry. Apart from a brief ferry trip from Rock, Jess was not used to boats, and I wondered how she would fare with the journey from Fowey to Polruan on the other side of the estuary. I needn't have worried. On board, she happily tagged behind a woman with a spaniel, more interested in the dog than the rocking boat.

It was cold and choppy on the water; spray splashed us every time the bow dipped into a trough and I put my arm around Jess to keep her warm. The woman with the spaniel and the ferry boatman obviously knew each other, and while we chugged towards the quay, they gossiped about mutual friends. Ten minutes later, we came alongside the jetty at Polruan, and I climbed out, with Jess behind me.

I knew the next seven miles would be difficult; all the guide books described the stretch as particularly onerous. Sometimes I wondered if it would be better not to know what lurked around the corner. I obsessively read and reread each day's route, fixating on the tricky bits and building them up to be something far worse than ever materialised. I remembered having the same discussion weeks before with Kelly. She'd said she would rather not know what the Coast Path might throw at her and, for that reason, didn't pack a guide book, only a map. As much as I admired her let's-just-see attitude, I couldn't emulate it. I do think the more you know, the better prepared you'll be. Unfortunately, the side effect of knowing was the fear of the known thing. As I led Jess up the road out of town and back onto the secluded cliffs, my mind raced with all the possible outcomes of the next few miles.

From Lantic Bay, we began the steady hike up to Pencarrow Head, with views of Gribbin Head. Between ascents, there was barely time to catch my breath before another flight of steps loomed. The rain forecast for the afternoon duly arrived, catching up with us a few miles from Polruan. We backed into a gap under a bush, and in our nest stayed dry and warm. So warm, in fact, Jess fell asleep, cuddled up to me like a cat. Sitting back on my heels, I had an excellent view of the path. A number of bedraggled and fed-up looking walkers passed by, shoulders hunched, hair plastered to their faces. If they found the sight of a grown woman hiding in a bush with a dog odd, they hid their feelings, giving us a thumbs up or a wave.

We waited until the rain eased. Then, splashing through newly filled puddles, we pushed on to East Coombe. Two men in hi-vis vests repaired a rotten bridge at the foot of the valley. Nearby, a pile of sawn wood was stacked ready to replace the old planks. How many times had those dedicated men scaled the vertical flight of steps leading out of the valley, encumbered by armfuls of wood and tools? I laboured to climb up those same hundreds of steps carrying only a rucksack with a map and a packet of nuts in it. The thought of doing it over and over again caused my knees to clack together.

Fortunately, the ground levelled off and, after one last push above a series of bite-shaped coves chomped out of the cliffs, we reached Polperro. Yet again, the six-mile stretch – although tough – had not amounted to the terrible ordeal I'd conjured up in my mind. We scrambled past a newly restored net loft perched on a jagged promontory, and followed a lane above Polperro Beach to the harbour. Trawlers, crabbers and punts lined up in rows, secured to their moorings with seaweed-encrusted ropes. In amongst the boats, swans presided over squabbling ducks and seagulls pecked at barnacles glued to the hulls.

Our B&B for the night stood behind a beautiful old humpbacked bridge at the far end of the harbour. I knocked on the door of what appeared to be a fish restaurant, to be greeted by a jolly man in an apron. "Do come in," he boomed and showed us to our room at the top of the building. As he left, he mentioned Jess and I were the only guests and he lived elsewhere in the village, so we would have the entire building to ourselves. Our room looked down on the harbour, and after settling Jess into her bed, I made a cup of tea, sat on the window seat and sketched the boats. Later, I rang Jack and filled him in on the walk.

As the day drew to a close, Jess and I ventured into the empty streets. For me, Polperro out of season was far nicer than in the throes of summer. With no crowds to jostle, no screaming kids or kamikaze seagulls, I took my time, peering into the mostly closed shop windows and poking around the back alleys and side streets until we arrived back at the harbour. A choice of pubs overlooked the water, and I made an arbitrary decision based on liking the look of one building over another.

Once seated at a table, I perused the menu. Surprised and delighted by its offerings of home-cooked food, I ordered pasta in a garlic and tomato sauce. Although early, a bunch of inebriated locals stood around the bar. They happily included Jess and me in their banter, and when they found out about our walk, they shouted questions across the room. "How many times have you cheated and got the bus?" "What do you do if you need a wee?" "Where's your husband while you're on your walking holiday?" (this said with a theatrical wink). And so on.

The food, when it arrived, tasted wonderful. I ate with relish, mopping up every last vestige of sauce with mounds of garlic bread; such a welcome change from the frozen food I'd grown used to. I ordered a coffee and sat back, watching the locals become more raucous, enjoying the disapproving looks of my fellow diners.

The sun slowly set as we left the pub and made our way back to the B&B. Jess attempted to engage a swan in a lighthearted game of chase, but the bird refused to cooperate and hissed its disapproval while unfurling its wings. Jess, the lion hunter, cowered between my legs until the swan waddled away.

We climbed the stairs to our room and, after a bit of television, turned in.

13.9 miles • 34,552 steps • Grading: Moderate/Strenuous

DAY 32 – POLPERRO TO PORTWRINKLE

The next morning, we woke early and left the B&B for a stroll before breakfast, the cloudless sky a watercolour wash of blue. I threw oatcake crumbs from my jacket pocket to the ducks then Jess and I pottered to the end of the outer harbour wall and back.

After the calm start, the day descended into mayhem. In the downstairs restaurant, I found a table laid for one, so I pulled up a chair and studied the breakfast menu. From somewhere above us came the sound of a door slamming. The owner appeared at the top of the stairs. He lurched down, juggling a tower of Tupperware boxes, and tripped at the bottom. The top tub fell with a splat onto the flagstone floor. As the lid flew off on impact, coleslaw shot out in all directions. Jess sprung forward but, just in time, I held her back, aware a breakfast of onions, carrots, cabbage and mayonnaise would mean a whole heap of trouble later. The owner, meanwhile, fetched a mop and bucket. After washing the floor, he used copious paper towels to remove coleslaw from the walls, paintings and furniture, before calmly taking my order for a full English breakfast.

We left later than usual, due to the discovery in my pocket of the front door keys to the previous B&B. When the post office opened, I popped the keys in a jiffy bag with a thank-you note and sent them on their way. By the time I finally got myself together, the rest of the village showed signs of being well and truly awake. Fishermen readied their boats while the idling engines belched clouds of diesel. Hordes of dog walkers took to the cliffs for their morning stroll. Jess and I joined the exodus on a concrete path, accompanied by birdsong and the sound of booming waves. One by one, our fellow dog walkers turned back while Jess and I continued on through fields dissected by streams.

Rounding a headland, we caught our first sight of Looe, and St George's Island, once owned by two sisters – Babs and Evelyn Atkin – before being bequeathed to the Cornwall Wildlife Trust. For most of the year, the island can only be accessed by boat, but a couple of times a year, on a big spring tide, you can get there on foot. A promenade swept around Hannafore Point, and through the trees I caught sight of the beach and pier at the mouth of the river that separates East from West Looe. The Banjo Pier bristled with fishing rods, each presided over by an expectant fisherman.

A short tramp along a road above the pier brought us into East Looe, but we swiftly turned onto the bridge spanning the river to West Looe. I squinted my eyes, almost blinded by the sun as it bounced off the surface of the water and played in amongst the moored boats. On the other side of the river, we wandered to the beach, through streets lined with shops and cafés. The sun worked its magic here as well, creating dramatic shadows. I stopped for a while to sketch the pier, with the dark headland behind and the bright light glistening on the sea.

We left the beach reluctantly; our late start meant we needed to keep moving. With no luck locating the acorn signpost I asked for directions at an ice cream kiosk, and once they put me on the right track I took advantage of the situation and bought Jess and me an ice cream to eat on our way. And so began a torturous hike to Portwrinkle, along roads, through the abandoned holiday village of Millendreath, and in and out of densely wooded coombes. A brief respite came when the low tide at Seaton Beach and Downderry meant we could walk on the sand rather than take the route along a road.

At the end of the beach, we walked through residential streets and re-joined the rollercoaster path. With no let up from the gruelling workout, I started to tire and prayed for a glimpse of Portwrinkle. I stopped for a drink and pulled out my map to check how far away we were. Thankfully, it was only a short distance to Portwrinkle, but, to my dismay, I realised getting to our B&B would require walking further on, to a place called Crafthole.

Portwrinkle Harbour

Arriving in Portwrinkle, I knocked on the door of a cottage to ask directions to Crafthole. The woman who answered advised me to take the hill out of the hamlet, then go along the road. Of course, a hill. Always, when I reached my lowest ebb, there would be a bloody hill. And a road.

Grinding my teeth, I set off, my anger the only thing keeping me going.

At the top, Jess bore the brunt of my frustration as I dragged her along the verge, inches from cars whose drivers thought it fun to speed up when they saw us. Half a mile up the road, a hand-painted sign announced our hotel. We turned down a winding driveway, at the bottom of which loomed a faux gothic manor surrounded by a pine forest. I rang the bell. A slight, grey-faced man wearing a white shirt and jeans opened the door. With a nod, he stepped back and allowed us to cross the threshold. He offered no small talk. As he checked our details, he appeared uninterested in our arrival. Bored even. Judging by the empty car park, I would have thought our gracious visit would be cause for a twenty-four-hour celebration.

After I'd signed in, he waved a hand at the bar near the entrance hall and told me it opened at six. Then he took us to our room. Up carpeted stairs, through corridors and numerous fire doors, the silent man led Jess and me to a part of the hotel as far from the front desk and human life as possible. When he left, I locked the door, pulled the curtains over the fake lead-lined windows and sat on the bed. Two hours to fill before I could sample the delights of the bar. I rang Jack and left a message, then fed Jess, took a look at the shower – which triggered images of the film *Psycho* – ran a bath, then watched the weather. At six o'clock on the dot, we left our room.

Twenty minutes later, after losing our way among the identical corridors and stairways, Jess and I entered the cavernous bar. The owner, perched on a stool with his back towards us, was watching the news on TV with the sound turned down. Uncertain whether he was working or unwinding, I tentatively enquired about the selection of white wines on offer. "We have one," he replied, "Chardonnay." I settled on a gin and tonic.

With the entire room to choose from, I selected a table near the bar. Jess lay at my feet. Apart from the tinkling of ice in my glass as I swallowed my drink in three gulps, the room was silent. I got up to look at the blackboard menu, my boots squeaking on the linoleum floor. Then returned to the bar and ordered a cheese ploughman's and another gin and tonic. The man served me, then turned off the TV and walked out. I stroked Jess's head for comfort and fiddled with my cuffs; why hadn't I brought my notebook down to give me something to do? The man appeared from nowhere and plonked an ornate condiment dispenser on my table, along with a knife, fork and napkin, then withdrew again. I scratched my nose. All of a sudden my supper arrived, carried in by a young woman in an apron. My god, the relief: another person in the hotel. She smiled as she put the ploughman's in front of me, and it took all my willpower not to grab her hand and plead with her to stay.

She turned the TV back on and adjusted the volume as she left; an act of kindness that gave me at least the illusion of having human company. Once I'd finished eating, Jess and I fled. I didn't see another soul as I crept to my room. Rain hammered on the windows as I locked the door behind me. I quickly got into my pyjamas, scrambled under the covers, curled into a ball and closed my eyes. Deep in the bowels of the hotel, a door banged open and shut. My eyes flew open. I gripped the duvet to my chin. Jess, fast asleep, was oblivious to my situation. I was the only person staying in the whole hotel. The only person. Rain lashed the windows. The bed creaked as another thought made me sit bolt upright. No, I wasn't the only person here. Somewhere in the hotel lurked the silent man.

I sprang out of bed, switched on all the lights, heaved both suitcases in front of the door and got back under the covers, walking sticks at my side.

16.1 miles • 40,110 steps • Grading: Moderate/Strenuous

DAY 33 – PORTWRINKLE TO PLYMOUTH

I woke, weary after a difficult night, but happy to be alive. The silent man served my breakfast in a deserted dining room. Surreptitiously, I searched his face for signs he might be a murderer – horns, three sixes tattooed on his neck, a sinister sneer – and came to the conclusion he was probably just shy. He said goodbye after breakfast and even smiled, no doubt looking forward to having the place to himself again.

He was welcome to it. Jess and I ran up the drive in our haste to leave. When I say ran, I mean walked a little bit faster than normal. Back on the road – thankfully much quieter now due to the early hour – we traipsed along the verge before pushing through a gate into a field. Next stop, Plymouth.

We marched through farmland overlooking Whitsand Bay until rudely confronted by a wire fence topped with barbed wire. The land beyond, owned by the MoD, incorporated a firing range and was only open to the public on certain days. Luckily for Jess and me, we happened to arrive on an open day. Ever-cautious, I double checked that the red flag remained firmly down, then walked through the unlocked gate. I prepared myself for a ravaged landscape, scattered with shrapnel and unexploded shells, but found undisturbed green fields and a herd of chocolate coloured cows. We eventually came across the MoD's mark on the land in the form of the Tregantle Fort, built in the 1860s to protect Plymouth. Every inch a military building, the hideous construction could house a thousand soldiers and thirty large guns. Would it kill them to plant some geraniums or give the walls a lick of paint? Nearby, another gate with a barbed wire flourish led back into the civilian world. My phone buzzed, a text from Jack: *Sorry I missed you last night Sash, I hope everything is ok.* I sent an upbeat reply, not wanting to worry him: *All good, I miss you xx*

I put my phone away and concentrated on the walk. Beyond the fort, at Freathy, the clifftops were scattered with chalets, visible from the road; a whole village built right to the cliff edge. The Coast Path twisted in and around each dwelling, following the contours of the cliff up and down. Too late, I realised I could have stayed with the road rather than take the stamina-sapping route. However, the detour did have advantages. As I passed each one, I imagined which chalet I'd buy with a lottery win: the perfect artist's studio offering the ideal workout; hauling canvases and easels up and down the winding tracks from the road would soon sort out my fitness. Oh, to dream.

I left the chalets – and thoughts of ever affording one – behind, and pushed on to Rame Head. The diminutive St Michael's Chapel, sitting on a mound at the tip of the headland, dates back to the 14th century. In those days, a priest kept a beacon burning to warn passing ships of the proximity of land. I did a quick sketch of the outside and then Jess and I went in. The interior felt cold and smelt of mould, the curved celling remained unadorned, and the floor was made of earth. But the view from the arched window was nothing short of breathtaking.

The Coast Path curved towards Penlee Battery, overlooking Cawsand Bay. Around the corner, a new view opened up like the next page in a book and the vast entrance to Plymouth Sound stretched out in front of us. A Royal Navy ship sat at anchor, guns aimed out to sea: a reassuring yet menacing presence. Beyond the ship, three nautical miles away on the other side of The Sound, I could see Wembury Point and the Great Mewstone, the halfway point of the next day's walk.

Tramping through woods on the way to Cawsand, I fell into conversation with a man walking two spaniels, who happened to be going my way. He'd completed most of the UK's national trails, including the South Downs Way, the Pennine Way and Offa's Dyke Path. I enjoyed exchanging anecdotes with him, feeling for the first time like a bonafide walker. In Cawsand, he popped into a café for lunch, and Jess and I pushed on through Kingsand to Mount Edgcumbe Country Park and the ferry landing at Cremyll. The park is reputedly one of the area's most popular tourist attractions, but not, it would seem, today. With eight hundred and sixty-five acres of country park, a big house and formal gardens, the gorgeous setting appeared deserted. Jess and I saw hundreds of sheep, and even a deer, but no other signs of life. This proved a problem when, after walking around follies, across meadows and through woods, I became lost. Who could I ask for directions? After going around in circles, I happened upon a car park devoid of a single vehicle. On a stand in the middle of the car park, I found a map, but even after scrutinising the image I couldn't decipher the way out.

It started raining. Jess, tail between her legs, sought shelter in a thicket. While enticing her out, I saw a path that showed promise. Keen to get out of the park, I decided not to wait for the rain to stop but to push on. Jess harboured other ideas, and only by putting on her lead and leaving a trail of oatcake crumbs away from the bushes could I get her to move. After luring her into the open I put her coat on and we set off through the rain. My hunch about the path proved to be right, and we escaped the confines of the park for a road.

While squelching along the verge, a woman in a car took pity on us and wound down her window to offer a lift. I glanced through the back window at the pristine interior, then at Jess, plastered in mud up to her knees, and regretfully declined the offer, asking instead if we were heading for the ferry landing. She confirmed we were going in the right direction; I thanked her and watched wistfully as she drove away.

By the time we found the jetty at Cremyll, Jess and I were soaked through. A few other bedraggled passengers turned up, and we stood in a line, cold, wet and desperate to see the ferry chugging towards us from the other side. When the boat came alongside, Jess jumped on board like an old sea dog. I took her coat off and dried her as best I could, knowing as soon as we disembarked, she would get wet again. As she lay on the bench next to me, I draped the towel over her and then watched out of the window as we came into Plymouth. After two hundred and ninety-six miles, Jess and I were leaving Cornwall for the wilds of Devon.

We hopped off the ferry into another county, another world. My only thought: to get out of the blessed rain. What does a stranger in a strange town do? Find a pub. Yards from the ferry terminal I spied one. Inside, six men stood drinking around a pool table, and three more sat at the bar opposite the door. An Alsatian dog lay at their feet and gave Jess a deadly stare. We quickly moved to a seat at the end of the bar and I asked the barman for a glass of lemonade, a packet of pork scratchings for Jess, and help with directions. Overhearing, the owner of the Alsatian moved to the stool next to mine, pulled out his phone and brought up a map of the city. "Listen, it's simple, you go right out of the pub then left at Durnford Street, or should that be right? DAVE! Left or right at Durnford Street to get to Elliot Street?" I switched off as he rattled on, nodding when I thought I should, until he exclaimed, "See, easy. You'll find it in no time."

He refused my offer to buy him a pint, so I placed a pile of pork scratchings on the bar for his dog, finished my drink and, shaking his hand, left in search of the hotel. Outside, overwhelmed by traffic, noise and rushing pedestrians, I tried to recall his directions. Did he say left or right at Durnford Street? Then I came up with an idea: if I could locate Smeaton's Tower, a significant landmark in the city, I would be all right; I knew the hotel was on one of the streets nearby. I set off again, this time heading for the waterfront, and stuck to the road all the way around to the Hoe and the red-and-white-striped Smeaton's Tower.

From the Hoe, I easily found the hotel on a nearby side street. Signing in at the reception, I apologised to the girl behind the desk for leaving puddles on her floor. She smiled, "What awful weather. You must be soaked through, but nothing that a hot shower won't fix. I'll show you to your room."

Whilst small, the room had a high ceiling and a tall, elegant window looking over the rain-drenched street below. Most importantly, the softest, comfiest bed I'd ever sat on dominated the tiny space. I pulled my boots off and sank into the mattress. It took all my willpower to get up to dry Jess off and sort out her supper. Once she'd eaten, I put her bed in front of a radiator and hung our sodden coats off another, folding a towel underneath to catch the drips. Jess fell into a deep sleep while I fell onto the bed and listened to the comforting sounds of the hotel. A far cry from my experience of the night before at the Bates Motel, this building hummed with life. People ran up and down the stairs slamming doors, a baby wailed in the next room, and muffled talking and laughter seeped through the walls.

I took a shower to warm up and, wrapped in towels, stared out of the window at the miserable weather. I wanted to eat, but the thought of getting wet again did not appeal to me. What's more, I didn't have a clue where to go and might spend hours hunting for somewhere dog-friendly to have supper. I glanced at Jess and the irresistible bed. We'd stay right where we were.

14.6 miles • 36,364 steps • Grading: Moderate

I woke early after a wonderful night's sleep, and made a mental note to ask the girl at the front desk where the hotel sourced their mattresses. Once dressed, I left my room in search of breakfast. On my way through the reception, I noticed a man sitting on a bench with a stick clasped in one hand and a plastic bottle of honey in the other. Even Jess gave him a curious look. "Would you mind escorting me to the breakfast room?" he asked as we drew near, "I can't see." That would explain the stick, but why the honey? I took his elbow and we drifted around the ground floor until I spied a sign pointing to the dining room. With Jess's lead in one hand and the arm of the man in the other, I backed into a fire door and pushed it with my bum while trying to pull them both through.

"Would you mind giving me a hand?" I asked the waitress who stood on the other side of the door. She ignored my plea and instead focused on Jess. "Please, could you help me with this gentleman?" I repeated slowly and loudly. With an exaggerated sigh, she grabbed the blind man's elbow, pulled him through the door, marched him into the restaurant and shoved him into a chair.

Not yet finished, she whipped around to face me and shrieked that dogs were absolutely not allowed in the dining room. I put my hands up and meekly enquired where, in that case, we should go. She growled and stomped off, abandoning Jess and me in the doorway. The blind man, unconcerned by his rough treatment, whistled a tuneless melody while expertly pouring himself a cup of tea and adding a blob of honey. Ah, the mystery of the honey solved. Jess and I hovered in the doorway, neither in nor out. Two other guests brushed past us into the dining room: the first, a short pale-faced woman with dyed black hair and rouged cheeks; the second, a bulldog of a man with well-muscled shoulders, wearing tight jeans. They sat on opposite sides of the dining room, leaving space around the blind man, but greeted him warmly, and he returned the salutation. "Morning Rose, morning Stan." I cleared my throat and fiddled with Jess's lead. Another employee came through from the kitchen and asked me where I wanted to sit. She ignored Jess and laid me a table near the door.

Once seated, Jess and I were included in the joshing between the three guests. The blind man asked the bulldog to describe me to him. "She's got brown hair. She's short. Oh, and she's with a big dog."

I ordered my usual full English breakfast, and we ate in companionable silence until the blind man thought to enquire about the bulldog's health. "Not bad," he answered, "apart from being beaten up last night. Someone bashed my bonce in. I'm off to hospital after breakfast to get my head stitched." He pushed back his chair, walked over to the blind man and encouraged him to feel the gash on his head. Gently, the blind man explored the wound with his fingers, letting out a high whistle. "Yep," the bulldog remarked, and walked back to his table to finish his cornflakes.

I pushed my plate away, regretting slathering my sausages in tomato ketchup. Time to go. I said goodbye to the three friends and returned to my room to pack.

The day began as the one before had ended, with a ferry ride. We left the hotel for the Barbican Landing Stage, taking the scenic Plymouth Waterfront Walkway. From the Hoe, we walked past Tinside Lido, the water an exquisite blue. Outside the Liner Lookout Café on the other side of the road, rows of tables and chairs awaited those hankering after an alfresco breakfast. Joggers, dog walkers and suited businessmen made the most of the beautiful morning, soaking up the sun. I thought back to the afternoon before. With the rain and the misery of getting lost, I hadn't taken in any of the sights of the city. Thank goodness I'd been able to see some of it under a blue sky.

I found the landing stage and, in a stroke of luck, the ferry turned up at the very same moment. Jess had to be restrained from bounding on board; the ferry boatman held her back while two students and an elderly woman were helped on first. She'd definitely got the hang of floating things and was in danger of becoming a bit of a show-off. The trip to Mount Batten Point lasted just long enough for me to get comfortable and exchange pleasantries with the other passengers.

After disembarking, I pulled out my phone to ring Patricia, our host for the night. She lived on the other side of the River Yealm, at Newton Ferrers, and had kindly offered to pick us up in her boat. Walking the SWCP in October could be tricky because most, if not all, of the ferries stop running for the winter. This would be a problem in the days to come, but for the time being, Patricia's private boat would sort me out. She arranged to meet us in three hours on the banks of the River Yealm.

Three hours. I hurried away from the breakwater fearing it would be a close call. The Coast Path wound its way along wooded cliffs with broken views of The Sound. Near Jennycliff Bay, I stopped to take a photo of a bright blue sign informing me of the mind-blowing fact that Poole was one hundred and seventy-five (and a half) miles away. Blimey. I ran my fingers over the raised numbers. For the first time since setting off from Porlock, I allowed myself to consider the idea that I might actually finish.

At the start, just reaching the next B&B presented enough of a challenge. Now, with the end in sight, I began to anticipate the emotions of going home. I imagined setting foot on familiar paths as I crossed into Dorset, paths I ran along as a child. Strange to look back and realise that, without knowing it, I'd forged a deep connection with the SWCP years before reading the book that inspired me to set off on my journey. Sunday walks around Durlston Country Park, fossil hunting in Kimmeridge, snorkelling in the tidal pool at Dancing Ledge: all were beloved memories from my childhood, and all took place along the SWCP. Two more weeks until I would revisit my childhood haunts and experience them as part of the whole. But for now, I had just two hours before my rendezvous with a woman and a boat, and the clock was ticking.

We continued, at a fair clip, around Bovisand Beach and into a community of chalets. We passed a sign asking people to keep their dogs on leads and off the beach. Fair enough, I thought, and clipped Jess's lead on. Two yards on, another sign, this one next to a dog bin, telling me to pick up after my dog. Then another, next to another dog bin, telling me not to park. Further on, another dog bin between a sign telling me what to do with my dog's poo, and a sign reminding me (in case I'd forgotten) dogs were banned from ALL beaches. And finally, another dog bin and a sign telling me when the gates to the community closed. Then, to cap it all off, I trod in dog poo.

As I scraped my boot clean on the grass verge, I awaited the sound of sirens and my immediate arrest. Nothing. Maybe the residents were at a meeting to discuss the installation of more dog bins or a watch tower with a machine gun. Time to go. As happy to leave a place as I'd ever been, I walked through the open gate and away.

With no time to dawdle, Jess and I rushed on to Wembury Point, where the Great Mewstone rose from the sea in front of us, dark grey with the sun behind it. Today, the island is a National Trust bird sanctuary, but centuries ago it served an entirely different purpose. In 1744, a local petty criminal was incarcerated on the island for seven years. He liked the experience so much that when he came to the end of his sentence, he elected to stay. The unusual dome-roofed house he built can still be seen from the mainland with binoculars. Given a choice between imprisonment on the Great Mewstone or living in the community of chalets Jess and I recently escaped, I knew where I would rather be.

We carried on through fields until we reached Wembury Beach. My shoulders dropped; after hours of checking my watch and hurrying, I knew we were now close to the river. I bought a cup of tea from the Old Mill Café, and a lolly for Jess, and relaxed on the sand, legs outstretched. After a while, I heaved myself up, shrugged on my rucksack and wandered back to the Coast Path. "Right Jess, the river should be on the other side of this hill." We began climbing. The sound of church bells filled the air. One last push and … at the top, the Coast Path receded into the distance through yet more fields. In a dither, I pulled out my map. Where was the bloody river? The Yealm – my map made clear – still lay

Wembury

two miles away.

I dashed off, yelling at a bemused Jess to "bloody well keep up, we're late!" Legs a blur, I ran through the fields, my rucksack jiggling up and down like a toddler needing a wee. Finally, dishevelled and sweating, I saw the river through trees and soon found the stone jetty that Patricia had described over the phone. I glanced at my watch. Thirty minutes late. I struggled to get my rucksack off, dumping it at my feet, then stood hands on hips, looking across the river to the houses on the other side. Unsurprisingly, I could see no sign of Patricia or the boat. I took out my phone, then remembered there was no signal on the river. Bugger. I tried waving and jumping about, much to Jess's embarrassment. Still no sign. I sat at the end of the jetty, at a loss. A young couple, arm in arm, appeared. After hearing my dilemma, they offered me the use of their phones. I didn't hold out much hope, but thankfully one of them worked. When Patricia picked up the phone, I sheepishly explained my mistake: "I, um, misjudged the whereabouts of the firmly established River Yealm …" She graciously dropped everything to come and pick us up.

We didn't have to wait long before I spotted her in the distance, with two other passengers: a Dalmatian dog and a woman. She came alongside the jetty and pulled the oars in while I grabbed the gunnels to steady the boat. I clambered in first and called Jess, who barked and wagged her tail furiously, but refused to budge. Leaning out of the boat, I seized the end of the lead and persuaded her in using half an oatcake. The boat rocked madly as we all shuffled around trying to get comfortable, and with a shove from an oar, we were off.

"Thanks," I gushed, relieved everything had worked out.

"No problem," Patricia smiled and pulled on the oars. The dogs weighed each other up from opposite ends of the boat, tails wagging. The last thing we needed was two dogs charging around, so I kept a firm grip on Jess's collar. Patricia, concentrating on fighting the current in the middle of the river, remained quiet, but her friend introduced herself and we shook hands. With so many souls on board, the rowing boat proved hard to control, so Jess and I jumped off at a pontoon on the other side of the river and walked the rest of the way to the B&B while Patricia, her friend and the dog carried on to her boathouse.

Strolling along the river bank, I grinned. "I think we'll be all right here, Jess." Detached houses lined the road overlooking the river, each with a pontoon, boathouse or jetty. Generous garages housed expensive cars with gleaming paintwork. Patricia and her friend met up with us in front of a glass-fronted, forest-backed house – our B&B for the night – and we walked up the drive together.

My room looked out over the river, the best view of the whole walk so far. I unpacked, fed Jess, and went in search of my host, feeling the need to apologise once more for making her row across the river twice. She brushed off my grovelling and, perhaps to shut me up, invited me to join their late lunch. I hadn't eaten since breakfast, and gratefully pulled up a chair. The dining table was positioned in front of a glass wall encasing the front of the house. Sunlight poured in, warming my back and highlighting particles of dust in the air. While Patricia flew about the kitchen, her friend poured three glasses of chilled white wine and offered one to each of us. The dogs, meanwhile, lolled in a patch of sun on the wooden floor, getting on splendidly, as I knew they would. I sighed and sipped my wine. Two teenagers appeared and plonked themselves on the opposite side of the table, heads bowed towards their phones. Then the food arrived: a glazed ham, warm from the oven, homemade coleslaw with red cabbage (my favourite), homemade pickles and fresh bread. Overwhelmed, I reverently tucked in, every mouthful delicious. How would I ever go back to eating frozen scampi and chips after this?

With lunch over, the household scattered, leaving Jess and me to our own devices. I wanted to walk off lunch, so persuaded Jess to mosey along the river with me to the village. When we got there, I popped into the village shop, stocked up on snacks, and enquired about the odds of finding a pub nearby. There were two: the imaginatively named Swan Inn and the Ship Inn. I plumped for the latter, and – after ordering a pint and a packet of crisps – found a table at a seating area overlooking the river and settled down to spend some time writing in my diary.

We stayed for a couple of hours, after I engaged in conversation with the man and woman sitting at the next table. Acknowledging my muddy boots, the woman asked if I'd walked far. I replied I was two thirds of the way through walking the SWCP. "That's on my list!" she exclaimed. "You must do it," I enthused. I met so many people who said they wanted to walk the whole path in one go, but were waiting to retire, or win the lottery, or for their children to leave home, or to get divorced. Consequently, the majority of fellow walkers I met were either retired or young enough to have no responsibilities. Whatever excuses people came up with, I always said the same thing: "You MUST do it!"

Wandering back along the river, with the sun low in the sky and the wind dropping, I decided to collect my rod from my room and indulge in an hour of fishing. I unpacked my perfectly made and little-used travel rod and assembled it in my room, then chose two lures, left the B&B, crossed the road and wandered out to the end of a wooden pontoon. Jess lay with her head on her paws and watched the comings and goings of a family of ducks while I flicked the iridescent lure into the fast-flowing water and slowly reeled it in, keeping an eye out for the telltale shadow of a bass. Gradually, the light faded, the ducks waddled onto the far bank looking for a safe place to sleep, and I retrieved my final cast. The perfect end to a wonderful afternoon.

We returned to our room, where I fed Jess. After our late lunch and a couple of packets of crisps in the pub, I didn't need supper. Instead, I ran a hot bath, watched TV and went to bed early.

12 miles • 29,888 steps • Grading: Easy/Moderate

DAY 35 – NEWTON FERRERS TO BANTHAM

The next morning, over a breakfast of eggs from chickens in the garden, butchers sausages and homegrown tomatoes, I went over the day's itinerary. The walk to Bantham included two rivers – the River Erme and the River Avon. Neither ferries were running, and going around both estuaries by taxi would cost £40. The sensible, and cheap, option was to take the day off.

I rang the luggage transfer company and arranged for Jess and me to travel to Bantham with our suitcases. The perfect solution. They planned to arrive at Patricia's around midday. I checked my watch; plenty of time for a walk. Jess and I left the B&B and turned left, away from the village, through the woods that grew to the edge of the river. Without the weight of my rucksack pressing on my shoulders, I skipped through the trees as nimble as a deer, effortlessly racking up one mile, then two. At Shortaflete Creek, we turned and retraced our steps, but instead of going into the B&B we continued to the village shop. I craved the Sunday papers and hoped to buy at least two to take to Bantham, but the locals had beaten me to it.

Patricia's car was gone when we got back to the B&B. I wrestled my suitcases out of my room to the front garden and sat on the steps waiting for the luggage transfer company, hoping I would get a chance to say goodbye. My lift turned up at the same time as Patricia, giving me the opportunity to say thank you for the lift and lunch and the view from my room and the marvellous breakfast. We hugged, then Jess and I clambered into the back seat with our suitcases and I waved goodbye.

An hour later, we pulled up outside the Sloop Inn. The scent of woodsmoke and roast meat wafted out of the door as I went in search of someone to help me with our cases. The barman left his post to heave Jess's case up three flights of stairs to an attic bedroom, while I dealt with mine. On the way out, he asked if I wanted lunch. I decided to wait; after my heavenly breakfast I wasn't hungry. I unpacked, fed Jess and left the pub to investigate the beach.

A straight road led directly to Bantham Beach. Camper vans, VW Beatles and people carriers filled the car park behind the dunes. The enticing smell of grilled burgers and hotdogs coming from a snack van made me drool, but I fought the urge to snaffle one; I'd hold out for a proper meal in the pub later. We traipsed onto the sand and walked along the shore. Twenty-something hipsters with sun-bleached hair wearing flip-flops, and fresh-faced parents with photogenic kids, populated the beach like extras in a sunscreen advert. Beyond the kite flyers and surfers, the prominent Burgh Island loomed offshore, attached to the mainland by a sand causeway, and accessible by tractor at high tide. Dominating the island, the restored Art Deco Burgh Island Hotel has reputedly hosted a plethora of famous guests, including Winston Churchill, Edward VIII and Wallis Simpson, Noel Coward, and even the Beatles.

The sea air triggered my appetite so I called Jess and we returned to the pub for a late lunch. The bar heaved with people, and wet dogs lay under chairs, their paws sticking out. Pushchairs laden with coats drifted rudderless about the tables on a floor that felt gritty with sand brought in from the beach. Exactly right for a Sunday afternoon pub lunch in autumn.

I fought my way to the bar, keeping a tight grip on Jess's lead, and asked if any tables were available. The barman indicated a table by the fire. "If you hurry, you can have that one." I bolted towards it, tied Jess's lead to the chair leg, and hung my coat over the back before returning to the bar to order a glass of wine and a local crab on granary sandwich.

With my back to the wall, I surveyed the room. In all the chaos, the staff kept smiling and knew precisely what to do. They swayed past the pushchairs while sidestepping the dogs' paws, picking up empty glasses and dirty plates as they went. My sandwiches came in good time and tasted delicious. I wanted to stay and have another glass of wine, but there was a queue of people waiting for tables. In the time it took me to untie Jess's lead, four women swooped on my table and made it their own. I hiked up the stairs at the back of the bar to my room. During the drive from Newton Ferrers, I'd asked the driver to stop at a shop so I could buy the papers. Now, I sprawled on my bed listening to the radio and reading the Sunday supplements.

Later, during the lull between lunch and supper, I left my room in search of the bar manager, hoping to ask about an early breakfast. He explained I could have breakfast in my room – a tray of bread, jams, milk and cereal would be left outside my door later that night. I returned to my room, and the papers, before turning in.

I rose at the crack of dawn and opened my door to find the tray of breakfast goodies and a toaster. Sadly the toaster didn't work, so I ate a round of bread and jam instead. By the time I'd finished eating, and packed, my early start had evaporated. Outside, a fine drizzle began to fall. I unpacked my waterproof jacket and trousers, pulled them on, Velcroed Jess into hers, and we shuffled down the stairs and out of the back door.

The drizzle grew steadily worse on the way to the beach, as a milky fog swept in from the sea. I pulled my hood up and strode towards a grassy cliff to the left of the car park. A fellow dog walker mirrored our progress for a mile or so, then melted away. Out at sea, a fleeting image of Thurlstone Rock dissolved into the mist, along with every object within a fifty-yard radius. My world shrunk. I put Jess back on her lead, as much for the comfort of having her near as to protect her from stumbling off a cliff. Side by side we pushed on, until I lost track of our place on the coast. I turned to my guide book for clues but the descriptions were no help, portraying incredible views of Burgh Island, a golf course and a string of sandy coves – none of which I could see.

A brief window of clarity came when we walked into Hope Cove. The fog shifted to reveal a huddle of houses in the crook of a grass-backed promontory. Jess and I walked through a car park and past a row of holiday cottages to a beach with a thin harbour wall, wooden boats lined up above the high-water line. The fog hovered above the spine of Bolt Tail, the next headland, threatening to roll over the sea towards us at any minute. I shivered as we stalked towards it.

At the top of the headland, the noise of waves crashing against the cliffs became muffled. Distant sheep sounded as if they were bleating into pillows. The air grew clammy and cold. I kept my eyes on the ground, obsessively checking that I was going the right way, but in a moment of panic, the well-worn path simply evaporated in the middle of a field. I froze. What now? Squinting, I could just make out the ghostly outline of a gate and a low stone wall. I groped towards it and – with my hand on the stones – made my way, by touch, to another gate and a signpost pointing to Bolt Head.

My knees felt suddenly weak. A flock of sheep appeared like wraiths, all around us, staring as we trudged past. When I glanced back, they'd dissolved. A frisson of apprehension shot through my body. I replayed in my mind the moors scene in

An American Werewolf in London, the part where two friends on a hike get caught in the fog on the moors and hear a howl. Bloody hell. I shook my head, trying to think about something else, anything. The theme tune to *The Waltons* began to play in my head. Much better. I latched on to the repetitive melody like a drowning woman grabbing a life ring, hoping to dispel my morbid thoughts.

After an hour of hearing the same catchy ditty ringing around my head, I yearned for respite. Then, at the end of Bolt Head, the fog at last cleared, taking *The Waltons* with it. Suddenly, everything around me vibrated with colour. My normally poor eyesight picked out the smallest details in the landscape. I could see the sea! I let Jess off her lead and she bounded away, glad to be free. We crossed a stream and walked around Starehole Bay, then climbed a flight of stairs through a jagged rock formation. On the other side, we enjoyed a fine view of Salcombe.

On the way into the town we skirted around two coves, South Sands and North Sands. For a fee, you could hop from the South Sands Ferry sea tractor onto the South Sands Ferry and be dropped off in Salcombe. Or, you could stand next to the selfsame tractor, looking up and down the deserted beach for the driver, give up, and plod along the cliff road instead. Which is precisely what Jess and I did.

My father knew Salcombe well and had recommended a pub on the waterside. Luckily for me, it happened to be the first one I came across. I ordered a crab sandwich on brown bread and a pint, and sat outside, overlooking the river. After the fog and drizzle, the clouds had cleared and the afternoon felt warm. My sandwich, when it came, turned out to be a disappointment: not a patch on the one I'd eaten the day before. I forced down a few bites but found the excessive use of brown meat too rich. I drank my pint and made a mental note to ignore my father's recommendations in future. Resolving to find a better pub later, I went in search of my B&B.

We arrived at a smart townhouse and I rang the doorbell. The lanky woman who answered lookedme up and down, then saw Jess and exclaimed: "Gosh, it's big."

"I know," I laughed. "But SHE is well behaved."

The woman narrowed her eyes at Jess, then at me. Puzzled, I

thought perhaps my muddy boots were the problem and quickly took them off, leaving me standing on her doorstep in socks. She ignored the gesture.

"There's no electric in your room."

"No electric? Um, don't worry. I only want to unwind. I don't need electric."

"Well, you're not supposed to be here until five o'clock. I never take anyone before five."

"I have never heard of a B&B that insisted people arrive after five."

"Well, you have now." She glared down at us, physically barring our entry into her house.

My bottom lip wobbled.

"I've changed my mind," I said. "I wouldn't stay here if you were the last B&B on the planet."

At that moment, I noticed our suitcases in her hallway. I felt my cheeks burn.

"I will return for our suitcases later," I told her, and with trembling hands I put my boots on, called Jess, and marched down the hill.

Heart racing, I fought back tears. The company that had booked the room for me made sure everyone knew I owned a ridgeback dog. To be snubbed so blatantly! I took a few deep breaths and reassessed our situation. Dog-friendly places to stay were few and far between in Salcombe, and I conjured a vision of Jess and me shivering in a doorway for the night.

Time to start looking. I began by asking in a couple of pubs, as in my experience pubs are normally dog-friendly. No luck. Rather than traipsing around the whole town, I then thought I'd try the tourist information office. We pushed through the door to be greeted by two smiling faces and a "how may we help?" Wrestling with tears, I explained our predicament. They knew the B&B woman – or The Harridan as I now thought of her – and were genuinely perplexed by her behaviour. While they got on the phone to find a dog-friendly place for us to stay, I began to formulate Plan B. On our way into Salcombe earlier, Jess and I passed by two smart hotels on the beach. I'd drooled over the menus and fantasised about booking a room. Well, now I could.

When the women ran out of options, I asked them if they could ring both hotels and enquire if they had a room and didn't mind a dog. The first hotel allowed dogs but cost a lot of money. Despite the price, I did give it a second's thought before saying, "Let's try the other one." The second choice allowed dogs and, although expensive, cost less than the first. I readily agreed, and they organised the booking. "What about our suitcases?" I wanted to know. The two angels sprang to the rescue and phoned for a local taxi to pick us up, liberate our bags from the clutches of The Harridan, and take us to the hotel. I thanked them both from the bottom of my heart, woke Jess, and we went outside to wait for the cab.

When the taxi arrived, Jess clambered into the boot and I sat up front with the driver. I told him what had happened. He swore under his breath and confided that the B&B owner had a bit of a reputation, telling me that he never recommended her to his customers. We pulled up outside the house, engine running, and he dashed through the open door, grabbed the suitcases and scarpered without seeing a sign of her. Next stop, the hotel.

A short ride later, I thanked the taxi driver and pushed through glass doors into the reception. The decor reminded me of the day room in a nursing home, with heavily patterned carpets, thick curtains and well- padded armchairs; dated, but comfortable. Our room overlooked the beach and felt snug and warm, the radiators turned up high. The ensuite included a rolltop bath: perfect. I fed Jess, and she fell asleep pressed up against the radiator while I luxuriated in a bubble-filled bath with a cup of tea and complimentary biscuit.

I rang Jack. He answered straight away. "Hey, Sash, how is everything?"

"Couldn't be better. We are staying in a hotel right on the beach."

"You lucky so-and-so!"

"I feel lucky. It's funny how things work out sometimes."

Later, feeling a thousand times better and squeaky clean, I roused Jess and pottered down to the bar to see about a bite to eat. Dogs weren't allowed in the restaurant but I could order room service and eat in my room. I ordered a starter of tuna pâté, a main of John Dory, and a fruit salad for pudding, to be sent to my room in an hour. That gave me ample time to enjoy a civilised drink. While waiting at the bar, I peered through the glass of a large saltwater fish tank set into the wall with bass, pollock and flatfish cruising around. The barman told me the salt water came directly from the sea via a pump. Our native fish were as beautiful to me as any tropical species, but I couldn't help thinking they'd be better off in the sea than in a tank in a hotel bar.

I carried my drink and bowl of complimentary crisps into the conservatory and lowered myself into a heavily upholstered armchair while Jess lay at my feet. A couple I'd met earlier recognised me and sidled over with their drinks. Pulling up two chairs, they started telling me about their two spaniels, their holidays in Salcombe, their holidays abroad, the difficulties of taking pets away, the joy of staying in this country, and on and on. I listened while sipping my wine and munching my crisps, then rose to leave.

"Are you having another glass of wine? Good idea, we will too. Jonathan, be a love and get three glasses of wine."

I slumped back in my seat. The barman, realising I'd been hijacked, came over and asked if I wanted to postpone my supper. I waited for a beat, hoping the woman would realise they were holding me up, but no, she wholeheartedly agreed that I should delay my meal. An hour later, they wished me a good night and waltzed off to the dining room. The barman came over to clear the glasses. "Your food's on its way," he reassured me. Thanking him, I woke Jess and we bolted upstairs to our room.

When I heard the gentle knock and muffled "room service" I nearly tore the door off its hinges in my haste to get at the food. I carried the tray to the bed, sat back on the pillows with my legs stretched forward, and wolfed down all three courses, finishing off with another packet of complimentary biscuits.

12.2 miles • 30,391 steps • Grading: Moderate/Strenuous

The next morning, I ate breakfast in bed, feeling extremely spoilt. As I chomped on my muesli with fruit and yoghurt, I looked out over the beach. Dog walkers marched up and down the shore, shoulders hunched under a steady drizzle. I tuned in to the weather forecast: low cloud in the morning, with clear skies later.

I fed Jess, packed, and traipsed down to the reception to pay the bill. With everything settled, I turned towards the glass front door and the unwelcome sight of torrential rain. Bloody hell. I changed into my wet weather gear, strapped Jess into her coat, and we left the warm, dry hotel lobby. As soon as she felt the first drops of rain, Jess strained on her lead to go back, her claws scrabbling on the slick pavement. "Come on Jessy," I encouraged. "We've got to get to Slapton."

We crossed over to the beach and trudged along the road into Salcombe. Our first obstacle of the day? Finding the ferry crossing to East Portlemouth. Protected from the rain by a covered walkway, I consulted my map and located the ferry landing mere metres from our spot. Poking my head out into the rain, I recognised the ferry further up the riverbank. I waved my arms above my head and soon heard the engine wheezing into life as the ferry chugged towards us. The ferryman looked as miserable as I felt and barely uttered a word during the short journey to the other side. Once across, I paid my fare, clambered off the boat and ran with Jess into an open-fronted shelter. I sat on a slatted bench and rooted around in my rucksack for anything I could use to help dry Jess off. My spare pair of socks worked a treat, but the gesture was futile; as soon as we left the shelter, Jess would get soaked again. I looked across the estuary and wondered if I'd made a bad choice to leave the hotel in the first place.

Heads down, we plodded along a residential road parallel to the river. A car sidled up beside us and the driver wound down her window, offering to give Jess a lift. I lay my hand on the top of Jess's head and assured the woman we were okay. She scowled. "You shouldn't be walking your dog in these conditions." In response, I laughed – how dare she tell me when and how to walk my dog – and again insisted we were fine. She shook her head and drove off.

I took a deep breath, my heart racing. In truth, the awful weather did concern me. The rain seemed set to stay, and I knew it would be worse on the cliffs. I debated turning around, but the spectre of Bess, laughing at my pessimism, drove me on. "I'm sorry, Jess," I said, not knowing what else to do.

We squelched across Rickham Common then struck out for the desolate cliffs. A thick sea mist gathered around us, rolled over the cliffs then pulled back. The path twisted in and out of gorges and around eruptions of rock. The rain continued to fall. Should we go on? Should we turn back? I fought with the two options at every step. Just a bit further, I told myself. The rain will clear and all will be well.

We climbed a rough track fringed with saturated grasses, and arrived at Prawle Point, with a coastguard station on the summit. From there, we trudged downwards, past a row of coastguard cottages and onto a plateau at the edge of the sea. Away from the cliffs, the fog dissipated and the rain eased. I pushed back my hood and brushed my wet fringe from my eyes, then, using the sock, dried Jess's face and ears and gave her an oatcake. Moments later, I unearthed a sign for East Prawle pointing away from the coast, up a hill. I paused for a second. Surely the worst must be over? I pored over my map and set my sights onward to Peartree Point.

Flat fields provided a welcome respite from the arduous cliffs, but the ground was sodden and in places the water reached the top of my boots. Jess, head low, sloshed through the waterlogged fields, looking utterly forlorn. I imagined the woman who'd offered her the lift rushing home and placing a call to the RSPCA. Poor Jess.

Suddenly a lump of a man stormed past us, wearing a gigantic backpack and army surplus clothing. He ignored us totally, fixated on some faraway point. A hundred yards behind him, a petite girl in unsuitable clothes slipped and slid in his wake. She offered me a wan smile as she passed us and vanished into the distance. Following on in their wake, Jess and I found ourselves at the edge of a completely flooded field, with no way around. I supposed Action Man and his limpet girlfriend had simply waded through. The thought of that poor girl, blindly following her man, no matter what … Wait, wasn't that what I expected of Jess?

No more. I spun around, called my long-suffering sidekick, and marched back to the sign pointing to East Prawle. According to the map, the village wasn't far, and from there I hoped to find a bus stop. We set off up the hill. Halfway up, Jess threw up her breakfast. Jess is never, ever sick. Appalled, I tried to encourage her, "Come on, Jess. We are so nearly there. Then you can have a sleep." When we at last got to East Prawle, the comforting smell of woodsmoke led me to a pub at the edge of a square. Thank goodness. I opened the solid old door and we stepped into the dark interior. A crackling fire – surrounded by antiquated armchairs pulled up to the hearth – took up one side of the low-ceilinged room. On the other side, a wooden bar offered the choice of just two beers on tap and a pot of pigs' noses for visiting dogs. I didn't plan to stay, so I kept my jacket on and enquired at the bar about buses. The barmaid shook her head.

"No buses come out here. We're in the sticks, you see."

"Oh. How about taxis?"

"Well, no. No one will come all the way out here. We are in the back of beyond, you know."

"So what can I do?"

"You'll have to walk to Beesands or Torcross and get a bus from there."

I looked at Jess, trembling in front of the fire. "Surely someone will come and get us?"

The barmaid served a customer, leaving me to stew over what to do. I shrugged off my wet rucksack and helped Jess out of her coat, laying it on the hearth. With no other choice, I'd give Jess time to warm up, try and get her coat dry, and then we would return to the Coast Path to walk the six miles to Torcross. The barmaid suddenly rushed over to me and said, "I've thought about it and there is a taxi driver who lives in the village and might be able to help."

Feeling buoyant for the first time all day, I rang the number she gave me and asked the taxi driver if he could pick us up and take us on to Slapton. He said he could, but not for an hour. "No problem," I said. I could think of far worse places to be than an eccentric old pub. Now we could relax. I peeled off my coat and lay it over a chair by the fire, then used the sock to dry Jess's legs and belly. I asked for a cup of tea and bought a pig's nose for Jess,

Pigs' Noses

then perched at the bar looking out at the pouring rain, feeling safe, warm and dry.

Exactly an hour later, a dark blue people carrier pulled up in front of the pub. The model looked familiar. The driver strode into the bar and, as he lifted his head, I immediately recognised him as our saviour from the day before. Enthusiastically, I shook his hand and explained to the baffled barmaid how we knew each other. They chatted while I retrieved our coats and coaxed Jess away from the warmth of the fire and out to the taxi.

"You're our knight in shining armour," I told the man once we were settled. "That's twice you've come to our rescue."

During the half-hour trip along narrow lanes, he regaled me with anecdotes about all the famous people he'd picked up over the years. According to him, the "back of beyond" teemed with celebrities. When I described the pub I'd be staying in that night, he knew it well and sang its praises, especially for its fabulous food.

In no time, we pulled into a snug car park and I hopped out, joking he would no doubt see us again tomorrow.

"Try not to get yourselves in any more trouble, you'll be leaving my patch soon," he said laughing, and drove away.

I introduced myself at the bar and explained that Jess and I were booked in for the night, but we'd arrived much earlier than intended. No problem. The barman asked if I wanted a drink and something to eat while waiting for my room to be ready. I glanced at the superb menu and ordered crab fishcakes.

After my late lunch, Jess and I tailed the barman to our room, up a flight of wooden stairs on the outside of the building. I fed Jess and tucked her into bed then arranged our damp clothes on and around the lone radiator to dry off overnight. With nothing else to do, and nowhere to go, I stretched out on the bed and fell asleep. Later, feeling groggy after my nap, I showered, dressed and returned to the bar for supper.

We found a prime spot in front of the fire, and I wrote up my diary then read the menu and ordered squid with capers. A foursome at a table nearby chatted to me while I waited for my food, then politely left me to eat in peace. The food tasted so good that any conversation would have been an unwelcome distraction.

As the bar filled up with other diners and drinkers, Jess and I climbed the wooden stairs to bed.

5 miles • 12,455 steps • Grading: Strenuous

DAY 38 – SLAPTON TO DARTMOUTH

The next morning, the view from my window did nothing to inspire me. A steady drizzle dripped from dark grey clouds. In contrast, the weatherman was predicting a dull-but-dry day, causing me to remain optimistic. I packed, and we went downstairs to the bar for breakfast. The foursome I'd met the night before sat at a table covered in the remnants of a substantial breakfast, drinking coffee. Their banter created a cheerful atmosphere, enhanced by the addition of a flickering candle on each table. Breakfast by candlelight: terribly romantic. I tucked in to homemade muesli, yoghurt and toast and – on the recommendation of the friendly foursome – ordered scrambled eggs and smoked salmon.

After my delicious breakfast, I returned to our room to pack. Overnight, our wet weather gear had dried, and I pulled on my still-warm coat before strapping Jess into hers. A quick check to see I'd packed everything, and we left. So much for the dull-but-dry day; in fact, the adolescent drizzle simply matured into grown-up rain. I put the brolly up, held it as well as I could over Jess, and set off along a road that would lead us to the coast and Slapton Sands.

Nearby, a memorial for six hundred and thirty-nine American soldiers and sailors looked out over the shingle beach. The men had died during a botched rehearsal for the Utah Beach D-Day landings, due to a combination of friendly fire and a devastating attack by German E-boats on the navy ships offshore.

The shingle bank offered no protection from the weather, and Jess and I caught the full brunt of the horizontal rain as it drove in from the sea. I positioned the brolly on the right of me, but the wind was pushing so hard that I struggled to stay upright.

At the end of the beach we climbed a stony path through a tunnel of trees. A torrent of rainwater cascaded down the middle, forcing us to one side. At the top, I caught my breath by the side of a busy main road. I got out my map to check I hadn't missed a turning, and at that moment, a vale of fog fell from the sky and blotted out everything. Visibility dropped to a few yards, keeping us dangerously hidden from the sight of passing drivers. As we started to walk, staying tight in to the verge, oncoming cars weaved around us, blaring their horns. Jess struggled against the lead, refusing to keep close.

I snapped. "Right, enough of this. No further." I wasn't going to bloody well risk my life or Jess's for a walk. The map showed we were on the outskirts of a village called Strete, which promised all the local amenities, including, I hoped, a bus stop. Taking our lives in our hands and paws, Jess and I faced the traffic and walked further into the village. I squinted through the fog at a familiar shape up ahead of us. Could it be? Yes! A bus stop. We waited patiently for whatever turned up to get us off the road.

Eventually, a bus loomed out of the fog, heading for Dartmouth. I paid my fare and sat in a damp fug, staring out of the filthy windows while Jess lay at my feet. Twenty minutes later, we clambered off the bus beside the quay at Dartmouth and immediately ran for shelter under the Butterwalk, an elaborately carved Tudor building. The overhanging upper floors rested on a row of granite columns, creating a covered walkway. I peered out at the pedestrians dashing through puddles and clustered in shop doorways, and tried to decide what to do next. Lunchtime was still hours away, and the B&B didn't expect us until much later. Wandering further along the pavement, I spotted the entrance to the Dartmouth Museum. The ideal solution. In the time it would take me to see all the exhibits, the rain would surely ease? The friendly staff welcomed Jess and me, and a steward personally showed us around the main exhibits then left me to poke in drawers for treasures and squint through microscopes. By the time I was ready to go, my brain bursting with historical facts and figures, the pavements were drying and the clouds had moved on.

The day stretched before us, begging to be filled, so I came up with a plan. We would walk back on ourselves, towards Strete, for as far as time allowed. Obviously, at some point we'd need to turn back, but I felt confident we could rack up a few miles. We set off through the town, walking parallel to the River Dart. Turning off for Castle Road, we soon passed St Petrox Church and Dartmouth Castle. A red fishing boat steamed towards the mouth of the estuary and passed beneath Kingswear Castle on the opposite headland. Around the wonderfully named Sugary Cove, the path grew slippery with mud. I untied my sticks and used them to help me stay on my feet.

We trekked up and down a convoluted path and into a wood. Under the canopy, the ground was dry and leaves crackled as we scrunched through them. A fallen tree blocked the way; feeling adventurous, I took a run up and with a jump flung myself at it. Draped over the trunk, like a bed roll on the back of a horse,

I inched one leg across the top, then the other, until I lay along the back, embracing the tree. Now all I had to do was swivel around on my belly and slide down the other side. Ta-dah. Jess leapt up and launched herself off the top in one fluid movement. Thoroughly chuffed with ourselves, we both marched on with a swagger.

A little further on, we climbed down onto a plateau of limpet-coated rocks, the sea frothing at our feet. A wooden bridge over a ravine in the rocks led to fields above the sea. In a gateway on the other side of the field I recognised a familiar figure coming towards us: the Action Man from the day before. And, behind him, the same dishevelled sidekick. Once again, he paid no attention to me as he stomped past. I offered a "hello" to the tenacious girl, and received a weary "good afternoon" in return.

They raced off towards Dartmouth, reminding me that Jess and I needed to turn back at some point. I unfolded my map and checked our progress. We were near Stoke Fleming, and from there the Coast Path went inland then merged with a road through the village and on to Blackpool Sands. Bugger that. I'd experienced more than enough road walking, thank you very much. "Let's go," I declared to my muddy companion, and we returned to Dartmouth.

When we got to the town, bright lights from the shop windows reflected off the pavements as heavy rain began to fall. I sought out a dog-friendly pub so Jess and I could dry off and I could have an early supper before checking in to our B&B. Not far from the Butterwalk, I perused the menu of the Royal Castle Hotel, checking whether they served food all day. The intimidatingly grand façade hid a comfortable, dog-friendly bar. I ordered a ham sandwich, chips and a pint of local beer, and fell into a squidgy leather sofa, with Jess at my feet. Munching on my chips, I couldn't help thinking my SWCP challenge had somehow turned into a pub holiday. I felt a twinge of guilt, then reminded myself my sole purpose for doing this walk had always been to soak up enough inspiration to kick start my ideas when I started painting again. Unlike my fellow long-distance walkers, for whom every mile had to be completed, I had a different agenda. Three days of scoffing pub grub, afternoon siestas and taxi rides did not make me a failure.

As the light faded, Jess and I left the bar and huddled under my brolly in search of our B&B. When we found it, the building looked promising: a smart, black and white townhouse with an imposing front door. Perfect, I thought, and prepared myself for a treat. An elderly woman wearing a purple cardigan, slacks and slippers, answered the door. She ushered us in, introduced us to our ground floor room and scuttled away.

I hovered, open-mouthed, in the doorway. A single bed jutted out into the room, near a white melamine cabinet and a TV. From there, the furnishings deviated from what I'd come to expect when renting a place to stay for the night. I wondered at the assortment of domestic appliances arranged throughout the space: a stand up freezer with a scrap of tea towel hanging over the top, a smaller fridge (again with a tea towel on it, plus tea and coffee making facilities), a second fridge (no tea towel) and, finally, a dehumidifier. And all of them whirring, buzzing and clicking as if possessed.

"I think I may need earplugs tonight, Jess." She jumped a foot in the air as the dehumidifier shook into life behind her. "I'll put your bed over here," I reassured her, finding space away from the rowdiest of the appliances. Feeling a chill, I ran my hands over the radiator – stone cold. I hung our coats over it anyhow, praying it might turn on later. The longer I spent in the strange room, the colder I became. Poor Jess curled into the tightest ball she could, but I still detected a shiver. I put a blanket over her and added a towel from the ensuite. Now, my turn. I pulled on three pairs of socks, a jumper and pyjama bottoms, filled my hot water bottle, lifted the tissue-thin synthetic duvet, and slid into the bed.

As I feared, the night dragged out, long and full of surprises. In twenty-minute intervals, the fridge nearest to me clicked and whirred into life. Despite wearing earplugs, I jumped out of my skin. Every. Single. Time. The cold reached into my bones and didn't let go.

9 miles • 24,635 steps • Grading: Moderate

I opened my eyes at dawn and got out of bed, thinking if I moved around I might thaw out. Jess opted for a different strategy; she kept as still as possible and refused to leave her bed. I packed our belongings and turned on the TV for the morning weather: a wet start getting worse as the day progressed. Mmmm, time to make another plan.

While defrosting in the blessedly warm dining room, I decided to take another day off; a decision based on my aversion to being cold, wet and miserable, and on the guilt I felt at making Jess cold, wet and miserable. So, what to do in Dartmouth on a gloomy day in October? I picked up a handful of pamphlets on a side table and read them while drinking my second cup of coffee. Most of the tourist attractions advertised trips; boat trips, ferry trips, train and boat trips, ferry and train trips, and so on. To book a ticket, I merely needed to wander down to the harbour and ask a person in one of the many tubular booths.

Returning to our room, I peeled our still-damp wet weather gear off the radiator. Bugger. We couldn't go out without protection. Reluctantly, I pulled my waterproof trousers over my jeans, zipped up my jacket, and strapped Jess into her coat, feeling a shudder run through her body as I tightened the straps. Next, I shouldered my wet rucksack, wincing as the cold material pushed against my back, and we walked out into the rain. At the harbourside, I strode purposefully up to the first in a line of ticket booths and, on tiptoe, peeped through the window. "What," I asked the man inside, "can a person and their dog do on a rainy day in Dartmouth?"

The man proceeded to tell me, in impressive detail, exactly what Jess and I could do on such a day. Faced with a plethora of choices, I simplified my request. "What can we do right now, from this spot?" The answer? Hop on the next ferry across the river to Kingswear, wait a while for the steam train, hop on the steam train, visit Greenway – Agatha Christie's old holiday home – walk back to Kingswear along the riverside via an oak forest, catch a bus to Brixham and go to the pub for a glass of wine. The bus ride and glass of wine were not included in the ticket, but everything else was. I responded with an enthusiastic "yes!"

Our mini adventure kicked off with a trip on the oversized ferry to Kingswear. The train station sat on the water's edge but wasn't yet open. I found a bench under the eaves of the station roof and gawped as water cascaded down the road in front of us and bubbled up from the drains. A woman, dressed for the office and wearing very high heels, tried to cross over to our side and got caught. The water swirled around her ankles. She squealed and dashed for the train station, where she mingled with the growing crowd of people sheltering from the horrendous weather.

When the station opened, Jess and I pottered up and down the platform and waited for the steam train. I couldn't help feeling excited; I hadn't travelled on a steam train for years and the encounter would be a first for Jess. She stood to attention, ears pricked, as the lumbering engine coasted into the station, filling the air with steam and noise. We walked past the hissing boiler, the cab and the coal-piled tender, and climbed into a brown-and-cream-painted carriage. Jess sat on my knee, quaking, but settled down when we slowly pulled out of the station, calmed by the motion of the train. I sat forward in my seat to take in the view. The tracks ran right alongside the banks of the River Dart, and at times it felt like the train was flying through the water – an exhilarating ride. All too soon, the sound of escaping steam and screeching brakes signalled we'd arrived at Greenway Halt, a platform in the middle of nowhere, enclosed by trees. From there, a brisk walk through woods ended at the entrance to a driveway that swept up to a National Trust reception. I flashed my membership card and the attendant waved me through.

The cream Georgian mansion, complete with portico and symmetrical wings, stood in an extensive woodland garden. Sadly, dogs weren't allowed in the house, but I made do by pressing my face up to the windows to ogle the downstairs rooms. The gardens stretched all the way down to the river and included a walled vegetable plot, exotic palms, camellias and rhododendrons. In no hurry, and with the rain easing, Jess and I took our time, following the meandering paths until we came to a boathouse tucked into the river bank.

The two-storey brick building faced across the river to Dittisham on the opposite bank. The first floor felt light and airy, with thick weathered floorboards, a simple tiled fireplace and original pieces of furniture. I couldn't help thinking what a brilliant studio the room would make: light poured in through the large windows even on this dull day and, being secreted away at the bottom of the garden, there was a real sense of privacy. A veranda ran the length of the top floor, accessed by a wide arched door, which stood ajar. I wandered out, sucked in a lungful of salty air and took in the views up and down the river. Under the top floor lay

another room, dark and windowless. The attendant explained
a hole in the floor functioned as an indoor saltwater tidal pool.
I poked my head in and admitted to the woman that it looked
extremely uninviting. I could almost see how it might be a good
way to cool down on a hot summer afternoon, but it took a good
stretch of the imagination.

Agatha Christie's Boathouse

We left the boathouse and retraced our steps through the
gardens and down the driveway to the start of the six-mile walk
to Kingswear.

The path took us through farmland, with open views of the River
Dart snaking through lush countryside. Following signs for the
Dart Valley Trail, we slogged through Long Wood, a lovely walk
ruined by having to wade through thick, claggy mud. The bloody
stuff stuck to everything – my boots, trousers, socks, even Jess
– and made each step exhausting. Using a stick, I scraped the
sticky mixture of mud, leaves, twigs and gravel off my boots, and
immediately felt a difference in the weight.

The rain started falling again as we neared Kingswear. I tugged
up my hood and stomped along a grass verge that ran between
the river and the train tracks, behind a boatyard and into the
town. Twenty minutes later, Jess and I were bumping along on a
bus, headed for Brixham and the second half of our day off.

First stop, the harbour to check out the Golden Hind. The full-
sized replica of Sir Francis Drake's ship has been part of the fabric
of the town for over fifty years. Standing up close, I found it hard
to believe seventy men endured three years at sea in such a
confined space. The deck of the original measured a paltry thirty-

one metres. I expect by the end of the first month at sea, the crew scrambled to volunteer for lookout duty; the crow's nest, high above the deck, would have been the one blessed place on the ship to get some peace. I sat on the harbour wall and attempted to sketch the pocket pirate ship, but soon gave up. The rigging proved far too fiddly. As a fine drizzle began to fall, I stashed my sketchbook away and continued around the harbour to our B&B. I wanted to get into some clean, mud-free clothes, feed Jess and then pop out again for something to eat.

The B&B stood in the middle of a terrace of houses that looked down on the harbour. Jess and I were welcomed in by the owner, who introduced herself as Kathy and asked if I would join her for a cup of tea. Over Jammy Dodgers and a pot of Earl Grey, I admitted I'd cancelled my ten-mile walk from Dartmouth and now wondered if I'd made the right decision. She showed me two pairs of filthy walking boots in the hallway. "Those belong to a couple who turned up just before you. They'd walked from Dartmouth. He looked ready to collapse, and she seemed on the verge of tears." She winked at me over her cup. "I think you made the right choice."

Kathy showed us to our room and returned to the kitchen to make a pot of sweet tea for the traumatised walkers. I double checked for fridges and clicking dehumidifiers, and ran my hands over the two radiators – they worked. At last, I could dry our clothes. I immediately smothered the radiators with our wet weather gear, and balanced my boots, upside down, on top.

The ensuite shower room was fitted with a towel rail – the Holy Grail for someone with a limited amount of socks and pants. I spent the next hour washing my smalls and scrubbing my socks, astounded by the amount of mud coming out of the wool. Then I hung them from the towel rail to dry overnight.

With my chores completed, Jess and I popped into the pub two doors down for an early supper, looking forward to spending the night in a warm, silent room.

7.8 miles • 19,499 steps • Grading: Strenuous

DAY 40 – BRIXHAM TO BABBACOMBE

After a great night's sleep, I took Jess out for a wee before breakfast. We wandered down to the harbour, past the marina and out to the Brixham Breakwater. For the first time in days, I felt the sun on my shoulders. I returned to the B&B in good spirits, eager to crack on after days of inactivity. After breakfast, I thanked Kathy for the warm welcome and toasty room, and Jess and I set off for Babbacombe.

Returning to the harbour, we passed the Golden Hind and continued through a car park to the coast. Leaving the town behind, we walked through Battery Gardens, which led to a wood and a tiny beach. I swung my arms and inhaled lungfuls of air, thrilled to be unencumbered by my Gore-Tex jacket and trousers, which, although great at keeping off the worst of the rain, rustled infuriatingly when I moved. Jess obviously felt the same without her coat and bounded up and down the shoreline when we got to Churston Cove. While she let off steam, I trained my binoculars on the lighthouse at the end of the Brixham Breakwater, visible in the distance. Half a dozen fishermen stood with their rods out, waiting patiently for the sudden bend in the tip and the shout of "Fish on!" I added the breakwater to the ever growing list of "places I must come back to and fish" optimistically recorded in my notebook.

From the cove, Jess and I climbed steps into a wood running parallel with Churston golf course. In the dim interior, a profusion of sounds bounced around the trees, like golf balls from an over-zealous player: squirrels flung themselves around the canopy, dogs barked, chainsaws whined and lawnmowers spluttered. We added to the symphony of sounds, boots and paws rustling through leaves stacked high on the path.

Sometime later we emerged, blinking in the sunlight, and crunched along the shingle at Elberry Cove. I watched Jess, nose to the ground, her tail swishing, ears alert, a different dog from the one throwing up at the side of a rain-soaked road just days before. At the end of the beach, we mooched across a common and into a car park behind Broadsands Beach. Dogs weren't allowed on the sand, so we continued along the promenade in front of multicoloured beach huts. On the other side of the bay, Torquay dominated the coastline, a rash of concrete, metal and stone.

Before we experienced the delights of the jewel in the English Riviera's crown, we enjoyed a stroll along Paignton's seafront.

My brain took a moment to adjust to the abrupt change in the colour of the sand. From the creamy white shore at Elberry Cove, the grains turned a rusty red, as if they'd been rolled in food colouring. We headed for the pier, which jutted seven hundred and eighty feet into the sea. Brightly coloured attractions studded the walkway, including an outdoor slide and amusement arcade. The spindly legs holding the pier up looked to me as structurally sound as kebab sticks. However, my guide book assured me that the delicate metalwork had withstood over a hundred and fifty years of battering from the wind and waves – and what did I know about engineering anyway?

From Paignton, the Coast Path ran beside a busy main road. The once-familiar noise of traffic now sounded amplified, causing my heart to race. Jess didn't fare any better, the carefree dog – earlier dashing along the shore at Elberry Cove – was replaced by a pitiful creature slinking beside me. When I came across an opportunity to abandon the road, I gratefully detoured along the shingle shore at Corbyn Beach. After one last push, Jess and I arrived in the popular (with foreign tourists at least) seaside resort of Torquay – the birthplace of Agatha Christie.

I commandeered a bench near the marina, rooted around in my rucksack for a packet of oatcakes, and settled back to watch the world go by. After only ten minutes, I craved the calm solitude of the headlands and coves. We relinquished our claim on the bench and scarpered.

Freeing ourselves from the urban sprawl took more time than I'd hoped, but two unexpected sights, together with the views on the way, made it worthwhile. Just beyond the last of the hideous hotels on the waterfront, I came across a limestone rock arch, bewilderingly named London Bridge. Then, nearby, at Thatcher Point, I slowed down to study the Thatcher Stone: a limestone island with an uncanny resemblance to St Michael's Mount near Penzance. Pine trees writhed and twisted as if in agony, their dark silhouettes a dramatic sight juxtaposed against the bright sky. From Hope's Nose, which sticks out into Lyme Bay, I could see all the way back to Berry Head and Brixham, and ahead to Exmouth.

After the sedate start to the day, along promenades and beaches, the terrain changed. The Coast Path rose and fell with plenty of laborious sections, but nothing I couldn't handle. In fact, as I marched, sticks pumping, I realised I was mirroring the techniques of my old friend, Wind-Up Woman. Like her, I now

Pine Trees Writhed and Twisted

took delight in overtaking other people (a first) and I raced up hills and down dales like a demented robot. Bolstered by this epiphany, and as if to confirm my metamorphosis, I broke wind. Blimey.

Trumping sporadically, I carried on along Bishop's Walk, created by the Bishop of Exeter as "a place of quiet repose and for the good of the constitution". Certainly, my constitution had never been better. From Anstey's Cove we crossed a common etched with numerous tracks, then wandered through a wood, emerging behind the houses at Babbacombe Beach. A stone pier poked into the bay, and I watched a fisherman cast and retrieve a string of sparkling feathers, on the hunt for mackerel. One more fishing spot to add to my list.

A metal walkway between outcrops of rock linked up to a rough path around the base of the cliffs. As I set off, I saw a disturbance in the water offshore. Suddenly, hundreds of sand eels flew out of the water in a wave of spray and scales. Something must have spooked them: either a bass or a seal. The shoal moved out to sea, obviously being chased, making the surface of the water boil. In the aftermath, a lone cormorant popped up in the middle of the bay with an unfortunate fish in its bill. I glanced at the fisherman on the pier, still methodically casting and reeling in, oblivious to the drama playing out behind him.

We left the path for the red sand of Oddicombe Beach on the other side of the bay. An immense landslide dominated the far end of the beach. The remnants of the cliff smothered the sands, completely cutting off access to the headland. I could only assume there would be some sort of detour at the start of the next day's walk. For now, I grappled with a different kind of obstacle: Babbacombe is situated at the top of a precipitous cliff. In order to reach the delights in the heavens above, you can either stumble up an interminable path, zigzagging this way and that for hours, or, for a fee, you could step onto the Babbacombe Cliff Railway and wet your pants while being hauled up a vertical track with nothing to stop you plummeting to certain death but a bit of clever engineering. I debated the situation for a moment, then my extreme laziness outdid my fear and I plumped for the funicular.

Jess took it all in her stride and waltzed on board with barely a thought. I followed – gingerly – and settled myself in a seat, looking up at the sheer cliff. The journey went without a hitch until, two feet from the top, the carriage slowed to a crawl. We hung in mid-air as the contraption ever so gradually inched to the docking position. I wanted to scream, but being surrounded by other passengers I chewed my sleeve instead. Just as I thought, "This is it, we're going to run out of steam and fall to our deaths," a loud click signalled the end of the ride. I left in haste as the child beside me jumped up and down with excitement, asking her parents if they could do it again. My god.

We walked out of the ticket office and along Babbacombe Downs, a common with trees and benches placed here and there. The view across Babbacombe Bay took my breath away: mile after mile of deep blue sea stretched out in front of us. I felt as if I were standing on top of the world.

Our hotel boasted sea views with every room. A bubbly, blonde woman took us up to our room and proudly showed off the balcony. When she left, I swung open the door onto our own little deck, with a table, a chair, and a view to kill for. A fresh blast of sea air filled the room as I unpacked, fed Jess, and made a cup of tea to take back out. What a view. I only wished there were more hours of daylight left to sit and take it all in. When the sun dipped beneath the horizon, I reluctantly came inside, closed the door and pulled the curtains. Time for supper.

The hotel had a restaurant, but dogs were not allowed. Instead, a waitress set Jess and me up at a table in the bar. I ordered a glass of wine and opted for local plaice with a shrimp sauce. When the fish arrived, I gasped; the hubcap-sized Leviathan barely fit on the plate. My first forkful was disappointingly bland – the shrimp sauce merely shrimps and cream, no seasoning, no splash of lemon – but the fish tasted fresh enough to convince me it had been skimming over the sand in the bay only hours before.

After supper, I sidled up to the bar to order another glass of wine and began chatting to the amiable owner. Suddenly, the door to the bar burst open and a dishevelled woman staggered in and asked for a large glass of wine. In a staccato voice, she said she and her brother needed to find somewhere to stay. The hotel owner apologised, explaining that they were fully booked, but said she could recommend a place a few doors down. The woman took two gulps of wine, shook her head and asked if they could at least eat in the restaurant. Again the owner said sorry but the restaurant only catered for residents. The poor woman slumped her shoulders and got ready to leave, then changed her mind and ordered another glass of wine. I did the same, feeling too invested in this drama to walk out at the interval. She stayed for an hour, drinking, yet nothing further was said about her brother. I imagined him sitting on a bench somewhere nearby, next to a brown suitcase, waiting.

When she did finally leave, I felt frazzled. Her frenetic energy still crackled around the bar and the three glasses of wine I'd imbibed no doubt added to my muddled state of mind. I took Jess out for a pre-sleep wee, and texted Jack: *Hey Jack, I miss you, I had a terrifying ride on a funicular train today, I don't think I'm cut out for all this adventuring. Sash* ⌄

14.9 miles • 37,182 steps • Grading: Moderate/Strenuous

I awoke with a fuzzy head and made a cup of tea, adding two spoonfuls of sugar. As I stirred, I listened to the weather forecast on the radio: wall-to-wall sun. Perfect. Tea on my balcony in that case. I swept back the curtains, and … black clouds were jostling for space on the horizon. The sea, a deep blue the day before, now looked the colour of slate. Rain pinged off my table and chairs and pooled on the balcony. Tea in bed, then.

Later, Jess and I went downstairs and I made myself comfortable at the same table as the night before. I ordered a full English breakfast, and by the time I'd finished the last mouthful of mushrooms I was starting to feel human again. I propped the guide book open and read up on the day's walk while drinking a cup of strong coffee. The stretch from Babbacombe to Exmouth comprised two parts: the first half looked strenuous, but the afternoon's section would appear to be nothing more than a leisurely stroll through the seaside resorts of Teignmouth and Dawlish.

Time to get going. Outside, the last of the rain clouds dissolved on the horizon, to be replaced by the promised wall-to-wall sunshine. We walked beside the Downs, past the terminal for the funicular and into a residential area, searching for the Coast Path sign. Finding no clues as to where it might be, I asked in a shop. The shopkeeper came with me to the door and directed us up the street. Soon, we left the rows of houses with their perfect squares of lawn and shiny SUVs parked in the drive and headed for the cliffs.

We skirted around the edge of a golf course and stepped into the musty interior of a wood. Before going too far into the trees, I pulled on my jumper and unstrapped my walking sticks. Jess stayed at my side, unusually reluctant to run ahead. I knew we were close to civilisation, but the woods felt remote, somehow cut off from the nearby town.

The path plunged up and down, around tree roots and rotting trunks, until we came to the edge of a large basin scooped out of the earth and I slid down the side, scraping a track through leaves. At the bottom, a scruffy dog in a knitted jumper ran into the clearing, followed by a runner; the first signs of life I'd seen since entering the woods. They didn't stop, but we called out a greeting to each other before going our separate ways.

At last, we left the woods for open fields with views over Babbacombe Bay. There was no let up from the relentless climbs, and I slowed as we tackled a hill with a gradient that left my legs shaking from the exertion. So much for my transformation into Wind-Up Woman; I had a way to go yet until I filled those walking boots.

Jess made up for my shortcomings by catching (and releasing) her first ever rabbit. One minute she had her head in a bush, snuffling at something, and the next she turned to me with a young rabbit in her mouth. I yelled at her to drop it and, shocked by my authoritative voice, she let it fall to her feet. I crouched down to inspect it, thankful that apart from looking a bit soggy the youngster seemed fine. Jess dipped her head to sniff the rabbit and it sprung up and bolted down a nearby hole. I saw a worrying glint of the wild in Jess's eyes. She shook herself off and trotted on, tail held higher than usual. I would have to keep a close eye on her now she knew the thrill of catching a living, breathing animal.

Above Smugglers Cove, the view in front of us opened out to reveal the Shaldon Approach golf course and beyond that, the Ness headland – a bulbous red cliff topped with trees. As we strode down a sloping field peppered with trees, more of the coastline came into view: the stretch of Teignmouth Beach, the Grand Pier and, in the distance, the red cliffs and sea stack of the Parson and the Clerk. We walked around the stubby nose of the Ness and crunched over a shingle beach to catch the ferry across the River Teign. The ferry was waiting at the pontoon. I paid our fare and Jess and I joined the other people sitting on the slatted benches. No sooner had we pulled out into the river than we were stepping off on the other side.

We walked past the lifeboat station, cut across a thin peninsula and picked up the Coast Path on the other side. There were two possible routes, dependent on the tides. At high tide, a section of the route that dipped under the railway tracks at the end of the beach flooded. The only option, in that case, was to take a detour inland. I double checked my tide book: by happy chance the tide was on the way out, meaning Jess and I could walk all the way along the prom.

The London-Penzance railway line runs parallel with the sea wall, and its trains were cruising up and down, just yards from where we walked. I knew this stretch of coast well, but had only experienced it from the comfort of a carriage – en route to visit my sisters in the capital – never on foot.

Just before the entrance to Parson's Tunnel, which burrows through a short headland, a flight of steps took us beneath the railway line. On the other side, the path turned ninety degrees inland, away from the coast, then a wide semicircle around the headland, circumventing a knot of houses, brought us back to the sea, near the railway line. At Dawlish, the Coast Path and the train tracks ran side-by-side once more, and we walked along the top of the sea wall, sandwiched between the sea and the trains: an exhilarating experience. I kept Jess on her lead, wary that she might want to chase the speeding tubes of metal and glass, especially after her success with the rabbit.

At the end of the sea wall, Langstone Rock created a barrier across the beach. The lump of red rock had been attached to the land, until separated by the railway cutting. At the base, three caves and a tall archway were carved into – and through – the stone. We walked through the arch and were faced with another rock sitting behind it. Back on the Coast Path, Jess ran ahead and began begging at a table outside the unimaginatively named Red Rock Café. I apologised to a poor woman trying to enjoy her burger and hauled Jess away.

We crossed a car park and began a tedious two-mile tramp to the ferry terminal at Starcross, along pavements bordering acres of caravan parks and holiday homes. The soles of my feet stung, and my ankles ached with the constant slap of boots on tarmac. When we came to the pretty village of Cockwood, on the banks of the River Exe, I stopped to inspect Jess's paws. Walking on pavements and roads did far more damage than the varied terrain of the cliffs. Fortunately, her thick pads held up well, unlike the delicate soles of my feet. I took a couple of painkillers and limped on.

Finally, we reached Starcross and shuffled down a pontoon to the dapper blue-and-white ferry, with minutes to spare. I took us down into the belly of the boat and gratefully relaxed on a bench, my feet throbbing. As the engine spluttered into life and we pulled away from the mooring, I chatted to a couple returning from a walk and lunch at The Anchor pub in Cockwood. They loved walking, and when I said Jess and I were going to walk the stretch from Exmouth to Sidmouth, they enthusiastically described it as one of their favourites. After disembarking, they waved us off with a cheery, "Enjoy your walk tomorrow!"

A townhouse on the street set back from the beach provided our home for the night, and the owner showed us to a downstairs room with two single beds. I fed Jess, unpacked our belongings and, after a shower, went out to look for a likely pub for supper, finding one that served food all day just around the corner. The two young bar girls immediately made us feel at home, giving us a table next to the roaring fire and gesturing for Jess to curl up in front of it. I ordered a pulled pork sandwich and a glass of wine, and turned my chair towards the fireplace, stretching out my legs to catch the heat.

"Your dog is gorgeous. What is she?" I swivelled around to see a table of four sitting nearby. This was a standard opener; Jess received a lot of attention. My standard reply – "She's a Rhodesian ridgeback, bred to hunt lions" – never failed to get a response. There was something about her chilled-out demeanour, contrasted with the hair-raising origins of the breed, that tickled people.

My food arrived and I tucked in, ravenous after a day's walking. Unwilling, for the time being, to leave our prime spot at the fireside, I ordered a sticky toffee pudding and a coffee and settled down to write up my notes. Later, I relinquished our table to the next round of diners and drinkers, and the lion hunter and I wandered back to the B&B.

As I got ready for bed, I started to feel peculiar. My stomach lurched and I was shivering. I crawled into bed and lay very still, willing the nausea to subside. After a while, I dropped off, but throughout the night I woke many times in a sweat.

14.9 miles • 37,161 steps • Grading: Strenuous/Easy.

The next morning I felt much better. Jess and I went into the breakfast room and I decided on scrambled eggs: something gentle to soothe my stomach. The B&B owner took my order and, on the way out of the room, she switched on a TV tuned into Formula One racing. She fiddled with the volume and turned it up so high the windows shook. The cars screamed around the track like mutant hornets on steroids. With each lap, my blood pressure went up a gear. When she returned with my scrambled eggs, I shouted over the ruckus, "Could you turn the TV down, please?" Frowning, she adjusted the volume. "You're not a fan of racing then?" I wanted to say, "No, I'm not a fan of bloody racing at eight o'clock in the morning after a night spent on the edge of throwing up, thank you." Instead, I asked if I could "please watch the weather forecast, thank you very much."

Later, ears still ringing, I packed up our belongings and stepped outside into the blessed calm and quiet of an Exmouth morning. A smoky mist hung like a gossamer curtain over the sea. Rhythmic waves broke on the shore. I let Jess off her lead on the beach, where she ran amok. The other, smaller dogs scattered as she dashed in circles around them, play-bowing and swatting them with her paws. In no time Jess created a wide exclusion zone where no hound would dare set foot. In our bubble, we passed a lifeboat station and kept to the beach all the way to Orcombe Point. The headland cut across the foreshore and we abandoned the sand for a switchback path leading onto the cliffs.

A plaque at the foot of the cliff marked the start of the Jurassic Coast – and the beginning of the end of our great adventure. From here to Old Harry Rocks, ninety-six miles away, the cliffs would record one hundred and eighty-five million years of the world's history, and at the end of those ninety-six miles, Jess and I would have completed a piece of our own history and made it all the way home. A lingering look over Exmouth and the headlands beyond brought a vision of the coast peeking out from a curtain of mist for mile after mile: a magical sight. I did a sketch, accompanied by a soundtrack of church bells and birdsong.

We walked out to the end of Orcombe Point to inspect an obelisk. The correct term for the sharp monument (I read in my guide book) was the Geoneedle. Constructed from different layers of stone from the Jurassic Coast, the design was simple but it was beautifully made. The birds and bells continued to fill the air as I floated along in a reverie, breathing in the cold, crisp morning air. Low, red cliffs topped with green fields stretched in front us, inducing in me an *Anne of Green Gables* moment. I pictured myself, arms outstretched, running through the grass towards the handsome Gilbert Blythe, but was rudely jarred back into reality by the unexpected appearance of hundreds and hundreds of caravans and chalets hidden in a valley. There was no room for holiday parks in my romantic vision, so I pulled myself out of the daydream and picked my way in and around the identical boxes.

On the far side of the caravan park, the Coast Path shunned Straight Point, where the Royal Marines learn how to shoot, and continued past yet more caravans. As we neared Budleigh Salterton, groups of people out for a Sunday pre-lunch stroll began to appear on the path. The sound of boots crunching on the smooth pebbles that carpeted the ground preceded a variation of the same exchange: "Lovely morning," or, "What a beautiful day!" or, "What kind of dog is she?" Everyone we met was in high spirits, something about the weather and the beautiful surroundings.

I knew nothing about Budleigh Salterton and had no expectations. I certainly hadn't envisaged the delightful rows of brightly coloured beach huts, the smooth-pebbled beach, or the fishing fleet pulled up on the shore. I dug out my sketchbook and pencils, bursting with inspiration; everywhere I turned, I saw a potential painting. After I'd sketched for an hour or more, Jess grew bored, so we strolled over to watch the fishermen sorting out their catch of brown crabs. While I scribbled away, Jess stuck her nose in crab pots and hoovered up bits of goodness-knows-what from the ground around the boats. I took a few photos of crabs in big blue bins and noticed Jess had her foot on an escapee. I hissed at her, "Jess, come here NOW." But she remained on the spot, seemingly unaware there was a crab under her paw. A fisherman turned to see what the fuss was about. "My dog has trodden on one of your crabs," I confessed. He frowned. "You'll have to pay if he squashes it." I dragged Jess towards me, allowing the fisherman to scoop up the crab and pop it in the tub. The crustacean gave the impression of being okay, but it's difficult to tell with crabs; they are not ones for showing their emotions.

The pebbles on the beach were hard to walk on, so we transferred onto the prom, mingling with more Sunday morning strollers. Near the end of the beach a couple of cafés were doing a brisk business, with customers sitting out in the open, drinking tea and coffee. I wanted to join them, but – under the influence of the walkers' rules handed down to me all those weeks ago – I carried on, mindful of the possibility of a dramatic weather event.

At the end of the beach, we took a detour inland to ford the River Otter. The estuary of mud flats and salt marshes provides a haven for all sorts of wildfowl, including redshank, dunlin, snipe and shelduck. Not surprisingly, we passed plenty of twitchers on the river bank, eyes glued to the cameras on their tripods. A bridge spanned the estuary, and we crossed over and turned back to the coast, beneath a row of pine trees.

The afternoon drifted on. We walked through a string of fields above the sea. The coastline was unlike anything I'd ever experienced. The intense red of the cliffs made the green fields pulsate. Both colours, equally bright, fought against each other. At times I could see down to the shore, where the red cliffs leached into the sea like dye. Would the whole coast eventually dissolve away, given time?

The stunning views were interrupted by yet another holiday park at Ladram Bay. Rising into the clouds above the rows of chalets was our next landmark – High Peak. I ogled the summit in horror. This challenge would require careful planning. The most important thing was to conserve my energy for the climb ahead – I took off my rucksack and slumped onto the grass. Next, I required fuel – I ferreted around in my rucksack for a bag of mixed nuts and raisins. I calculated half a packet of nuts and three swigs of an isotonic drink would get me to the top. As I made my preparations, a fellow with a brown dog turned up and, apparently sensing my steely resolve, asked if Jess and I were about to climb High Peak. "It's not as bad as it looks," he said. "The Coast Path doesn't go all the way up to the top." Hurrah, I thought, but then he went on: "But you really must keep going; the views on the summit are too good to miss."

"Great," I muttered. He sauntered off, shouting, "Good luck!"

Once he'd vanished into the maze of chalets, I heaved myself up from the grass, shouldered my rucksack and squared up to the mountain. "Right, Jess, here we go." On the other side of the holiday park, we set off through fields, the gradient becoming progressively steeper with each step. As the path disappeared into woods, we scrambled up rugged steps that wound through the trees, up and up. Near the top, just as the man had said, the

Walking Into Sidmouth, With Salcombe Hill Ahead

Coast Path shied away from the summit, which had been cleared of trees and resembled a monk's tonsure. The dilemma: Do I take the easy option, ignore the summit and continue on my merry way? Or, do I embrace Wind-Up Woman's ethos and jump at the chance of a detour? Reader, I gave in to peer pressure and pressed on to the summit.

Blimey. The views were amazing – three hundred and sixty-five degrees, stretching for miles inland and far along both coasts.

Breathtaking. Buzzing with endorphins, and feeling terribly proud of myself, I skipped down the other side and headed for Sidmouth.

A hill led us down into the town and to the beach, which was full of people enjoying the afternoon sun, with a handful of kids braving the water.

Our hotel was set back from the promenade, and had an old-fashioned air that appealed to me. We were shown to our room, which had a door that opened out into a little garden. The room – well, cupboard – had so little space that once I'd unpacked Jess's bed and stored our suitcases under the hand basin, there was no carpet visible. I fed Jess in the garden.

Feeling claustrophobic, I decided to look around the town and find somewhere for an early supper. We walked along the esplanade and were spoilt for choice with hotels and cafés and plenty of pubs. I chose a gastropub and ordered a chicken burger and chips, and a beer to drink while waiting. The bun arrived on a wooden board with a scrap of rocket in one corner and a mound of hand-cut chips in the other. Ravenous after my exhausting detour, I devoured everything, even the rocket garnish, finished the beer and set off to find a shop selling the Sunday newspapers.

Four hours later, my eyes were sore with the effort of reading and my brain felt full to bursting with world news, fashion tips, expensive cars and meals for under a fiver. I let Jess out into the private garden, tucked her in for the night, rang Jack for an update, then fell asleep.

14.6 miles • 36,213 steps • Grading: Moderate/Strenuous

The next morning we rose early, and after extricating ourselves from our room we headed for the beach to stretch our legs before breakfast. Dogs were not allowed in the dining room, so the hotel staff set us up under the main staircase. We received plenty of puzzled looks as our fellow residents came down for breakfast, but I liked the spot; away from everyone else, I could read my guide book in peace. The words *severe* followed by *strenuous* jumped off the page. With a chuckle, I thought back to the start of the walk, when reading those words would have made me faint with terror. Not now. I actually looked forward to the challenge.

I finished my full English breakfast, packed up our belongings, and we set off. Jess was less than enthusiastic. She moped behind me as I strode along the deserted esplanade. We crossed a little bridge and took a detour through a housing estate to bypass a landslip. Ahead, Salcombe Hill dared me to try my luck. I sauntered towards the base, in no hurry. With a massive breakfast in my belly, the only option was to take my time, or else risk throwing up. I walked as if in slow motion, stopping now and then to chivy Jess, straightening my legs and locking my knees until we reached the top.

After taking in the view, which stretched all the way back to Budleigh Salterton, I pressed on. The guide book's warning of a *severe* first half of the walk proved to be a perfect description: a continuous rollercoaster of steep, wooded valleys. To help with my motivation, I played Kate Bush's *Running Up That Hill* on a loop on my MP3 player. The music lifted my spirits, and although I didn't mirror her lyrics to the letter, her melodious voice helped me focus.

Staggering down a flight of steps we came to the foot of a valley and Weston Mouth beach. Across a stream, tucked into the base of the cliffs, an old coastguard building and a white rowing boat caught my eye. I sketched, while getting my breath back in preparation for the thousands of steps out of the valley. I remembered reading in my guide book that the beach was popular with nudists. In my opinion, the effort expended in accessing the beach seemed excessive, merely for a chance to air certain bits and bobs.

At the top of the valley, I glanced back, and was startled to see the red cliffs had turned white; a dramatic and sudden change, and one that reminded me of the white cliffs of home. I'd never felt truly comfortable with the unfamiliar red sand and cliffs of

Devon, despite their striking appearance and notwithstanding the last few days' entry into my top ten favourite stretches of the trip.

On the other side of a wood, we came to Branscombe Mouth, a shingle beach with a car park and a café. The village of Branscombe lay about a mile inland. With the encouragement of Kate urging me to be a love and run up that hill, we'd made superb time so I decided to stop for a cup of tea and a piece of fruit cake. The café sold plastic cups full of dog biscuits; I bought one for Jess, which improved her dour mood somewhat. From a wooden bench outside the café, I scrutinised our next big obstacle: South Down Common, the proud owner of a hill that seemed to slope upwards at an alarming angle. However, on our way to the foot of the hill, I saw an acorn sign pointing straight through a collection of chalets at the base of chalk cliffs. I studied my map, feeling uncharacteristically averse to cheating, but in fact it turned out to be the official route, through Hooken Undercliff.

Almost as soon as we got going, I realised that hiking up and over the hill would have been preferable. Leaving the chalets behind, we scrambled around a jumble of tree roots, scrub and haphazard boulders scattered along a narrow track. Above us, a sheer wall of cream cliffs rose out of the vegetation, looking as if they might tumble down on top of us at any moment. I sped up, humming the melody of *Wuthering Heights* to take my mind off the possibility of being flattened in a trice.

Escaping the undercliff involved scaling a mound of rocks and plants as we worked our way up to the clifftop. Back on level ground, we approached Beer Head and its amazing previews of the next day's walk. In the distance, the summit of Golden Cap – at one hundred and ninety-one metres, the highest point on the south coast of Britain – soared above the undulations of the surrounding coast. Between here and that particular milestone, Jess and I had yet to tackle the daddy of all undercliffs at Lyme Regis: a seven-mile stretch of landslip that would make our battle through Hooken Undercliff feel like a skip to the shops.

Near Beer, more people appeared on the cliffs, some with dogs. I didn't engage anyone in talk but homed in on various conversations as I trailed behind or in front, even slowing down if I was interested in a particular topic. By far the most popular theme was food; a threesome in front of us spent a good half a mile debating what they would have for supper. This was by no means unusual – eighty percent of the conversations I overheard were food-based: the benefits of a light supper; needing to eat more if you are going to be walking up a hill; the joy of eating prawns when abroad; a late father's love of crème brûlée; whether cheese was good for dogs …

When at last we entered Beer village, we dived into a pub to escape a shower. Lo and behold, the majority of punters in the bar were discussing food. Once the shower stopped, we tramped up the street to another pub, this one our home for the night. The manager showed us to a nondescript room with generic furniture and ugly curtains. I quickly unpacked, fed Jess, and, with my fishing rod in hand, left for the beach. All the talk of food had brought out the hunter-gatherer in me and I set my sights on catching a bass.

Beer Boats

White chalk cliffs, speckled with vegetation, protected Beer's beach from the prevailing westerly winds. Along the shore, men dressed in daffodil yellow bibs-and-braces unloaded boxes of fish from a fleet of boats stranded on the shingle. A small crowd advanced on the scene, hoping for a spanking-fresh mackerel or pollack. I peeked in the boxes then walked down to the water's edge. Dead dogfish, scallop shells and crabs littered the tideline. Now and then, a wave snatched one or two and dragged them out to sea, where the waiting gulls squabbled over the scraps. I felt sure there could be a big old bass patrolling the shallows hoping for a free meal.

I made up my rod, tied on a lure and cast out into the waves. Out of the corner of my eye, I saw Jess, further up the beach, eating something that looked very much dead. As I stared, appalled, she dipped her shoulder, preparing to roll in the rotting remains. Dropping my rod, I marched across the beach shrieking, "Don't you dare!" A fisherman spun around, wide-eyed, as I stalked past and seized Jess by the collar. She didn't take kindly to the interruption and put up a fight as I yanked her away from the stinking carcass, warning her not to make a scene.

Returning to my rod, I clipped Jess's lead to my belt and commenced fishing. I cast out, and Jess – thinking I was throwing the lure out for her to fetch – leapt forward, nearly tearing my hip out of its socket. This fishing lark wasn't going to work. I reeled in my line, took off the lure, and we wandered up the hill back to our room, taking time on the way to peer in the various gallery windows full of local pottery and paintings of fishing boats.

Later, Jess and I went into the downstairs bar, where I asked for a glass of wine and grabbed a table. After looking at the menu, I ordered smoked haddock mornay and, as a treat, prawn cocktail to start. The prawn cocktail was everything a seventies-style starter should be: a pink sauce, a garnish of cucumber and lemon, and a side of buttered brown bread – the taste of my childhood. Next, the haddock, which came in a huge portion; what was it with oversized fish and Devon? I picked up my cutlery and got stuck in.

Only halfway through, I admitted defeat, heaved myself up and wobbled upstairs to our room, too full of seafood to do anything but lie down and breathe.

9.9 miles • 25,041 steps • Grading: Severe/Strenuous

Jess woke me at six in the morning with her "I need a wee NOW" whine. I was in no mood to leave my warm bed, but she wouldn't let up. "For goodness' sake, Jess, come on then." We crept out of the room and tiptoed downstairs, where I carefully unlocked the back door, expecting at any moment to hear the pub alarms go off. All remained quiet. I hopped from one foot to the other next to the bins in the car park while Jess mooched around as if she had all the time in the world, and then returned to me with a "cheers, just wanted to sniff the car park" look. My glare felt a lot less benign. Muttering to myself about how spoilt my dog had become, and vowing to be more firm-handed, we traipsed back up to our room. Unable to go back to sleep, I made a cup of tea, put the weather on, and sat in bed watching children's TV until breakfast.

At eight on the dot, I returned to the bar, Jess in tow, for something to eat. While talking to the waitress, I told her of our plan to walk to Seatown through the Undercliffs. She shook her head and wandered off with my order.

When she returned with my full English breakfast, she enquired, "Do you have a mobile phone?"

"Yes," I answered.

"Mmm," she responded and wandered away tutting. At the door, she spun on her heel. "You should know, the Undercliffs are extremely treacherous: muddy, slippery and very unpleasant."

"Okay."

"Whatever you do, don't stray from the path. And watch where you put your feet."

Feeling like Little Red Riding Hood, I let out a chuckle, trying to lighten the mood.

She pursed her lips and twisted the tea towel in her hands. "Just be careful."

Bloody hell, the woman was serious. Suddenly, my full English didn't look so inviting. I opened both of my guide books to see if the authors were on the same page as the waitress: one depicted the Undercliffs as an untouched jungle; the other said they felt eerie. Great. I forced down my breakfast and packed, ready to begin the perilous mission.

Returning to the beach, we climbed steps onto the cliffs and skirted around a headland to Seaton Hole. At low tide, it was possible to walk along the beach and link up with Seaton's seafront. However, our arrival coincided with one of the highest tides of the year. We retraced our steps and turned right onto Old Beer Road, running along the top of the cliffs. Not far ahead, a red sign in the road depicted a chap tumbling from a cliff and warned us not to take another step. I investigated and saw, to my astonishment, that about twenty metres of road beyond the sign had been swept away in a landslide. Bugger. Everything, it seemed, was conspiring to keep us away from the Undercliffs. Was it a sign?

"Right," I declared to a confused Jess, "let's try again." We walked back to Seaton Hole, and I asked a woman setting tables outside a café how to get past the landslip. She plonked her tray of cutlery down, and in a weary tone redirected us to the main Beer Road. "It's an extra mile, but it's the only way to get to Seaton if you're on foot." I thanked her, and we set off once more.

Thirty minutes later, we reached Seaton unscathed and, after cutting through a park, continued along the esplanade. The River Axe flowed into the sea at the end of the beach, and we passed a boat yard and harbour then crossed over a bridge to the far bank. From there, a driveway through an avenue of trees led to Axe Cliff Golf Club. We struck out over the manicured fairway, keeping a wary eye out for runaway golf buggies and rogue balls.

On the edge of the golf course, farmland butted up against a wood. The Coast Path melted into the gloom beneath the trees. To the side of the path a sign read: *Please note it takes approximately 3½ to 4 hours to walk to Lyme Regis. The terrain can be difficult and walking arduous.* In all the miles I'd walked, I'd never come across such a sign. I reread it. A spark of competitive spirit ignited in my mind, and rather than interpreting the words as a warning, I took them as a challenge. I made up my mind to walk the seven miles in less than the time stated. After all, I wasn't a greenhorn; I could finally call myself a long-distance walker. I made a note of the time in my sketchbook, and we plunged into the "jungle" of the Undercliffs.

Protected as a National Nature Reserve, the Axmouth to Lyme Regis Undercliffs came about after a devastating landslide on Christmas Eve, 1839. Eight million tons of rock, soil and vegetation slid from the cliffs into the sea. Untouched by the meddling of man, the eight hundred acres has thrived ever since as an isolated ecosystem. After witnessing plenty of evidence of the unstable local coastline, I prayed there wouldn't be another landslide while Jess and I carried out my challenge.

From the start, the woods felt different from others I'd walked through. Three squirrels and a pheasant crossed our path in the first few minutes, and multiple layers of birdsong rang out from the trees. Hazel, ash and field maple sprung from a forest floor strewn in ferns, the gloom under the canopy creating the perfect conditions for the shade-loving plant. Tree roots writhed in and out of the earth, snaked across the path and dived into the leaf litter. I watched every single step for potential hazards, navigating around rocks, fallen branches and tangles of ivy.

Undeterred by the harsh terrain, I set a punishing pace, more from nerves than to prove I was fitter than the average person tackling the route. Rather than enjoy the experience, I wanted to get through it as quickly as possible. A mild feeling of claustrophobia crept over me as we pushed deeper into the wood; the foliage and tree cover grew so thick, both sky and sea vanished from view. After an hour, and despite my best efforts, I started to lag. Every step became an effort. We stopped in a clearing. While Jess crashed through the underbrush after a squirrel, I got my breath back and munched on an oatcake. All around me, the Undercliffs rustled with life. Blackbirds grubbed around in the fallen leaves, searching for worms and bugs. Squirrels jumped above my head, dislodging twigs that fell around me. I could hear the croak of pheasants, getting fainter as they retreated into the trees. Jess returned, her tongue lolling out of her mouth. I gave her a drink and, feeling better, pushed on.

For a while, we walked down the middle of a broad track that cut through the trees, until the path changed course into dense woodland once more. I stumbled along narrow ridges and crouched under the branches of fallen trees, losing track of where we were and how far we'd come; the landscape as disorientating as navigating through fog. Eventually, the trees thinned, and we rejoined the world. I looked at my watch. Blimey, we'd walked the entire Axmouth to Lyme Regis Undercliffs in two hours and ten minutes. "Yes!" I gave Jess a thumbs up. At last, I could be proud of my fitness levels – and it had only taken me six-and-a-half weeks of full-time training.

After a morning without seeing a soul, Lyme Regis came as a shock. The sun was out and the town teemed with people sipping coffees and teas and slurping ice creams. I ordered a takeaway tea at a café on the Cob and sat on the beach with my back to the sea wall. Jess stretched out on the sand to recover from her morning of harassing squirrels. I unfolded my map and mulled over the next half of the day's walk. A thick red line – representing a detour – travelled for miles inland, then back to the coast, then inland again at Charmouth, followed by a lengthy stretch along a road to Cain's Folly. Bugger that. Jess and I could hop on a bus to Chideock (the location of our B&B), a mile inland from the coast. From there, we would walk to Seatown – the official end of the day's walk – and take on all one hundred and ninety-one metres of the mighty Golden Cap.

I drank my tea, woke Jess, and we mooched into the town centre to find a bus stop. When the bus pulled up, we shuffled on behind a group of chattering women of advanced years. They bagged the back seats and produced packets of sweets, knitting and magazines from their handbags. One of them offered me a sherbet lemon and asked if she could stroke Jess. After they'd made a fuss of her, Jess slept by their stockinged feet. At Chideock, Jess and I left them guffawing like a gang of school kids; they even waved from the back window as the bus pulled away.

Chideock is a pretty village with honey-coloured cottages smothered in roses, thatched roofs and plenty of green space. Unfortunately, the village is cleaved in two by the horrendously busy A35 trunk road. Our first challenge of the afternoon was to get safely across. Lorries, buses, vans and cars streamed past, inches from our feet. "Wait for it … NOW!" We dashed to the other side. A pick-up blared its horn and left a cloud of dust and fumes in its wake. "Come on, Jess," I grumbled. "Let's get back to the coast."

We scuttled through a park and down a pot-holed lane to a privately owned beach and the hamlet of Seatown. The sparse collection of buildings around the beach comprised a few holiday homes, a holiday park and The Anchor Inn. I marched towards the pub then remembered my mission to conquer the Golden Gap. On the left of the pub, a sign pointed back along the coast. I tightened the straps of my rucksack, adjusted the grips on my walking sticks and we set off. A hundred yards on, a fence blocked the way forward. For goodness' sake, what now?

A nearby sign informed me that the path to the Golden Cap no longer existed, due to a landslip. I looked up at the sky; what was it with the coastline around here? The one bloody time I actually wanted to take part in some extreme exercise, I was stymied by coastal bloody erosion. Back to the pub, then?

I opened the satisfyingly creaky door and stepped into the bar. While ordering half a pint of bitter, I became aware of a man wearing a leather waistcoat and cowboy hat sitting on a bar stool. He squinted at me for a long moment then asked, "Are you one of Rob Harding's daughters?"

"Um … Yes?" I replied.

"I've known your family since you were tiny. How is your old man?"

I smiled. "Fine, thank you."

"Tell him John with the white Jag says 'Hi'."

"Will do."

We shook hands, and he left.

The bar girl said, "We all know Rob, but we haven't seen him for a while."

Of course, the nearer I got to home, the greater the likelihood of bumping into one of Dad's drinking buddies in any – or indeed all – of the pubs. I'd have to start brushing my hair if I didn't want to show him up.

"I'd like to climb the Golden Cap," I said, to change the subject, "but the way seems to be blocked."

"Oh, there's another way up from around the back of the pub."

"Really? That's great." I swallowed the last half of my beer, roused Jess, and we set off once more.

A path beside the pub took us to the foot of the hill. Sticks at the ready, I began the ascent, keeping up a steady plod and taking my time as always. With Jess at my side, I tramped through fields and around patches of scrub, the gradient progressively becoming steeper as we rose higher. I didn't need to rest on the way up and didn't get out of breath, and in no time we scrambled up the last rise and stood on the summit. I stared at Jess. Was that it, the mighty Golden Cap? I untied my hair, letting it blow about in the wind, placed my fists on my hips and surveyed the miles of ocean below me. I was on fire! To my left, towards home, the butterscotch sand beneath Dog House Hill, the harbour wall at West Bay and the ghostly outline of the Isle of Portland. To my right, I could see the vast stretch of Lyme Bay, all the way back to Berry Head. I rang Jack. "Guess what? Jess and I have triumphed over the Golden Cap!"

"Sounds like you're playing a video game."

"Actually, it's the highest point on the south coast of Great Britain and we are standing on it right now."

"Do you know, I think I can just make you out. Give me a wave."

I stuck two fingers up in his general direction. "Bye, Jack."

One more obstacle to cross off the list: the not-so-mighty Golden Cap. "All right Jess, let's call it a day." We made short work of the descent and returned briefly to the pub.

I popped my head around the door and gave a thumbs up to the bar girl. "That was worth the effort, thanks."

"Say 'Hi' to Rob from me," she replied.

In no time, Jess and I were once again standing at the side of the road playing chicken. I saw a gap. "Quick Jess, RUN!"

Our B&B was only a few doors away, a handsome manor house with a thatched roof and a thick covering of wisteria – much too grand for two scruffs like us. I knocked, and the door opened to reveal a lady in a cream polo neck and burgundy slacks. "Do come in." She gave us the once over and focused her gaze on my boots. "You can leave those in the hallway."

"Of course, I'm so sorry." Flustered, I quickly undid my laces. "Follow me," she said, then took us upstairs and showed us into a beautifully furnished room. "You get settled. There's a pub up the road that does good food if you're hungry. I'll see you later." I flopped onto a four-poster bed clad in sumptuous bedding.

"Wow, Jessy, now this is what I call a B&B." I unpacked, folded my clothes into a pile on an antique armchair, and put my suitcase on a carved wooden chest at the foot of the bed. Jess ate, then curled up for a nap while I ran a bath, pouring in a cap of lavender bubble bath.

Later, the skin on my fingertips nicely puckered after a long soak, I dressed, woke Jess, and we left for the pub. A brisk wind bit into us. I wrapped my arms around myself and kept my head down, while Jess used my legs as a windbreak. When we got to the pub, the landlady took pity on us and opened a few minutes early to let us in from the cold. I ordered a glass of wine and a bowl of chilli. The bar was empty, but before long an American family burst in, filling the low-ceilinged room with their booming voices and inane questions. Jess and I retreated to a snug at the back.

The chilli was spicy and warming, perfect fodder for a cold night. I returned to the bar and asked for a portion of sticky toffee pudding. The waitress soon appeared with a bowl the size of a sink, filled with a lake of custard and a family bible-sized slab of toffee pudding. What WAS going on with portion sizes in this county? And for that matter, why were all the cliffs sliding into the sea? And who on earth was White Jag John? I nibbled the edges of the pudding and left before the staff could ask me why I'd bothered to order it.

Back at the B&B, I snuggled into the layers of soft bedding and pillows and watched cookery on TV before falling asleep.

9 miles • 23,101 steps • Grading: Strenuous

DAY 45 – SEATOWN TO ABBOTSBURY

I woke, stretched, and turned on the Roberts radio on my bedside table. The weatherman predicted gale force winds and hazardous conditions around the coast and at sea. Our route to Abbotsbury included a section of lofty cliffs, and I started fretting that Jess and I might get blown off. I wasn't going to take any chances, so I rang the coastguard, explained my plan to walk to Abbotsbury via the coast, and asked if they thought we would be okay. Surprisingly, it wasn't the wind as much as the likelihood of a landslide that prompted her to tell me not to go – apparently, the recent rain had made this part of the coast extremely unstable. You don't say.

I took my guide book and map down to breakfast. Sitting at the end of an ornate dining table with my map laid out in front of me, I smiled at the B&B owner standing in the doorway.

"Good morning, did you sleep well?" she asked.

"Yes, thank you, that bed!"

"My grandfather commissioned it to be made. Isn't it beautiful?"

"And so comfy."

She took my order for coffee and returned with a pot. I showed her the map. "I'm hoping to get a bus to Abbotsbury this morning. Do you know if there's anything to do there?"

"Well, there's the swannery."

"Hmmm, Jess is wary of swans. Any good walks? Away from unstable cliffs?"

She opened a drawer and handed me a pamphlet showing local walks. "Have a look in there at the South Dorset Ridgeway."

While she cooked me a hearty full English breakfast, I read up on the route.

The South Dorset Ridgeway, accessible from Abbotsbury, is, in fact, part of the South West Coast Path, and although inland, has stunning views of the Jurassic Coast. Running from West Bexington to Osmington Mills, the route is seventeen miles long and passes close to historically important long barrows, round barrows, bank barrows – and for all I knew, wheelbarrows.

I packed, and Jess and I scurried up the road to the bus stop, where we didn't have long to wait. As we boarded the bus I couldn't help but notice a man and a woman in full hiking regalia sitting on the back seats. With my clothes giving me away as a fellow rambler, they wasted no time in introducing themselves – Angela and Dave from Nottingham – and we fell into conversation.

"So," began Angela, "what kind of footwear do you prefer? I like a mid-cut leather boot with a high traction vibrate outsole, whereas Dave swears by a high-cut soft-shell boot with a padded tongue."

I blinked. "Um."

"I can see you're old school. You can't beat leather, and they get better with age."

I considered my boots: the last six hundred miles etched into the leather, the toes scuffed and worn, the stitching frayed, deep laughter lines spreading out from each side of the bridge, the laces barely holding together.

"I'm not sure about improving with age," I said. "My pair is ready to go into a home."

They went on to tell me they were doing part of the South Dorset Ridgeway, from Abbotsbury to West Bay, not far from Seatown.

"Me too," I said before thinking it through.

"Lovely," beamed Angela. "Let's go together."

Well, it had been a while since I'd walked with anyone, so …
"Okay," I said.

The bus driver dropped us off on the main street in Abbotsbury. We spent a few moments putting on rucksacks and untying walking sticks. "Ready? Let's go," Angela said, then sped off, shouting over her shoulder, "We need to find the start; it's near Cowards Lane." A turning off the main road revealed the sign, and I insisted on bringing up the rear as we began our hike up to the ridge through farmland and a wood. Angela kept up a steady stream of conversation, while Dave murmured in agreement here and there and I battled to hide my laboured breath.

On top of the ridge, a tempest whipped my hair across my face and shoved me from behind. "The wind!" I shouted, fighting to stay upright. I put Jess into her coat and we pushed against the wind like forwards in a scrum. "GREAT VIEWS," Angela yelled. "YES," I agreed, scraping my hair from my eyes. Below us, West Fleet, a brackish lagoon trapped behind Chesil Beach, shone like polished steel. Angela screamed in my ear, "THERE'S THE SWANNERY!" She pointed to a mound surrounded by a ditch, and yelled, "THAT'S ABBOTSBURY CASTLE. SHALL WE TAKE A LOOK?" On the way, a gust of wind took me off my feet and I landed on Jess in an embarrassed heap. I'd honestly never known wind like it. Neither of us was hurt, but Jess kept her distance from me for a while.

The shouting and the wind started to take a toll. We stopped for a break, hunkered behind a stone wall, and able – at last – to talk normally. Angela opened her rucksack and produced two warm sausage rolls. She gave Dave one and broke the other in half to share with me. Crouched there, high on an exposed ridge, seeking sanctuary from a gale, in the company of two generous strangers, I'd never tasted a better pastry product.

As much as I was enjoying their company, I told Angela and Dave I wanted to go back. I didn't like the wind at the best of times, and all the shouting had tired me out. They planned to head for the coast to escape the worst of the weather, and continue along Chesil Beach to West Bay. We packed up and prepared to go our separate ways. "Take care," I said as I shook their hands. "Don't worry about us," Angela said. "Dave used to be a Wall of Death rider. Nothing scares him." Dave raised his eyebrows at me, and I laughed. "Well, well, it's always the quiet ones, eh?" We came out from behind the wall. "GOODBYE, DAVE. GOODBYE, ANGELA. THANKS FOR THE SAUSAGE ROLL."

They pushed through a nearby gate and set off over the fields. I watched them for a while. "Come on Jess," I sighed, and we retraced our steps to the village, where the biting wind had kept most people barricaded indoors. As Jess and I walked alone down the main street, a church clock struck one – time for lunch. We happened upon the Ilchester Arms, where a fire crackled and spat in an inglenook fireplace to one side of the bar. Jess sat on the hearth, mesmerised by the flames, while I ordered a cheese ploughman's and half a pint of local beer. I flopped onto a sofa next to the fire but found I couldn't relax. I missed the feeling of exhaustion that rolled over me at the end of a hard day on the trail. Somehow, the food and drink didn't taste the same; if I hadn't worked for the nourishment, it came with a side order of guilt.

After I'd eaten, I ordered a pot of tea and read the papers, filling in time before checking in to the B&B. Outside, the weather deteriorated. A man sporting mutton chops and wearing a flat cap came into the bar. He shook rain from his hat and rubbed his hands together. "Brrrrr, 'tis filthy out there, Pam. I'll have a brandy, thank you." The wind blew down the chimney, splattering the hearth – and Jess – in soot. Time to leave, before the conditions got worse.

Our B&B was on the edge of the village. A short woman, wearing a pinny with a picture of a Great Dane on it, opened the door. "My goodness, come in, come in. Are you soaked through?" She picked up a towel from a radiator. "Here, dry off your poor dog." I removed my soaked jacket and hung the toasty towel over Jess's back. "This way," the short woman beckoned, leading us to a bijou bedroom with an ensuite. The room's single window perfectly framed the fourteenth century St Catherine's Chapel, sitting stolidly on its hill. As I admired the view, the building vanished before my eyes, lost behind a curtain of rain. The wind drove the raindrops horizontally across the sky, lashing against the window with such force it sounded like hail. "Will you be going out again in this?" asked my host, wringing her hands. "I shouldn't think so," I replied, and resigned myself to an afternoon indoors, drinking tea and reading through the pile of *Hello!* magazines thoughtfully left by the bed.

As the sky darkened, I fed Jess and turned on the news and weather, then had an early night.

7 miles • 16,151 steps • Grading: Moderate

DAY 46 – ABBOTSBURY TO WEYMOUTH

The next morning, I ate my usual full English breakfast in a dining room festooned with horse brasses. When I'd finished, the owner cleared my plate and we discussed the walk to Weymouth. "When you get there, whatever you do, don't go down any side streets," she warned me. "Weymouth is overrun with lowlifes just waiting to prey on the unaware." I had no reason to disbelieve her; my only prior knowledge of the town came from a chaotic coach trip to the beach in my teens, and falling asleep in front of the sailing on TV during the 2012 Olympics. "I'll keep my distance," I promised. We returned to our room and I packed. On our way out, the kitchen door stood ajar, revealing a fawn-coloured Great Dane sprawled on a mat by the oven. In the whole of our stay, we hadn't heard a peep from him.

We headed out into the blustery day. Leaving the village, we walked around the base of Chapel Hill and I looked towards the summit at the compact chapel. From the window of the B&B, the stone had appeared a drab grey, but up close I could see the walls were built of the same buff limestone used in the village.

Near the entrance to Abbotsbury Swannery, we climbed through fields and onto a grass-backed ridge. Up high, we were pummelled by a bitterly cold and blustery wind. My right ear throbbed. My cheeks burned. I put up the hood of my jacket and pulled the zip to my chin. At Merry Hill, the ground sloped down into farmland encircling a wood. Jess, loping in front of me, disturbed dozens of pheasants. They shot into the air with Jess in hot pursuit. She raced over a ploughed field, leaping the furrows until she became a mere speck in the distance. After an anxious wait, her lithe form materialised at the edge of the field, hurtling towards me. She landed in a heap at my feet, panting. "Bloody hell, Jess," I scolded as I poured a bowl of water and waited for her to get her breath back.

My phone buzzed at the bottom of my bag – a message from my Dad:

Darling, I'm trying to sort out some press for you and get you in the papers, do ring back.

I put my phone back in my pocket, too preoccupied to deal with PR.

We set off over more fields, and on the approach to a farm came to an open gate. Hoof prints churned up the earth and formed hundreds of water-filled impressions around the entrance. Feeling somewhat resigned, I began to pick my way through. Tentatively, I put a foot out, added my weight, and sank to the top of my boot, frigid water soaking my socks. Wincing, I put my weight on my other foot and sank further. Jess paced up and down on dry land, refusing to get her paws wet, and I decided on a change of tactic. Using my sticks for leverage, I lumbered as fast as I could through the mire, trying to minimise contact. I called Jess from the other side, waving a packet of oatcakes, but she wouldn't budge. Time for Plan B. "Bye then, Jess," I chirped and strode away. In a panic, she leapt over the quagmire and bounded up to me. "You clever girl." I proffered an oatcake as a reward.

My boots squelched as I walked. Leaning on a post, I took them off, pouring out a cup of soupy liquid from each. Then, balancing on a tuft of grass at the base of the post, I tugged off my socks, wrung them out, and stuffed them into a side pocket of my rucksack. I unearthed a clean pair, put them on, and forced my feet back into my cold, damp boots with a shudder.

From the farm, the Coast Path travelled along the banks of West Fleet. On the other side of the lagoon, Chesil Beach kept the sea at bay. The land that fringed the lagoon was sodden and more mud clung to my boots as I fought to keep them from being sucked off my feet. My phone buzzed again. I lent on my sticks and read the message:

Darling, please do call me back. I need to know where you started on your walk and where you will end up. I have emailed a few contacts, and I think I can get you in the Daily Echo.

This time, I rang him back. "Listen, Dad ..."

"Sasha, I'm doing this for you. You should be thrilled to have a write-up. Remember, any press is good press."

I sighed, gave him a few details and hung up.

Ahead, a wooden boardwalk bridged a swollen stream to more fields on the other side. The scrubby remnants of a crop stuck out from deep furrows. After only a few yards, my boots had tripled in weight, a prickly mass of clay and straw surrounding each sole like a rustic snowshoe. The effort to heave my feet from the clutches of the sticky clay left me frustrated and out of breath.

Jess lifted each paw as if she was wading through something unspeakable. Further on, at East Fleet, the lagoon had breached the land, flooding the entire area. I shook my head, exasperated. A bridge rose above the water thirty yards away, offering no help to anyone. I stepped into the frigid water and my foot plunged into the gloopy layer of mud at the bottom. "Bugger this." I waded, up to my knees, through the flood to the bridge.
Jess tried everything she could think of to bypass the water. She ran around the flood, but a hedge blocked her exit route. I encouraged her to try: "Come on, Jessy, you can do it!" With no choice, she braved the water and scrambled onto the bridge. Two women appeared on the shore and in raised voices asked how deep the water was. I showed them the tide mark on my trousers. "I think we will find another way around. Good luck!" they called over their shoulders, leaving Jess and me stranded. I clenched my jaw and stalked over the bridge. Near the end, the wooden slats began to sink, and then vanished below the water. Dry land taunted us: so close. Well, we couldn't get much wetter. I stepped off the bridge, all hopes of staying dry replaced with a perverse delight in getting wet. Jess attempted to jump the gap and nearly succeeded. I dried her off as best as I could with my spare fleece, apologising over and over.

My phone buzzed.

I told the man at the Echo you were an art scholar at Marlborough College and got your art A Level at fourteen years of age. If that doesn't get you a write-up, nothing will.

I stuffed the phone into the depths of my rucksack and tried to block from my mind my father's bizarre campaign to get me featured in the local papers.

We reached the Rodwell Trail, a cycle path on the outskirts of Weymouth. I shook with cold. My boots rubbed, my ears throbbed, my dog no longer trusted me. I texted Dad to apologise for being less than enthusiastic about being in the paper and went on to say I'd nearly finished a particularly awful walk and felt sorry for myself. The phone buzzed.

I've just had eight teeth removed at the dentist. Now you know how I feel.

I turned my phone off. All that mattered now was to get out of the cold and dry out.

The trail continued past an extensive marina and over Westham Bridge. On the other side, we found ourselves in the middle of the high street, and headed for our seafront B&B. I kept us to the main thoroughfare, peering into every alley for beady-eyed ruffians. The closest we came to being accosted was a perky youth with a clipboard prancing about us, pleading with me to sign up for some charity or other.

Relatively unscathed, we came out onto the esplanade and trekked along the pavement looking for our home for the night. A terrace of Georgian buildings overlooked the beach; their smart, understated, architecture gave the impression of genteel elegance, but as I travelled further along, the façade crumbled. Weymouth is a tourist town, and the shops on the seafront reflect that: gift shops full of plastic tat, amusement arcades and fancy dress shops. The air smelt of rubbish and old cooking fat. Empty crisp packets pirouetted in doorways, in amongst fag butts and sweet wrappers. There was no sign of the gloss and shine I'd expected from a town basking in the kudos of hosting the Olympic Games Sailing Competition.

Weymouth Seafront

Struggling to find any sign of our B&B, I retraced our steps and spotted it on the corner: a dapper, red brick property, with window boxes and a porch. A woman with an immaculate blonde bob, wearing a trouser suit, answered the door and let us in without a moment's hesitation, despite our grimy appearance. Apologising for the state of us, I took my boots off and set them in front of a radiator in the hallway, then trailed behind her up the stairs. She showed us into a spacious room with a low double bed, modern furniture and a large flat screen TV. "And, in here, a bath." She raised an eyebrow. "You look like you could do with a soak."

I fed Jess. She flopped into bed while I ran a bath and peeled off my trousers and socks and put them over the radiator. I wallowed in the soothing water and sipped a cup of tea, relieved to be warm and out of the wind. After my bath, I felt a little more human and decided to go out and find somewhere for supper. I didn't have the will to travel far, so Jess and I crossed the road and headed for a café on the beach. After reading the blackboard menu I ordered a prawn sandwich and chips at a hatch then found a table. The wind whipped off the sea, picking up sand on the way and hurling it at the café. I turned my back to the view and hunched my shoulders against the chill. Jess curled up in a tight ball at my feet and was soon coated in a light dusting of sand. When my food arrived, I stared at the sandwich in dismay. A thick coating of mayonnaise suffocated a handful of prawns between two flaccid slices of bread. I risked a bite. The synthetic mayonnaise coated the roof of my mouth and wouldn't come off. Pushing the plate away, I filled up on chips, gave Jess the last few, then left the beach for our room.

I made a hot water bottle and a cup of tea and took both to bed. After a bit of TV, I burrowed under the covers and fell fast asleep.

15.5 miles • 38,498 steps • Grading: Moderate

DAY 47 – WEYMOUTH TO LULWORTH

After our early night, I woke at the crack of dawn and lay wide awake in the darkness. Today, Jess and I would set off on the last thirty miles of our six-hundred-and-thirty-mile adventure. Lulworth Cove, Durdle Door, Kimmeridge Bay, Chapmans Pool: I reeled off the familiar names in my head. Going home. Coming home? Too jittery to stay in bed, I woke Jess, snuck out of the B&B and crossed the road to the beach. A slither of light peeked out from the horizon, but Weymouth was wide awake: a rubbish truck lumbered past, beeping and clattering; buses lined up beside the pavements, their engines ticking over; seagulls squawked and squabbled on the rooftops. We dropped down onto the sand and I walked to the water's edge and watched the lights from the town twinkle on the surface of the sea.

Back at the B&B, dogs were banned from the dining room, so Jess and I made ourselves comfortable in the communal sitting room, overlooking the beach. I helped myself to cereal, yoghurt and stewed fruit before tucking into scrambled eggs and bacon. Replete, I poured a cup of coffee from the pot on a sideboard, added a dash of cream, then stood in the window for a moment, drinking my coffee and looking at the waves. My stomach fluttered. Time to get going.

I packed and said goodbye to our host, and we embarked on a three-mile tramp along Weymouth's seafront. Thankfully the wind had died down, but storm clouds obliterated most of the headlands in front of us, and the ghostly outline of White Nothe faded away as low clouds rolled in from the sea. We walked on the sand for a while, then, when we grew tired, moved onto Brunswick Terrace, a wide walkway lined with communal gardens, tennis courts and Greenhill Bowling Club. My phone buzzed.

Darling, I am trying to sort out a press photographer for you. The Echo has your mobile number and has promised to ring you for an interview. I think I might be able to get you a column on page five.

We reached Bowleaze Cove at the other end of the beach and climbed up and over a grass-topped cliff. A caravan park spread out before us, with a fun park, a restaurant and an assortment of bars. We skirted round the complex and struck out for Redcliff Point. The path became thick with mud and I gritted my teeth – here we go again – untied my walking sticks and waded through the mire. At least there was no wind, and the clouds had retreated. An uncomfortable thought popped into my head:

in three days, all my concerns about mud and wet socks and the adverse weather conditions wouldn't matter. I resolved to savour every last moment of the next few days, even those spent trudging through mountains of mud.

Near the village of Osmington Mills, I became aware of children's screams and shouts. Through gaps in the bushes, I made out an outward bound centre. Children – wearing bulky knee pads, elbow pads and helmets – crawled, dangled and jumped off an array of lethal contraptions. Every time a child did anything, they let rip with a shriek: "Oh my GWAD!" or, "AWESOME!" or, bizarrely, "MY HEAD IS LIKE A SAUCEPAN!" Now there's a child with an imagination.

Gradually, the racket faded away, and my attention fell to the next headland: White Nothe, or White Nose. As we launched our trek to the nose's tip, the Coast Path wriggled upwards, through woods, past isolated houses and a shed … I stopped in my tracks. What at first glance appeared to be a garden shed was in fact the church of St Catherine by the Sea. The only giveaway was an understated cross attached to the gable end of the building and half a dozen gravestones. On reaching the top of the headland we continued above Burning Cliff. The evocative name came about after a fire broke out in 1826 and smouldered for years due to the highly flammable bituminous shale. Before I forgot, I wrote *The Church of St Catherine by the Sea and the Burning Cliff* in my notebook – the title of a novel if ever I saw one – and pressed on to White Nose. (Another book title?)

At the end of the headland we passed in front of a row of austere coastguard cottages. A nearby sign for Lulworth Cove gave me the shivers: whenever I pictured my homecoming, the dramatic scenery and white chalk cliffs around Lulworth formed the backdrop, the doorway to my return. In my head, I played a fanfare as I prepared to walk into my past.

On the other side of the "doorway" stretched three miles of horrendous, torturous coastal footpath (next time I'll go through the back door – less dramatic, but easier on the knees). The clifftops plunged to sea level then rose, like waves in a swell. Bloody hell. I paused by an obelisk and chewed two dextrose tablets, swallowed a handful of nuts and took a glug of my isotonic drink. Jess launched herself down the first precipitous slope, bounding through the prickly grasses on either side of the track. I called after her, "Do be careful, Jess." She barked, spun around and dashed off again.

Sticks at the ready, I gingerly made my way down the hill and then slowly inched back up the other side. Heeding my own advice, I revelled in every moment: I gazed at the stark white cliffs and their reflections in the still water surrounding them; I took time to appreciate the turquoise shallows, the swooping gulls and the monstrous blanket of grass rolling into the distance. As we approached Durdle Door, gatherings of people appeared on the cliffs. From total isolation, Jess and I became part of the throng. Yappy kids, day trippers, couples and dogs of every description swarmed over the grass and spilled down to the beach opposite the iconic cliff arch. I steered clear of the steps down to the beach and contemplated the landmark from a safe distance.

The limestone arch of Durdle Door is part of the vast Lulworth Estate, privately owned by the Weld family. Over the years, musicians and directors have used the unusual topography in their creative endeavours; Cliff Richard, Billy Ocean and Tears for Fears all lip-synced in front of the arch. Durdle Door hovered on the border of my family's territory when we were growing up. My one memory involved the steps leading up to the cliffs from the car park in Lulworth. As Jess and I made our way down those same steps, I recalled kicking up a fuss as a child when my parents told me we were all going to walk up the steps to look at what I referred to as "Durdle's Door." I'd always disliked hills.

We crossed the packed car park and plodded along the road into the village to find a pub. Plumping for the first one we came to, and without much of an appetite, I ordered a starter and a beer. I discovered an unoccupied table tucked away in a booth by a window, took off my rucksack, dropped it on the seat next to me, shrugged off my jacket and rubbed the tension out of my neck.

Through the window I watched packs of people wandering past the pub on their way to and from Lulworth Cove: another landmark to tick off. Jess put her head on my knee and I distractedly scratched her ears. What did the other people in the bar see, if they even noticed us? A dog walker out for lunch? No one knew how far we'd come. I wanted to get up on the table and shout, "Hey everyone, we've walked six hundred and twenty miles to get to this pub." Instead, I dipped a battered prawn in a pot of mayo, bit it in half and gave the rest to Jess. "Cheers to us!" I declared.

We left the pub and walked away from the crowds, leaving the village for our B&B. A white-haired woman in a maroon cardigan answered the door. "I'm Dot. You can leave your boots and jacket in the porch." I did as requested and stood in my socks in the cream-carpeted entrance hall. "Would you like to meet Henry?" she asked and opened the kitchen door. A chocolate brown spaniel, wiggling with excitement, dashed out and raced around us then sped off on a series of laps around the house. "Henry, please! Do calm down." Jess batted him with a paw as he flew past her, and he abruptly stopped. "Please excuse him," Dot said. "He's not had a walk today and is uncontrollable."

"We'll take him out," I blurted. Jess looked at me in total disbelief. "In return," I added, "could you wash some of my clothes?"

"Of course." Dot was delighted with the barter. "Now, let me explain where I normally take him."

There and then, I put my boots and jacket back on and left the house with Henry and Jess. It started to rain. We crossed over the road and went up a lane that led onto open farmland. Henry ran hither and thither, flushing out birds from the bushes and finding sticks, while Jess moped along at my heels. The rain got heavier. My phone rang.

"Sasha, hi! It's Fran. How are you getting on? You must be getting close."

"I'm in Lulworth walking someone's dog."

"Blimey, you're keen! I've been thinking about you."

"I wish you were here to wave a flag or throw some confetti. It's not the homecoming I'd imagined."

"You've got a way to go yet. I'm sure you'll feel different tomorrow when you get to Swanage and see all your family."

She wished me luck, and we said goodbye. Henry disentangled himself from a thicket, his fur festooned with twigs and bits of leaf. Mmmm, time to go back.

Dot and I dried the dogs off and they retired to the sitting room. I brought a pile of grubby clothes down and popped them in the washing machine. Then we drank tea and munched through a plate of custard creams. Later, Jess and I went upstairs. I ran a bath in the bathroom down the hall, leaving Jess asleep in our room with the door open. Five minutes later, she nosed open the bathroom door and lay on the mat with a sigh. "I love you, Jess," I said. I couldn't have wished for a better sidekick. She'd never baulked at the tiring days and strange places, taking everything in her stride. As long as we were together, she was happy. And so was I.

We returned to our room. Jess climbed into her bed and I lay on mine, listening to the rain on the window.

11.9 miles • 29,588 steps • Grading: Easy/Strenuous

I slept fitfully and woke when the light of dawn seeped under the curtains. Jess's gentle snores filled the room. I went over the day in my mind. The walk to Swanage would be the longest of the whole seven weeks: over twenty miles. The first few miles cut through the Lulworth Ranges, which, by a happy stroke of luck, were open to the public. From there, the part of the coast I knew so well growing up would unfurl before me: Chapman's Pool, Winspit, Dancing Ledge, Peveril Point. These weren't just names on a map; they were memories offering a chance to relive time spent with my mum while she was alive.

I jumped out of bed. After taking Jess out for a morning wee, I returned to find Dot making toast. At one end of the sitting room, a table was set with a coffee jug and an assortment of cereals and yoghurts. I pulled up a chair and tucked in, while Jess and Henry rolled around on the floor at my feet. When I finished, I discovered my neatly folded clothes, still warm from the dryer, at the foot of the stairs. I put on a top-to-toe clean outfit and pranced around in a haze of washing powder fumes, feeling pristine for the first time since leaving Portloe.

Gathering my belongings for the last time, I hugged Dot, scratched Henry's ears, and Jess and I tramped down the road to the famous Lulworth Cove. The cliffs and beach, which almost encircle the cove, form the shape of a scallop shell, one of the world's best examples of an eroded concordant coastline (where bands of different rock types run parallel with the coast). Five hundred thousand people a year visit the cove and the surrounding area, none of whom were on the deserted beach that morning. With no crowds to spoil the experience, we delayed our departure and pottered along the white pebble shore. I skimmed a few stones. Jess nibbled on a dead crab.

Leaving the beach, we climbed a wooded trail onto the cliffs above the cove then struck out for the Lulworth Ranges. The gate to the site stood ajar. I double checked for any red flags, and we pushed through. A leisurely stroll over white chalk cliffs led to Mupe Bay, a poor cousin in relation to the magnificent Lulworth Cove. A row of sea stacks – Mupe Rocks – formed a broken barrier offshore. Nearby, a herd of brown cows popped up from behind a thicket beyond the yellow posts marking the safe zone. Presumably, the cows acquired a sixth sense while grazing on the ranges and left the unexploded shells well alone. Unequipped with that superpower, Jess and I stayed safely within the posted route.

This laid-back start ended abruptly and irrevocably when we found ourselves at the foot of Bindon Hill. Every part of my being shouted, "Run, run away and never return." The gradient was so severe I feared the weight of my rucksack might tip me backwards. Knees trembling, I hauled myself up the flight of steps hacked out of the chalk, stopping to catch my breath every few yards. At the top, the grey outline of the Isle of Portland peeked above the horizon. I hobbled down the other side of the hill to sea level and almost immediately began climbing again to the brow of Flower's Barrow before descending to low cliffs above Worbarrow Bay. Plastic buckets, bottles and barnacle-encrusted ice boxes littered the shore: an ugly sight. My phone rang.

"Hey Dad, I haven't heard from the paper."

"There's been a slight change of plan, darling. They don't need to interview you and don't want to take photos. You might get a paragraph on page sixteen if a cat doesn't get stuck up a tree, but don't hold your breath."

"What a relief. Thanks, Dad. I'll see you later." I rang off.

At Worbarrow Point, we sat on the grass and I watched a bright yellow fishing boat chug towards us from Weymouth. A troop of pubescent boys carrying colossal backpacks turned up and collapsed around us, red-faced and sweaty. The air grew heavy with the overpowering odour of a boys' changing room. One of them laid out his map and produced a compass. "Right, listen everyone. We are here, and we need to be here." He prodded at the paper. "So if we take this path …" A small boy spoke over his shoulder: "That goes to Tyneham you berk." They began to wrestle. "Give the map to someone who knows what they're doing," shouted another boy, and he snatched the map from the first boy, who was momentarily distracted by the small boy chewing his ear.

I left them to it.

Jess and I continued along the mercifully flat and easily walkable Gad Cliff. As we drew near to Kimmeridge, we passed a stone marker with *Swanage – 11 miles* carved into it. I looked at my watch. If we didn't stop, we would make it to Swanage before the light faded. With renewed determination, I pushed on through fields and came to a headland with views across Kimmeridge Bay to the distinctive Hen Cliff, crowned with Clavell Tower, a

Tuscan-style folly built in 1830 and now owned by the Landmark Trust.

During my childhood, a family trip to Kimmeridge meant just one thing: a fossil-hunting competition on the beach. Mum would set up a blanket, make herself comfortable and pour a coffee from a flask, while my siblings and I got to work. The sheer numbers of fossils lurking in the cliffs and scattered on the shore guaranteed everyone a find. I always hoped for a Tyrannosaurus Rex tooth, but had never unearthed anything more exciting than an ammonite.

Nearby, a gate topped with barbed wire marked the end of the ranges. I turned the handle and pushed. Nothing. I put my shoulder into it. The gate held firm. I tried again, yanking the handle down and rattling the gate. No luck. Through the wire fence and thick bushes, I could see a concrete enclosure the size of a tennis court, with a nodding donkey, a holding tank and a lorry. I shouted, "Hey in there, the gate's locked! Hello, anyone, hello!" The place looked deserted. I stalked the perimeter, searching for a way out, but the fence stretched as far as the eye could see. I returned to the gate. What now? How the hell were we going to get out of the Ranges?

My stomach lurched. Would we have to go all the way back to Lulworth Cove? Jess nuzzled me with her nose. "All right girl," I told her. "I need to think." I pulled out my map to see if there was another way out and saw a phone number for the Lulworth Ranges. Okay. I got out my phone, praying the battery wasn't flat. It wasn't. I had plenty of juice – but no signal. A faint track to the left of the gate rose towards the brow of a hill. I set off, phone in hand, seeking one or two bars. No sooner had I started up the track than the gang of boys from earlier turned up and went through the same pantomime as me. When they realised they couldn't get through, they walked along the perimeter. I turned around to meet them.

We came together in a storm of outrage. How could the gate be locked? What now? Where now? I explained I had a number to ring and asked if anyone's phone worked. Not one of them had a signal. As a group, we carried on up the hill, staring at our phones. "It's working," I cried out, twenty minutes later. The boys gathered around me, and I rang the number. After three rings, I heard a click: *This is an automated message; for information on the opening times of the Lulworth Ran …* I hung up.

The boys shrugged off their backpacks and gathered in a huddle to consult their map. Immediately, a quarrel kicked off.

"Look, you twerp, if we are here then we need to find the crossroad and turn down there."

"But our campsite's over there."

"That's not a campsite. It's a farm."

"What are you on about? There's a picture of a tent on it."

"That's not a tent, moron. It's a teepee."

I wandered away, needing space. What now? In a flash of inspiration, I decided to call the coastguard. Surely they could open the gate? I rang 999 and asked to be put through. When I described the situation, the operator said he would ring the local coastguard, who had a set of keys, adding, "I can't guarantee when he'll get there though." Deflated, I rang off. The search for a signal had stranded Jess and me a mile or more inland. I couldn't risk going all the way back to the gate only to have to wait hours for it to be unlocked. Our only choice was to find another way out of the Ranges and make our way home by a different route.

I shoved a handful of nuts in my mouth and chewed. "Right, Jess, let's go." We continued walking away from the coast, sticking to the fence, until we found an open gate. Why did whoever was responsible unlock this one but forget to unlock the other one? Could they not be bothered? Did they think no one would notice? Did they think it would be funny? I kicked the gate, feeling my eyes well up. All this bloody way.

I scrutinised the map; we were near a hamlet called Steeple. From there, a footpath led to Smedmore Hill, a ridgeway running parallel with the coast. There didn't seem to be a way to get to the coast but at least we were going in the right direction. Up high, the landscape stretched for miles around us in all directions. Behind us, a flash of white chalk cliffs – Bindon Hill? – peeked out from behind the headland of Worbarrow Point. In front of us lay Kimmeridge Ledges and St Aldhelm's Head, with its tiny Norman chapel. On the other side of the ridge, Poole Harbour and Brownsea Island formed a shimmering backdrop to the iconic silhouette of Corfe Castle.

I'd lived in Corfe for a while with my sister Nina, before I moved to Cornwall. From her house, a trip to the corner shop for a pint of milk required a stroll through fields of buttercups at certain times of the year. I never tired of the walk – we got through a lot of milk. When my siblings and I were young, from the moment the ruin came into view after a car trip, we would sing, "I can see Corfe 'a' Castle, I can see Corfe 'a' Castle." For years, we'd all thought Corfe Castle had an "a" in the middle.

At Swyre Head, we came down from the ridge, slogged across fields and tramped along a road that cut through a wood. Finally, we reached the village of Kingston. I sat on a bench at the bus stop and unfolded my map. A footpath linked the village to the coast, but the extra miles, combined with the time it would take to get there, meant we wouldn't reach Swanage before the light faded. Who was I kidding? The truth was, the moment the gate from the Ranges didn't open, I lost my drive to complete the walk to Swanage. That one misstep had shattered the carefully choreographed homecoming I'd envisioned. It changed everything. My phone buzzed, a text from Sophie:

Hey Sash, how are you getting on? We are in Corfe visiting Nina, we're going to get the steam train to Swanage in a couple of hours, see you there!

I couldn't face texting her back. What would I say? *Hey Soph, I've decided to call it a day, I'm over this walking lark. See you soon, Sash xx*

A bus for Swanage pulled up, and without thinking I boarded it with Jess. That was that then. No reliving the picnics at Dancing Ledge, nor the long walks around Durlston with my mum and our dog, Sunny; nor slow worm hunting around the cliffs at Durlston Bay; nor crabbing at Peveril Point … I stared through the bus window as my old school went by, and I felt the familiar butterflies in my stomach. Home.

We got off the bus and made our way to my friends' B&B. I'd booked all the rooms at Joe and Sarah's house; three of my sisters were travelling down from London and Sophie and Dad had driven from Cornwall, all to celebrate the penultimate day of the walk together. Jack was driving up the next day to walk the final seven miles to Poole with Jess and me. I knocked on the door. Joe opened it, explaining, "Sorry, Sash, we're on our way out; the kids are late. Choose any room you want!" The door slammed shut.

After a moment, I lumbered up the stairs and went into the first room off the landing. Jess sniffed every inch of the carpet and all the corners while I slumped onto the bed, utterly exhausted. My phone buzzed.

Hi Sash, I hope you are nearly there and not too tired! We will be with you in two hours. Bee x x

Sash, nearly there, you did it xxx Daisy

Well done Sash. Fran xxxx

I fed Jess, took a shower and dressed in clean clothes. The essentials of my day-to-day life on the Coast Path lay about me, soon to be redundant. I wouldn't need my rucksack, stained and ripped in places, or my maps, plastered in scribbles and notes, or my sticks (how did I ever do without them?) I'd continue to wear my boots for as long as they lasted. But I'd no longer need to dress in my uniform. Back to jeans then. No more scampi and chips with a clear conscience. No more glasses of wine as a reward for seven hours of exercise.

My sketchbooks lay on the bed and I flicked through them. The pages were crammed with drawings of boats and beaches and windswept cliffs, seagulls and seals, twisted pine trees and every shape of island. Between the covers were enough ideas and detailed notes for months, if not years, of work. I shook my head and smiled. What a plum. While I'd been obsessing over what I saw as a failure to complete the walk to Swanage, I'd missed the bigger picture; my seven-week search for inspiration was an unequivocal and absolute success. I couldn't wait to get back in the studio and start painting. I gave Jess a big hug. "We bloody well did it, my girl."

I heard a knock at the door and bounded down the stairs with Jess. On the doorstep, my sisters greeted us with hugs and excited whoops. "Well done, Sash. Well done, Jessy." "You look great. Have you lost weight?" "When did you finish? Have you been here long?" I invited them in, and we settled around the kitchen table. Sophie produced a bottle of champagne and while I searched for glasses, Cara poured crisps into a bowl. Another knock. I opened the door to my dad, who, to my mortification, welled up. "Come in, Dad. Everyone's here." Right behind him, Joe, Sarah and their two kids burst through the door, and the greetings started all over again.

We sat around the kitchen table until late, catching up. One by one, my sisters turned in. I went outside to say goodnight to Dad, who was having a fag in the garden.

"I forgot to tell you," I said, "White Jag John says 'Hi'."

"White Jag John? Oh! White Jag John! I could tell you a few stories about him."

"Another time, Dad. Good night."

Jess and I went to our room and I quietly closed the door. I sat on the bed, overwhelmed by the change in my circumstances. For it to end so suddenly. I heard Dad closing the patio door downstairs and going to his room. But what a wonderful homecoming.

13 miles • 34,080 steps • Grading: Severe/Moderate

The next morning, I rose early, and Jess and I left the B&B. We walked past my childhood home, a beautiful old rectory hidden in a walled garden behind black gates. We passed the stream where I spent many hours as a child wading up and down in my wellies, catching eels and even flatfish. On the seafront, Jess and I jumped off a low wall onto the sand. I stalked along the shore, my hands in my pockets, then I faced out to sea. Twenty or more years before, Mum and I had driven to the beach and parked on the seafront. We didn't jump off the low wall. I held her elbow and helped her down the stone steps. We stood, touching, at the water's edge and stared across the bay. What was she thinking, I wonder? She knew she was dying, we all knew, but we rarely spoke about it. I wish I'd known what to say to her at that moment. Was she scared? Angry? But I was eighteen, and clueless, and now the chance was long gone. I picked up a pebble and flung it at the sea.

We left the beach and returned to the B&B. Any dark thoughts evaporated the moment I opened the door. Joe hovered in front of the grill, keeping an eye on the bacon. Sarah fried eggs. Daisy made mugs of tea. Dad drank coffee and read the paper. Sophie and Bee laid the table while Cara applied mascara at a mirror in the hallway.

"Where have you been?" Cara wanted to know.

"I took Jess for a walk, to warm up for the last seven miles."

"Blimey, a pre-walk walk? What did you do with the old Sash?"

Over breakfast, we discussed the day. Jack hoped to get to us by midday, in time to join Jess and me on the walk to South Haven, the official end of the SWCP. The girls were heading back to London in the early afternoon, and Sophie and Dad would return to Cornwall soon after. Meanwhile, we had all been invited to Daisy's old friend Katie's house for lunch, which gave us the whole morning free.

"How about a stroll along the seafront and a coffee at the café at the end, keep those walking legs warmed up?" Cara suggested.

Dad declined. "I'll see you all later. I've texted White Jag John, and we're meeting in the Red Lion."

Off we went, the five sisters and Jess. For the first time, I felt self-conscious wearing my walking clothes. On the seafront, Daisy and I fell in together.

"Do you remember our swims before breakfast when I was little?" she asked.

"I remember the water was freezing, but so clear – do you remember the shoals of sand eel?"

"And having a cup of tea in the café afterwards?"

"That was the best bit!"

"What about the beach hut?"

Throughout our childhood, Eileen, our grandmother, had owned a painted wooden beach hut on the far side of the bay: the epicentre of our summer holidays. In amongst the fishing nets, wet towels and buckets and spades, Eileen had kept a bottle of tonic water on a shelf in the corner.

"Why were we never allowed to touch the bottle of tonic water?" asked Daisy.

"That was for Eileen's gin and tonic after her swim," said Sophie.

"Oh," I laughed, "so that's why the beach hut smelt of lemons."

At the café, we sat outside and drank coffee. Jack rang to say he was nearby. I gave him directions to Katie's house and said we would meet him there. The walk along the seafront shaved a mile or so off the last seven miles, and getting to Katie's house, which by chance sat right next to the SWCP, would take care of another one, leaving just five miles to get us to the finishing line.

I waited outside the house for Jack. My white Volvo soon appeared at the bottom of the drive, and in no time Jack was clambering out of the driver's seat. "I've missed you!" I said, embracing him, while Jess ran around us in circles.

Once again, we gathered around a kitchen table. Katie brought in bowls of soup and a wooden board with bread and cheese. After the main course she gave us wedges of chocolate cake and mugs of tea, saying to Jack and me, "That'll set you up for the last stretch." I glanced at Jack. What with the drive and the filling lunch, he was fighting to keep his eyes open. "We'd better get going," I said. Jack blinked and rubbed his face. "Right, yes, of course; a five-mile walk, how wonderful." We left my siblings sitting around the table calling, "Good luck," and, "Well done!"

The final five miles.

A steep lane beside the house met up with the Coast Path going to the top of Ballard Down. Jess and I set off at a moderate pace. I turned to talk to Jack, only to find him catching his breath a bus length behind us. "Are you okay?" I shouted.

"Do I look okay? Slow down, will you?"

"I'm sorry, I didn't realise I was rushing."

"You're like a machine."

"Wow! What a lovely thing to say. Thanks, Jack."

A white chalk track ran through fields along the top of Ballard Down. After the tough start, the clifftops were flat. Jack got his breath back and used it to say, "That's better. Don't ever ask me to walk with you anywhere again."

I laughed and glanced down at Jess. I'd definitely chosen the right sidekick.

A gentle grass slope above a string of half moons carved out of the chalk cliffs led us to Old Harry Rocks. The row of sea stacks, pitted with caves and holes, rose from the sea, cut off from the mainland. We inched towards the lip of the cliff, and watched seagulls skimming over the water far below.

I chivvied Jack along. "Nearly there." My phone buzzed; a text from Joe:

The kids and I are coming to meet you, where are you?
I let him know we were near Middle Beach car park, and he arranged to leave his car at South Haven and walk back along Studland Beach towards us.

Jack held my hand. Squeezed it. "How do you feel?"

"Sick."

He laughed. "Me too after that hill. What joy do you find in this walking lark?"

I punched him in the arm. "Thanks for coming."

We passed a sign for the nudist beach. "Keep your eyes down, please," I instructed.

"Why do the men always wear socks and sandals?" Jack asked. "If you're going to get it off, get it all off."

"We used to come to Studland Beach for an annual school picnic when I was young," I told him. "The highlight was seeing a person with no clothes on."

"How juvenile."

In the dunes, I could make out the odd figure here and there, popping up and then disappearing, like meerkats. Further on, a sign told us we were now leaving the nudist beach and, in immaculate PG-timing, Joe appeared from behind the dunes with his two children. The kids ran about with Jess and skimmed stones. Jack and Joe talked rugby. This was it. A few more steps and the walk would be over.

I called Jess to me and put her on her lead. Blocking out the sound of the kids playing and Jack's raised voice, I moved out in front. "You and me, Jess," I said, and we marched forward, ignoring Jack's shouts of, "Wait, Sash." As we got closer to the ferry landing at Shell Bay, the unmistakable SWCP sign came into view. Glancing back at Jack, I strode towards the blue metal sculpture and ran my hand over the carved letters: South West Coast Path. In front of the queue of cars waiting for the ferry, I crouched beside Jess and kissed her cheek.

"We did it."

7 miles • 17,437 steps • Grading: Moderate

THE END

ABOUT THE WALKERS

Sasha Harding is an artist and author living and working in Cornwall. Born and raised on the south coast of Dorset, Sasha's love of the sea was nurtured from an early age. She studied for her Fine Art degree at Falmouth College of Art and quickly put down roots, marrying a Cornishman and buying a kayak.

She has exhibited all over England and has had numerous One Man Shows. Her work has been published as limited edition prints and cards. This is the text from a revised edition of her first book, A Brush With The Coast, originally published in 2015.

Jess is an eight-and-a-half-year-old Rhodesian ridgeback. She was born in Exeter and now resides in Cornwall. After completing the South West Coast Path, Jess was hoping to return to doing nothing all day. However, Sasha had other plans: in 2016 the pair embarked on a 140-mile stroll around Anglesey and Sasha published *A Brush With Anglesey*. Jess was relieved not to have to walk anywhere when Sasha published her first children's book, *Plop!*, in 2017.

If you would like to know more about walking the South West Coast Path, visit:
www.southwestcoastpath.org.uk

Thanks to:
www.walkthetrail.co.uk
www.luggagetransfers.co.uk

RÉALISATION : IGS-CP À L'ISLE-D'ESPAGNAC
IMPRESSION : MAURY IMPRIMEUR À MALESHERBES (45)
DÉPÔT LÉGAL : MARS 2017 - N° 132541 (215807)
IMPRIMÉ EN FRANCE

dans ce chœur de femmes, mais il s'est lui aussi laissé prendre par l'harmonie qui régnait dans la pièce. Puis tout a basculé. Izou a passé son CD de Deva Premal. Les *mantras* ont envahi la salle de travail. Silence, douceur, gravité. Puis, un éclat de rire qui a fait hurler la machine à laquelle j'étais reliée. Les sages-femmes ont accouru. L'enfant allait naître. J'avais eu une pensée rapide pour Babaji. Son dernier rire. Le rire qui donne la vie.

Le premier cri de Perceval. Son petit corps. Puis on me l'a retiré trop vite. L'arrachement sans son odeur. Pendant que je désespérais de ne pas le voir, Domnin s'était déshabillé pour coller son bébé à sa peau. Izou et ma mère prenaient des photos de Perceval et Domnin, Perceval et ma mère, Perceval et ma tante. Elles venaient me les montrer en riant telles des bonnes fées papillonnantes. Deux heures plus tard, Domnin m'a enfin amené mon fils. Il avait un peu souffert de l'accouchement, je me suis écriée : « Oh, mais tu as une drôle de tête petit ange ! » Domnin a répondu avec force : « Mais non, tu es beau mon fils, tu es magnifique ! » Sa petite bouche a cherché mon sein. Je l'ai respiré de toutes mes forces. J'ai enfin compris ces mots de Babaji : « Regardez, le monde est magique. »

*

En donnant la vie, j'ai découvert l'amour viscéral, total, animal, mais aussi le service envers ce petit être exigeant qui possède et bouleverse. L'enseignement de Babaji ne cesse de fleurir dans ma vie de famille. Il insistait beaucoup sur la nécessité d'agir dans un esprit de service, je trouvais l'idée belle, sans la comprendre. MA disait : « Servir présuppose que l'on se sacrifie, et nul vrai service n'est possible lorsqu'on attend du plaisir, ou une récompense ou des résultats quelconques […]. On peut servir par le corps, par l'esprit et la parole. » J'ai découvert qu'il était finalement très beau de consacrer ses journées à les donner…

J'étais libre sur les routes, seule, rêveuse, je suis libre entre les horaires de crèches et de nounou. Je m'étais juré de partir souvent en voyage et laisser mon fils à ma mère. Le quitter est une souffrance. Son rire, ses yeux, ses premiers mots sont aussi un voyage que je ne pouvais imaginer. Je me suis perdue dans cette nouvelle fusion, toujours déchirée entre les petits bras rondelets et l'appel de l'ailleurs. Mais MA et Babaji m'ont montré chaque jour le chemin : entre dans le courant de la vie, donne-toi, lâche tes résistances, tes questions, tes pensées, aime. Et laisse faire les anges.

Après la naissance de Perceval, Domnin et moi avons traversé de grosses tempêtes. Je me plaignais, questionnais MA et Babaji chaque matin en méditant : pourquoi nous éprouver à ce point alors que ce petit être grandit à nos côtés et n'aspire qu'à la joie ? Un jour, la réponse est venue. Elle était déjà en moi depuis longtemps puisque Babaji n'avait cessé de m'encourager dans ce chemin. Mais je n'étais pas prête. Ou peut-être n'avais-je pas assez aimé et souffert pour ressentir le besoin d'emprunter cette voie de façon radicale : faire le choix de la joie. Malgré tout. Non une joie qui dépend des événements extérieurs, mais une joie intérieure, une attitude mentale, une décision de ne pas se laisser happer, éteindre, éreinter par la vie. Dans un monde désenchanté, la joie comme résistance. La joie comme ultime transmission. J'ai trouvé sa source dans le souffle du Maître.

LEXIQUE

Arati : rituel consistant en plusieurs offrandes réalisées à la déité.

Ashram : lieu où vivent les fidèles pour se consacrer aux pratiques spirituelles autour d'un Maître.

Bhav : attitude mentale.

Bidis : petites cigarettes indiennes en forme de cône constituées de feuilles provenant d'un arbre tropical.

Brahmanes, brahmines : hommes et femmes de la caste des prêtres, caste la plus élevée au point de vue religieux dans le système hindou.

Darshan : littéralement « vision ». Lorsqu'on a la grâce de voir un grand Sage, on reçoit son *darshan*.

Dharma : loi éternelle.

Diksha : initiation spirituelle.

Ghat : marches qui descendent dans un fleuve sacré pour les ablutions des hindous. C'est aussi un lieu où sont déposées les offrandes.

Karma : conséquence des actes, paroles et pensées d'un individu.

Karma yoga : yoga de l'action désintéressée.

Kirtan : chant dévotionnel.

Mantra : son sacré.

Pandit : lettré spirituel hindou.

Pranam : prosternation devant les pieds du Sage.

Prasad : nourriture sacrée.

Puja : offrande rituelle.

Pujari : officiant de la *puja*.

Rickshaw : petite voiture à trois roues motorisée.

Rishi : instructeur de l'humanité.

Sadhu : moine.

Samadhi : état de supraconscience ; ou tombeau d'un grand Sage.

Shaktipat : éveil de l'énergie.

Shilom : pipe à haschisch.

Shivaïte : dévot du dieu Shiva.